282
Dul

Dulles, Avery

The reshaping of Catholicism

THE RESHAPING OF CATHOLICISM

THE RESHAPING
OF CATHOLICISM

Current Challenges
in the Theology of Church

Avery Dulles, S.J.

1817

Harper & Row, Publishers, San Francisco

Cambridge, Hagerstown, New York, Philadelphia, Washington
London, Mexico City, São Paulo, Singapore, Sydney

All acknowledgments for previously printed material are included in the Sources section unless otherwise noted.

THE RESHAPING OF CATHOLICISM: *Current Challenges in the Theology of Church*. Copyright © 1988 by New York Province, Society of Jesus. All rights reserved. Printed in the United States of America. No part of this book may be used or reproduced in any manner whatsoever without written permission except in the case of brief quotations embodied in critical articles and reviews. For information address Harper & Row, Publishers, Inc., 10 East 53rd Street, New York, NY 10022. Published simultaneously in Canada by Fitzhenry & Whiteside, Limited, Toronto.

Library of Congress Cataloging-in-Publication Data

Dulles, Avery Robert, 1918-
    The reshaping of Catholicism.

    Bibliography: p.
    Includes index.
    1. Catholic Church—Doctrines—History—20th century. 2. Catholic Church—History—1963-   . 3. Church and social problems—Catholic Church.   4. Vatican Council (2nd : 1962-1965)   I. Title.
BX1755.D85   1988   282′.09′04   87-46205
ISBN 0-06-254856-5

88 89 90 91 92 RRD 10 9 8 7 6 5 4 3 2 1

Contents

Preface

Catholic theology in the past twenty years—and to some extent in any period—is the story of the interaction between the church and its changing environment. What is distinctive to the past twenty years is that the problems have been confronted in the light of the Second Vatican Council (1962–1965). This council concentrated on the church as its central theme, and thus ecclesiology has remained at the center. As an ecclesiologist I have frequently been asked to speak and write on problems arising out of Vatican II. Looking over the articles I have published since 1984, I find it possible to assemble a collection of twelve pieces that deal with a rather typical range of questions. Without claiming that these essays touch on all the key problems of our time, I believe that they give a fair sampling of the issues that the Catholic Church has had to face in the two decades since the council. I have arranged the papers in such a way that the early chapters of this book are more general in scope and more popular in style and content. The later chapters are, on the whole, more specialized and analytic and thus, in a few cases, more technical.

This collection begins with a background paper dealing with the sociocultural situation of American Catholicism before, during, and after the council. In this chapter I suggest what the United States has been able to contribute to the council and its interpretation, and what the council could bring as a corrective to certain typically American tendencies.

In the second chapter, I conduct a brief survey of the central teachings of Vatican II, especially with reference to the church. I take the position that the basic principles of the council constitute the essential framework for fruitful discussion of other problems in the church. I try to show how the council took mediating positions that need to be interpreted and applied with discretion and balance and thus without blind partisanship.

Chapters 3 through 9 deal with a series of themes to which Vatican II made significant contributions. Each of them deals with a tension-filled area in which the authority of the council has been invoked on behalf of two or more conflicting positions.

Chapter 3 takes up the question of the so-called "world church"—the truly global community that began to emerge with Vatican II. I discuss whether the church can simultaneously inculturate itself in the various regions of the world and still retain its visible unity as a single community of faith and commitment. I argue that it can do so but not without conscious effort to preserve certain shared symbols and structures of unity and continuity. Thus cultural autonomy must not be absolutized.

In chapter 4 I turn to a problem arising from the ecumenical orientation of the council. Vatican II called the body of Christians in union with Rome the "Catholic church," but at the same time it described "catholicity" as an attribute of the "Church of Christ," which it depicted as a reality transcending any given ecclesiastical body. In this chapter I argue that Catholicism is not exclusively proper to the Roman communion, but that it "subsists" in that communion, which is preeminently Catholic. Catholicism, I maintain, is not in need of being supplemented by some countervailing property, be it Protestantism, mysticism, or whatever.

Chapter 5 deals with the question of continuity and innovation. Vatican II is frequently said to have marked an official acceptance of historical consciousness in the Catholic church. Does this mean that the church gave up its previous claims to identity with the church of apostolic times and accepted a kind of chameleonlike adaptability to its changing environment? In this chapter I seek to affirm both permanence and adaptation by relying on a vital, realistic, and dynamic theory of tradition.

Then in chapter 6 I address one of the more notorious internal problems faced by Catholic Christianity since the council. Vatican II, while firmly asserting the teaching authority of the hierarchical magisterium, also stressed the principles of religious freedom and personal authenticity. Some look upon the doctrinal vigilance of the Roman authorities under John Paul II as a betrayal of the spirit of Vatican II, while others consider that dissenting priests and laity are flaunting the clear teaching of the council. I set forth some principles that, if followed, would render dissent rare, reluctant, and respectful.

Chapter 7 concerns a question of immense importance that has been all but overlooked in contemporary theological literature. By issuing a Decree on the Instruments of Social Communication Vatican II showed an awareness that the church must enter fully into the new electronic age. The council did little more than to identify the problem, but some further progress has been made in postconciliar documents. I suggest that the complexities of the question can be illuminated by considering what the various models of the church imply with regard to communications.

My eighth chapter takes up a traditional question too little explored in recent theological literature—the purpose for which the church exists. Many seem to take it almost for granted that Vatican II backed away from the church's claim to be an instrument of eternal salvation and raised human and social goals to parity with those that are divine and everlasting. Yet a close inspection of the council documents does not seem to support this popular impression. We have here a paradigmatic case of how the teaching of Vatican II has been overlaid by the commentary.

The problem of the church and politics, treated in chapter 9, has received no lack of attention in recent years. The literature is vast; the disagreements are sharp and bitter. I here adopt a middle course. On the one hand, I strongly affirm the competence of the church to issue authoritative social teaching, but on the other hand I caution against plunging the church too deeply into concrete sociopolitical issues. Ecclesiastics, I believe, should respect the proper competence of secular disciplines and refrain from canonizing their preferred solutions to disputed policy questions.

Chapter 10 differs from the preceding seven insofar as it focuses not on a problem but on an event, the Extraordinary Synod of 1985. This meeting, called by John Paul II with the purpose of assessing the meaning of Vatican II for our day, issued two consensus documents that can be of great value for preventing arbitrary and selective interpretations of the council. The Synod also flagged several key problems that will occupy the Catholic church for some years to come.

One of the problems noted by the Extraordinary Synod is taken up in chapter 11, on the teaching authority of bishops' conferences. Drawing on the arguments of certain theologians who support the authority of the conferences and of others who warn against exaggerating that authority, I attribute a limited authority to conference statements, depending on a great number of variables to which I call attention. We have here an example of a complex question that has been obfuscated by polemical writing that slurs over necessary distinctions.

The Catholic church is not a fully self-contained unit. It embraces in some sense not only its own members but all who are mysteriously linked to it by the grace of Christ. In a special way the Catholic church is related to other Christian churches and communities, with which it stands in "imperfect communion." This concept, proposed in Vatican II's Decree on Ecumenism and confirmed by the Final Report of the 1985 Synod, raises the question whether the doctrinal divisions among separated Christians can be overcome through ecumenical dialogue. In the last chapter I summarize, in broad strokes, the results of the dialogues of the past twenty years and speculate on the prospects for further progress. There is no reason, I believe, for complacency, impatience, or discouragement.

The twelve chapters of this book have all been previously

published, but I have reworked them somewhat to fill in gaps, minimize repetitions, and update the references to current literature. As I bring these articles together, I am more convinced than ever that Vatican II has lost none of its actuality in the past quarter of a century. On the contrary, its insights and directives become clearer and more evidently practical when viewed in the perspectives of the postconciliar experience. As Bishop James W. Malone, then president of the National Conference of Catholic Bishops, said in his report for the Extraordinary Session of the Synod of Bishops in 1985: "Disputes about the meaning of Vatican II and even failures in its interpretation and carrying out neither cancel nor outweigh what has been accomplished on many fronts in these two decades. Overall, the council still stands as the best, necessary foundation for Catholic renewal in the closing years of the twentieth century."

The council spoke with a balance and circumspection that are increasingly appreciated with the passage of years. Those who are too eager to fault the council and go beyond its achievements have often fallen short of the council's insights. In this book I take a new look at what the council really said with reference to certain debated questions of our day. Like every historical achievement, Vatican II had its shortcomings. But I am convinced that unless its members allow themselves to be instructed by that council, the church will not be able to find the inner coherence and dynamism needed to deal constructively with the tensions and crises that lie ahead.

I cannot here name all the individuals who have helped to make this book possible, but I wish to mention in a special way the Reverend Patrick Granfield, O.S.B, and the Reverend Walter J. Burghardt, S.J., both of whom read the manuscript and offered helpful suggestions. In addition I thank the Committee for Research of The Catholic University of America, which awarded me a grant for the expenses of typing the manuscript and preparing the index. Pauline Bellesky did the typing and Kevin Forrester compiled the index.

I dedicate this book with special gratitude to my colleagues and students, past and present, at The Catholic University of America, as I complete my fourteenth year of teaching there. The centenary year of the university and its theological faculty provides an auspicious occasion for me to give this sign of my esteem and of my cordial good wishes for the years and the century to come.

December 31, 1987   Avery Dulles, S. J.

1. American Impressions of the Council

The American Catholic Experience Before Vatican II

Since the seventeenth century American Catholics have had many experiences of church, most of which were only faint memories by the end of World War I. With the condemnation of the so-called Americanist heresy by Pope Leo XIII in 1899 and the rejection of modernism by Pius X in 1907, many earlier trends were simply crushed. The large Catholic immigrations from western Europe in the latter half of the nineteenth century and the early years of the twentieth, together with the influx of European priests and religious, brought about, by 1920, an era in American Catholicism that was somewhat discontinuous with the preceding history. In the period between the First and Second World Wars, certain common features became characteristic of the Catholic church in this country. These features correspond to my own experience of Catholicism, when I first came into contact with it in New York and New England during the 1930s. The Catholicism of this period has recently been described in historical works by William Halsey[1] and James Hennesey.[2]

Relying on my own impressions as well as on sources such as these, I characterize the Catholicism of the 1930s somewhat as follows. First, the church in this country was, as I have said, predominantly immigrant and ethnic. Apart from a few areas such as Louisiana and southern Maryland, it did not include, unless by way of exception, the established American families but rather was made up of minorities who vividly remembered the old country from which they hailed.

The Catholic population, having come in many cases to escape persecution or oppression, appreciated their new environment, with the freedom and opportunity it offered. They tended to be patriotic and were proud of their participation in the various wars of their adopted country. But at the same time, they were not fully at home, since they still suffered from prejudice, social discrimination, and economic exploitation. They clustered together defensively in ghettos that were simultaneously religious and ethnic. The large urban ghettos provided avenues to prosperity, power, and success in certain callings. Because of the important position of the pastor, as teacher, guide, and defender of the flock, the clergy enjoyed great power and prestige. This in itself assured an abundance of vocations to the priestly and religious life. In some major cities, such as New York, Boston, and Chicago, Catholics played a prominent role in politics.

Within the relative isolation of their own communities, Catholics were well provided for, partly through the efforts of their church. Summarizing this religious situation, Andrew Greeley has written, "The rigid, often oversimplified, unquestioningly self-confident Catholicism of the first half of the present century was the result of an effort to provide poor and frequently uneducated immigrants with a simple and serviceable response to the trauma of adjusting to an unfriendly—and frequently anti-Catholic—host society."[3]

The American Catholic community of those days was not conspicuous for its intellectual and cultural life. Its cultural features were borrowed for the most part from the Catholic countries of western Europe. With the encouragement of Rome, American Catholics tended to look upon the Middle Ages as the golden age of faith. The title of James J. Walsh's popular book, *The Thirteenth: The Greatest of Centuries* (1907), summarized the prevalent mood. French neo-Thomists such as Jacques Maritain and Etienne Gilson, both of whom lectured frequently at American secular universities, gave respectability to medievalism in philosophy.[4]

In the period between the two world wars Protestant converts flowed steadily into the Catholic church. They were attracted by the cohesiveness and self-confidence of the Catholic community, by its manifest faith, and by the antiquity of its roots. Intellectuals who felt that the modern world had lost its way and that Protestantism had excessively diluted the Christian message turned to Catholicism for a stronger witness. The temper of such converts was reflected in the titles of their books; for example, *Rebuilding a Lost Faith* (1921), by the popular travel lecturer, John L. Stoddard, and *Restoration* (1934), by the history professor Ross Hoffman.

Although politically most Catholics were Democrats and were suspicious of big business they were in no sense radicals. They were nervous about the dangers of socialism and communism, but their Italian, German, and Irish extraction made them sometimes less alert to the dangers of fascism and nazism. Halsey catches this point when he writes, "An outbreak of 'minority-itis,' in [George N.] Shuster's view, gripped Catholics following Al Smith's defeat in 1928, the Mexican Revolution, and Catholic fears of the rising influence of Communism. In the 1930's Catholics were susceptible to the irrational appeals of anti-Semites, pro-Nazis, and Fascists."[5]

Religiously speaking, the church stood for centralized authority, tradition, and discipline. Catholics did not publicly, or even in most cases privately, question the decisions of their popes, bishops, and pastors. For them, the priest stood in the place of Christ. There was a sharp line of demarcation between clergy and laity. The liturgy reflected this distinction of roles. The priest was set off by the communion rail; only his consecrated hands were allowed to touch the sacred vessels as he offered sacrifice for the people in a language understood by himself and God. There was majesty and beauty in this liturgy, almost unchanged since the sixteenth century, and it embodied the spirituality and art forms of the medieval West. The Catholics of this nation showed no disposition to introduce into their religious life the characteristically American themes of democratization, pluralism, experimentation, and progress. To Catholic ears, any suggestion of this kind would have seemed close to blasphemy.

And yet, what I have said does not represent the whole story. A small segment of the American Catholic community was quite at home with the dominant culture of the land, moved easily among the cultured elite, and felt that the church should relate more positively to the American political and intellectual tradition. The layman George N. Shuster, who served as managing editor of *Commonweal* from 1928 to 1936, and many of the contributors to that periodical exemplify this tendency. In the 1940s and 1950s the New York Jesuit John Courtney Murray became the chief exponent of the thesis that there was a natural affinity between the perennial Catholic tradition and the American civil tradition. With some exaggeration he wrote in his most influential book, *We Hold These Truths*, "Catholic participation in the American consensus has been full and free, unreserved and unembarrassed, because the contents of this consensus—the ethical and political principles drawn from the tradition of natural law—approve themselves to the Catholic intelligence and conscience."[6] Pursuing this line of thought, Murray contended that Catholics were closer than other Americans to the original American consensus, for they still professed the principles that had inspired the founders of the republic, while other Americans were drifting away from the natural law tradition. Even the American principle of separation of church and state, according to Murray, was acceptable from the Catholic point of view, for it gave Catholics the freedom to exercise their religious mission without burdening them with a legally privileged status, which had proved an incubus in many European countries.[7] The Catholic church, Murray seemed to be saying, could do much to sustain authentic Americanism, and, conversely, authentic Americanism could make a valuable contribution to world Catholicism.

During the 1950s, the Murray thesis was rejected as all but

heretical by some watchdogs of orthodoxy, especially at The Catholic University of America. Rome itself frowned on Murray's writings and for a time restricted his freedom to publish in his field of specialization. But Murray had a wide and enthusiastic following among younger intellectual Catholics, both clerical and lay. This was so because the ghetto Catholicism was beginning to break down. Already in World War II the majority of young, American, male Catholics were torn out of their ethnic ghettos and thrown into the American melting pot, where they survived quite well. After the war, colleges and graduate schools became for the first time open to Catholics on a large scale, thanks to new programs of government aid. The high mobility of American business and industry in the postwar period affected Catholics as much as other Americans.

Inevitably, the time soon came when Catholics were eligible for the highest positions in government and in the professions. In a dramatic reversal of the defeat of Al Smith, John F. Kennedy was elected to the presidency in 1960, and his election symbolized the emergence of Catholics to full equality with Protestants in the American establishment. Speaking during the summer before the election, Gustave Weigel expressed what many felt:

The world is new. The situation of 1960 is revolutionary. It is quite unlike the world of 1900. Consequently, the relationship of the action of the laity and hierarchy must be seen in the light of the new world. We are living in a revolutionary moment.[8]

It was new, indeed, for the Catholic laity no longer to be dependent on their pastors for education, direction, and patronage. Now that they were fully accepted, they could dismantle their ideological barricades. This new situation, to be sure, gave rise to new problems. Since virtually all walks of life were now open to them, Catholics were less motivated to support specifically Catholic institutions such as schools, hospitals, and charities. These institutions, no longer needed strictly to take care of the Catholic community, had to face questions about their continued reason for existence. There was wide-spread questioning in the church, and the authoritative an-swers of the clergy were no longer automatically accepted.

In these changed circumstances the defensive, reactionary posture ceased to be appropriate. Catholics felt called upon to make a positive contribution to American life, and for this they were, as a group, ill prepared. Thomistic medievalism did not provide ready answers to the majority of present-day Ameri-can problems. For the first time, Catholics began to take a positive interest in modern thought and in the American tra-dition, with the expectation of finding not only errors to refute but lessons to be learned. Some younger Catholics were dis-satisfied with, and even perhaps ashamed of, the conservatism and parochialism of their church.

The weakening confidence in the Catholic tradition and the declining authority of priests and religious made it inevitable that soon there would be a shortage of clerical and religious vocations. Talented young men and women found that other walks of life would offer them wider opportunities for the exercise of their talents. The decline of vocations, however, was not immediate. It was partly offset by the religious boom of the 1950s.

In the 1960s a new generation came to maturity who remem-bered nothing of the ghetto Catholicism of their parents—a generation educated often, at least partly, in secular institu-tions, articulate, financially secure, and bent upon breaking down the last barriers that excluded them from the privileges enjoyed by scions of the first families who had graduated from the name schools of the Northeast. These young Catholics were conscious of themselves as a new breed. Their outlook was expressed by two prolific lay commentators: Michael Novak, who wrote in 1964 a volume entitled *A New Generation: Amer-ican and Catholic*,[9] and Daniel Callahan, who published in 1965 a symposium of autobiographical essays by his contemporaries under the title *The Generation of the Third Eye*.[10] Callahan's title was taken from an article by John Courtney Murray, under whom he had studied at Yale, and who regarded these young Catholic intellectuals as rootless, uncertain, and introspective. As Callahan's book illustrates, this generation was proudly confident of the American experiment, oriented toward experience and pragmatic results; it rebelled against the repressive structures of the church and the authoritarian style of parish life and preaching. It sought spiritual and intellectual nourishment from other fonts. Novak's and Callahan's books were published while Vatican II was in session, but their ideas were on the whole independent of the council. They prove, if proof were needed, that American Catholicism was on the verge of a crisis even before Vatican II began.

Vatican II and the American Agenda

The preconciliar experience of Catholics in the United States was paralleled to some extent in other countries. Since Gregory XVI and Pius IX had set their faces sternly against the liberalism of their day, Roman Catholicism had projected an image of medievalism and reaction. In France and Germany, Belgium and Holland, and to some degree in other countries, increasing numbers of intellectuals felt that the church was paying too heavy a price for continuity with its own past. Having in effect opted out of modern culture, it was in danger of becoming intellectually, culturally, and institutionally obsolete. When Pope John XXIII called for a more positive attitude toward the modern world, the advocates of modernization, who had been under a shadow under Pius XII, began to appear as leaders. At the Second Vatican Council, the bishops of Northern Europe, with their avant-garde theologians, arrayed themselves against what they had experienced as Roman repression and reaction.

The council proved to be a difficult struggle between the forces of the right and the left, between conservatism and progressivism. Reacting against the centralism and authoritarianism of Pius XII, many of the bishops pressed for more freedom and autonomy. For a variety of reasons, the hierarchies of the Third World tended to side with the European liberals. After some initial hesitation, the American bishops gravitated toward the progressive majority, at least if their speeches and voting are a reliable index of their thinking.

A surprising thing therefore happened. The very theologians who had been under suspicion as dangerous liberals came into favor and influence. In the United States this meant that advocates of Americanization, such as John Courtney Murray and Gustave Weigel, were allied with the hierarchy against Romanizing theologians such as J. C. Fenton and Francis J. Connell. Thanks to the council, the concerns of the Americanizers became in some measure official Catholic teaching. Michael Novak went so far as to write in 1965, "The Council has made the underground official."[11]

It will not be possible here to examine this development in detail. Some summary impressions must suffice. A prime instance, of course, is the Declaration on Religious Freedom, *Dignitatis humanae*, which was, more than any other document, the special American contribution to the council. This document formally abandoned the earlier Roman position that the secular state is in principle bound to profess the Catholic faith, and it admitted the concept of a religiously neutral state. Thus it accepted, in effect, the American principle of separation of church and state. The declaration also asserted that people must be free to inquire about matters of religion, that no one's conscience should be forced in matters of faith, and that in human society "freedom should be respected as far as possible, and curtailed only when and insofar as necessary" (*DH* 7).

A second theme of special interest on this side of the Atlantic was the democratization of the church, which had previously been perceived as a society sharply divided into rulers

---

*Full titles of works cited and their abbreviations may be found at the end of the text, on pp 246–247.

and ruled, teachers and taught. Vatican II brought about a wider distribution of power by giving all bishops a share in the supreme government of the church rather than allowing them to be perceived as mere deputies of the pope. The council sought also to upgrade the status of the laity by authorizing pastoral councils on which the laity would have representation. In its revision of the liturgy, a key principle was to increase the active participation of the laity, so that not even the sacrifice of the Mass could any longer be considered the action of the priest alone. David J. O'Brien, commenting on these developments, has said, "The stress on common Christian vocation exalted the dignity of the laity, asserted its responsibility for ecclesiastical decisions, and left the priest's role uncertain."[12]

In the United States, there was great concern for improving the relations between Catholics and other Christians. Here again the council offered help. In its Decree on Ecumenism, it emphasized the possibility for a person to be a Christian without entering the Catholic church, and, furthermore, it asserted that non–Roman Catholic communities, as communities, have an ecclesial status and a real salvific value for their own members.

Although American Catholics were not greatly concerned about relations with most of the other world religions, relations with the Jews were of great concern in some parts of the United States. In this matter the council followed, on the whole, the guidance of the liberals. It firmly asserted that the Jewish people ought not to be held collectively responsible for the death of Jesus.

A major grievance of the liberals had been what they viewed as the monolithic centralization of the church from Vatican I through the pontificate of Pius XII. On this point, too, the council seemed to offer relief. In its Constitution on the Church, *Lumen gentium*, and its Decree on Ecumenism, *Unitatis redintegratio*, Vatican II stressed the value of having different customs and observances in different countries, suited to the variety of natural gifts and conditions of life (*LG* 13; *UR* 14 and 16). In its Pastoral Constitution on the Church in the Modern World, *Gaudium et spes* the council stated that each nation should develop the ability to express Christ's message in its own way, and that a living exchange should be fostered between the church and the diverse cultures of peoples (*GS* 44; cf. 58). These principles were consonant with what Michael Novak was proposing when he wrote, "American Catholicism is becoming, and ought to become, different from any other form of Catholicism in history, because it is *American.*"[13]

In its teaching on the church-world relationship, the council seemed to give official endorsement to the secularization that had been experienced in the previous decade by American Catholics. In many texts of Vatican II, the church was depicted as a servant in the transformation of human society in the pattern of the kingdom of God. Mission was presented not simply as an effort to recruit new members but rather as the church's commitment to the work of the kingdom and thus as including the restructuring of human society according to the gospel.

Another major problem for liberal Catholics in the United States was that of reconciling the church's concern for continuity and tradition with the characteristically American desire for change and progress. In his references to the coming council, Pope John XXIII frequently spoke of *aggiornamento*, that is to say, "the adjustment of Christian discipline to the exigencies of modern day living."[14] In his opening allocution at Vatican II, Pope John stressed the importance of understanding the gospel message with modern tools of research and through what he called "the literary forms of modern thought." Following up on these directives, the Pastoral Constitution invited theologians to seek continually for more suitable ways of communicating doctrine to their contemporaries (*GS* 62). It also reminded all members of the People of God of their responsibility to take part in discerning the signs of the times and in assessing the many voices of our age in the light of the gospel (*GS* 4 and 11). Statements such as these seemed to allow for a dynamic and progressive understanding of the church's teaching, accommodated to the American spirit of exploration and change.

American Reactions to Vatican II

Because of features such as these, liberal Catholics in the United States and elsewhere interpreted Vatican II as a victory for their own cause—one that had seemed all but lost only a few years before. The four years of the council (1962–1965) were accompanied by a growing euphoria. Some American liberal Catholics spoke almost as though the parousia had arrived. But the council had hardly ended when difficulties began to appear. Some of the bishops, on their return from Rome, seemed unaware of what they had done and reluctant to implement what were being heralded by others as the conciliar reforms. Rome itself, while claiming to carry out the council, seemed to back away from the clear import of its decrees. The papal congregations reasserted some of their preconciliar powers and interpreted the documents of Vatican II, with the encouragement of the pope, in ways that the liberals viewed as restrictive. Pope Paul's own encyclical *Humanae vitae,* prohibiting artificial contraception, was symptomatic of a shift toward greater continuity with the preconciliar tradition.

Several reasons may be assigned for this official caution. For one, many adult Catholics, at least in the United States, were content with the church as they had known it before the council. The supposed conciliar reforms threatened to deprive them of what had sustained their religious life and devotion since childhood. The liturgical changes had a particularly painful impact. Many American Catholics had been deeply devoted to the quiet low Masses of early weekday mornings and to solemn Gregorian liturgies on Sundays and feast days. They were attracted to Benediction, Adoration of the Blessed Sacrament, private confession, the cult of the saints, and popular novenas. When all these treasures were suddenly swept away in favor of folksy guitar Masses, they felt cheated, bewildered, and distressed. Ecumenism and modernization, they protested, should not be allowed to destroy their beloved Catholic tradition. Understandably, church authorities were reluctant to upset their most faithful constituents any more than seemed inevitable.

Furthermore, the council documents themselves did not represent a clear victory of the liberal side. In every decree of Vatican II the conservatives had succeeded in safeguarding their own special concerns. For example, the Declaration on Religious Freedom deliberately "leaves untouched traditional Catholic doctrine on the moral duty of men and societies toward the true religion and toward the one Church of Christ" (DH 1). The Constitution on the Church, while encouraging the participation of the laity, kept all real power in the hands of the clergy. It reaffirmed the prerogatives of the pope as defined by Vatican I—including papal infallibility—and gave the bishops practically unlimited power over all who were not bishops.

The Decree on Ecumenism, while expressing polite esteem for non-Roman churches, made no dogmatic concessions. It insisted that the Roman Catholic church alone contained all the institutional features made necessary by Christ and that it remained in that sense the only valid realization of the one Church of Christ. The Declaration on Non-Christian Religions carefully refrained from recognizing that nonbiblical faiths were based on divine revelation. Nor did it unequivocally absolve the Jews of Jesus' time from the crime of deicide.

The Constitution on Revelation insisted that public revelation had become complete in apostolic times and that the magisterium of the Roman Catholic church alone was competent to interpret that revelation authentically. All the council's words about the signs of the times and the sense of the faithful had to be understood in terms of this position.

Confronted by these facts, the liberal interpreters of the council came to admit the presence of strongly hierarchical and conservative statements in the decrees of Vatican II. George Lindbeck, for example, addressed this problem in the introduction to his *The Future of Roman Catholic Theology*.[15] After acknowledging the existence of compromises and deliberate ambiguities in the council documents, he proposed as the proper hermeneutical procedure that the new theological emphases be regarded as the most significant and that the old be understood in terms of the new, rather than vice versa. In this way he found it possible to subordinate many certain traditional teachings of Vatican II as incidental concessions to the conservative minority rather than central or emphatic affirmations. Yet it was possible for other interpreters to argue, with equal plausibility, that in reaffirming the constant teaching of the church throughout the centuries, the council was at least as authoritative as in opening up new directions for the present day. Even the innovations of Vatican II were for the most part retrievals of an earlier heritage.

As the liberal interpretation of the council was increasingly challenged, a number of progressives began to insist that the church should move beyond the hesitant and ambiguous teaching of Vatican II. Inspired by the American dream, some radical Catholics developed specific programs, the general tenor of which can be summarized, without quoting chapter and verse, somewhat as follows.

In the name of religious liberty, all Catholics were considered free to select whatever dogmas they found meaningful and credible, without blind submission to external authority. In the name of democratic equality, the residual hierarchical elements in the church were judged unacceptable. In place of a governing class perpetuating itself by cooption, the church, it was asserted, should have freely elected representative leaders, accountable to the whole People of God.

In ecumenism, it was alleged, the council had stopped halfway. A truly generous and open spirit, according to the radicals, required full recognition of the ministries and sacraments of every Christian group, open communion, and the abandonment of any claim of special status on the part of the Roman Catholic church. Similarly, according to this faction, non-Christian religions should be recognized as being on a par with Catholic Christianity, so that nobody should be urged to convert from one religion to another.

Pluralism in the church, as seen by the radicals, required a major revision of the idea of papal supremacy. In place of a primacy of jurisdiction and personal infallibility, the radical progressives advocated, through drastic reinterpretation of the conciliar decrees, what amounted to a mere primacy of honor. The pope was sometimes depicted as the chief executive officer of the college of bishops.

Vatican II, these reformers held, had done well to broach the theme of the servant church, but consistency, they added, would require that such a church surrender all claims to superiority over the world it served. It should humbly take its place as an equal alongside secular humanitarian agencies working for the betterment of the world.

Finally, in its attitude to change, the council was accused of stopping short. Authentic modernization would demand that Christians listen to what God is saying today and not simply repeat what God was believed to have said in the remote past. Talk of irreformable teaching and immutable dogmas, according to these progressives, was anachronistic in a world of rapid flux.

This program, which I have called radical, perhaps never has been explicitly formulated. It has existed more as a tendency than as a platform. But in the American atmosphere it would have been almost impossible for such a program not to exist. The American experiment, as currently understood, rested on implied dogmas such as self-determination, nondiscrimination, unlimited self-correction, equal opportunity for all, free election and public accountability of officeholders. Applied to the church, these democratic dogmas involved the kind of program I have just sketched.

This radical revisionism was more vigorous in the late sixties, I would estimate, than it is today. It depended on two assumptions: first, that the American experiment had permanent and universal validity; and second, that Catholic Christianity could absorb this kind of change. Today, I suspect, many Americans are less confident of the democratic dogmas, because our national history has been, in recent years, a troubled one. Furthermore the Catholic church has shown unexpected resistance to this kind of radical reform. In some cases the reformers themselves, primarily intent upon social progress, lost interest in the church and channeled their energies into secular causes, retaining only tenuous links with the Catholicism they had sought to revamp.

This thorough revisionism cannot claim to be warranted by the letter of Vatican II. In fact, it can be shown to run directly counter to the council's teaching on each of the issues in question. The council, while advocating freedom, emphasized the imperative to seek and adhere to the fullness of revealed truth and thus to the total heritage of Catholic Christianity. Vatican II, moreover, adopted a strongly hierarchical view of priestly ministry, with the bishops as supreme judges in matters of doctrine. It reiterated the teaching of Vatican I on the primacy and infallibility of the pope. It insisted on the unique status of the Catholic church as the sole possessor of all the institutional features made necessary by Christ. The council was therefore reserved in its teaching on mutual recognition and on intercommunion between the Catholic church and other Christian bodies. In opposition to a purely secular understanding of the gospel, Vatican II repeatedly stressed the importance of evangelization and conversion. All these emphases were contrary to the postconciliar radical agenda.

Do these and other "conservative" teachings of Vatican II run counter to the American experience? It must be admitted that Catholic Christianity as interpreted by this or any other council has attributes markedly different from what Americans find congenial in their secular life. Whoever is convinced that the American political tradition of freedom, democracy, and reformability provide adequate norms for the church will in time encounter serious difficulties in being a committed Catholic.

Catholic Christianity cannot be governed from below by majority votes; it cannot allow its dogmas to be obliterated or reversed; it cannot absolve the faithful from their obligation to revere tradition and authority.

By acknowledging that values such as personal freedom, equality, and fraternity have a certain applicability in the church, Vatican II made it easier for native-born Americans to feel at home with their Catholicism. If Vatican II had not shown a certain compatibility between the concerns of the American liberal tradition and those of perennial Christianity, there would have probably been more alienation and defection among American Catholics than in fact occurred in the late sixties and early seventies. But it is important, also, not to give the impression that the church can be totally recast in the image of the American liberal society. There comes a point at which the church must say that it is different from any secular society. Unlike any social, political, or academic institution, it is committed to the faithful transmission of a patrimony that comes from God by way of revelation.

The American experience of church, therefore, should not be simplistically patterned on the American political experience. Political experience of any kind cannot be made into a norm for judging the gospel. The gospel must be allowed to generate in the church the special structures needed for the faithful transmission of the apostolic faith. A measure of conservatism is inseparable from authentic Christianity. Precisely in order to be a force for progress, the church must adhere to the gospel originally given in Jesus Christ.

Conclusion

During the 1930s the United States passed through a period of doubt and disillusionment. The ideals upon which the nation had been founded seemed to be crumbling. Immigrant Catholics, who had found in this continent a place of freedom and opportunity, became the chief heirs of what William Halsey calls American innocence. Appealing to the order and rationality of the Thomistic synthesis, they helped to shore up the structures of the American heritage. During World War II and the ensuing cold war, Catholics became full partners in the shaping of American culture and public policy. From their national experience they were able to make a positive contribution to world Catholicism, as attested by the performance of the American bishops at Vatican II.

Since that time Catholics, together with other Americans, have experienced new trials and disappointments. The Vietnam War, the student revolts, the race riots, and the brutal assassinations of the late sixties, followed by Watergate, the Iranian revolution, the arms race, worldwide economic depression, and the chaos in Central America and Lebanon, have sorely tested our national principles and goals. In the present crisis, Catholics are no longer naively self-confident. They have experienced bitter criticism and division within their own church. The aggressive, triumphal Catholicism of the post-Reformation period, severely censured at Vatican II, has continued to decay. Chastened by the experience of their own fragility, Catholics are groping for a new identity.

Can American Catholics, then, find in their own tradition the resources demanded of them by the present situation? Vatican II, I suggest, may provide grounds for an affirmative response. In the judgment of one priest-theologian, Robert Imbelli, the major theological achievement of the council is to have recovered an ancient, dynamic idea of tradition and thereby made it possible for the church to restructure itself in a manner that is both faithful to the past and adequate to the present.[16] Drawing on the "depth grammar" of this foundational reality, Imbelli is able to describe Catholicism in terms of its unique sacramental consciousness—bodily, communal, and historical. Other contemporary theologians have made similar assessments of Catholic roots.[17]

As this book proceeds we shall explore certain resources of Catholicism and of the Catholic tradition. We shall see how, thanks in great part to Vatican II, the church can take on new aspects suited to new times and cultures without loss of its true identity. We shall reflect on the possibility that it may foster authentic freedom, progress, and personal commitment, in harmony with our national heritage, without loss of authority, continuity, and solidarity. Catholicism, I shall contend, can bring important correctives to certain less desirable features of our contemporary culture while at the same time profiting from what is best in that culture. In place of religious privatism and aggressive sectarianism it can help to forge "a religiously informed public philosophy for the American experiment in ordered liberty."[18] Confronted by kaleidoscopic change and escalating demands from special interest groups, our society stands in need of the Catholic vision of the lasting, universal good. Catholicism can bring depth and integrity to human understanding and communication. By upholding a qualitatively diversified universe of symbol, sacrament, and mystery, it can combat the superficial reductionism of a purely quantified perspective. All this Catholics must do with genuine respect for other religious traditions with the hope of establishing a broad ecumenical consensus. These and similar themes will be touched on in the chapters to come.

If Catholicism, drawing on the potential of its own heritage, can do for America in our time something like what John Courtney Murray envisaged at midcentury, the church will remain healthy and vigorous. Exerting a sound influence on American religious life, it can likewise contribute to the church universal, as it did at Vatican II. We may even stand on the verge of what some have called "the Catholic moment."[19] In order to assess the present prospects we shall do well to review, in summary fashion, the horizons opened up by Vatican II.

2. The Basic Teaching of Vatican II

The Conflict of Interpretations

For reasons that have been to some degree indicated in the first chapter, Vatican II has become, for many Catholics, a center of controversy. Some voices from the extreme right and the extreme left frankly reject the council. Reactionaries of the traditionalist variety censure it for having yielded to Protestant and modernist tendencies. Radicals of the far left, conversely, complain that the council, while making some progress, failed to do away with the church's absolutistic claims and its anti-quated class structures. The vast majority of Catholics, ex-pressing satisfaction with the results of the council, are still divided because they interpret it in contrary ways. The conser-vatives, insisting on continuity with the past, give primary emphasis to the council's reaffirmation of settled Catholic doc-trines, including papal primacy and infallibility. The progres-sives, however, hold that the true meaning of the council is to be found rather in its innovations. For them Vatican II made a decisive break with the juridicism, clericalism, and triumphal-ism of recent centuries and laid the foundations for a more liberal and healthier Catholicism.

Like most other councils, Vatican II issued a number of com-promise statements. It intentionally spoke ambiguously on cer-tain points, leaving to the future the achievement of greater clarity. Many commentators, accenting these problematic fea-tures, give the impression that the council left nothing but doubt and confusion in its wake. It may therefore be time to acknowledge that, while leaving many open questions, the council did present a solid core of unequivocal teaching on matters of great importance.

Vatican II addressed an extraordinary variety of issues ranging from highly technical questions about the theology of revelation to eminently practical questions about marriage and family life. But its central focus was undoubtedly the self-understanding of the church, and this is the theme highlighted by the Extraordinary Synod of 1985. Before analyzing the results of the Synod in a later chapter, I shall here set forth, with a minimum of personal interpretation, the basic vision of the church as understood by Vatican II. I shall concentrate on practical and pastoral matters that have a direct impact on the lives of rank-and-file Catholics. For the sake of clarity I shall arrange my observations under the rubric of ten principles that I regard as unquestionably endorsed by the council. Whoever does not accept all ten of these principles, I contend, cannot honestly claim to have accepted the results of Vatican II.

Ten Basic Principles

Aggiornamento

This Italian term, which may be translated by English words such as *updating, modernization,* or *adaptation,* was popularized by Pope John XXIII, who made the concept fundamental to his own program for the coming council. Accepting this program, the fathers at Vatican II were critical of the hostility and suspicion toward the modern world that had characterized the Catholicism of the nineteenth and early twentieth centuries. Especially in the Pastoral Constitution on the Church in the Modern World, the council declared its great respect for the truth and goodness that had been brought into the world through modernization (*GS* 42). It stated that we are witnesses to the birth of a new humanism in which people are conscious of their responsibility to one another for the future of the world (*GS* 55). The faithful, said the council, must "live in close union with their contemporaries" (*GS* 62). Catholics must, moreover, "blend modern science and its theories and the understanding of the most recent discoveries with Christian morality and doctrine" (ibid.), so that the church may keep pace with the times and enter fully into the new age now being born. In so doing the church can enrich itself and better understand the treasures it has received from Christ. Far from clinging to ancient forms, the church as pilgrim must press forward toward the consummation of history, when God's kingdom will be revealed in its fullness. Neither Pope John nor the council, of course, held the absurd dogma that the new is always better than the old. In fact, they frequently pointed out that modern techniques can easily be abused so as to distract people from the lasting goods of the spirit. But that is no excuse for burying oneself in the past.

The principle of *aggiornamento*, like all the others we shall consider, is only a principle. To apply it requires prudence and discretion lest the gospel, in being accommodated to the spirit of the age, lose its challenging power. Still, the principle itself is sound and important. The church, glorying in its magnificent heritage, should not allow itself to become a museum piece. It must not become a relic of the Middle Ages or any past period but rather a vital part of the modern world as it presses forward into God's future. Confident that the Lord himself remains with his people down through the centuries, Christians can have the courage to live out the gospel and bear witness to it under the conditions of today's world.

The Reformability of the Church

In recent centuries it has been common to look upon the church as a divine institution without spot or wrinkle. Although Catholics have sometimes admitted the faults of individual believers, they have regarded the church itself as pure and holy. Vatican II, however, depicted the church in terms of the biblical image of the People of God. As we learn from Scripture, this people, though always sealed by its covenant relationship with God, was sometimes unfaithful. The Constitution on the Church, therefore, was able to admit, "The Church, holding sinners in its embrace, is at the same time holy and always in need of being purified and incessantly pursues the path of penance and renewal" (*LG* 8). Furthermore, in the Decree on Ecumenism, the council declared, "Christ summons the Church, as it goes its pilgrim way, to that continual reformation of which it always has need, insofar as it is a human institution here on earth" (*UR* 6).

The idea that the church might be reformable caught many Catholics by surprise. In the late Middle Ages several councils had as their express aim the reformation of the whole church "in the head and in the members," but after the Protestant Reformation the idea of reform came under suspicion in Catholic circles. Thanks to Vatican II, however, we are relieved of the burden of having to defend the whole record of the past. We can freely admit that not only individual Catholics, but the church itself in its official actions has committed errors and sins, such as the burning of heretics, the persecutions of Jews, and the excesses of Holy Wars. We can admit that Catholics had a large share of responsibility in bringing on the divisions among Christians that so weaken the Christian witness in our time.

Like the principle of updating, this second principle must be applied with discretion. Not everything in the church is suspect and fallible. The basic sacramental structures, its Scriptures, and its dogmas are abidingly valid. The grace of Christ, which comes through these channels, is more powerful than human infidelity and sin. The church, therefore, does not have an equal affinity to holiness and to evil. Evil is against its true nature. For this reason Vatican II, while speaking of the church of sinners, avoided the expression "sinful church." The difference is a subtle one but has a certain importance.

With regard to past historical events, we should be on guard against a kind of spiritual masochism that would transfer all the blame from the other party to our own. Often it is best to follow the principle of Pope John XXIII:

We do not wish to conduct a trial of the past. We shall not seek to establish who was right and who was wrong. Responsibility is divided.[1]

Still, to set the record straight, it is well to disavow certain errors. An example might be the present investigation to determine whether the papal commission erred by condemning the theories of Galileo in the seventeenth century.

Renewed Attention to the Word of God

In the Middle Ages, and even more since the Reformation, Catholicism tended to become the church of law and sacraments rather than the church of the gospel and the word. Catholics too often neglected the spiritual riches contained in the Bible. Emphasizing the precepts of the church, they allowed the proclamation of the good news to fall into some neglect. They celebrated the Mass in Latin—a language not understood by most of the people—and usually without any homily. In Catholic theology the Bible was viewed as a remote source of doctrine, hardly used except to find proof texts for later church doctrines.

Vatican II, especially in its Constitution on Divine Revelation, *Dei Verbum*, recovered the primacy of Scripture as the word of God consigned to writing under the inspiration of the Holy Spirit (*DV* 9). The teaching office of the church, according to the Constitution, "is not above the word of God but serves it, listening to it devoutly, guarding it scrupulously, and explaining it faithfully . . . " (*DV* 10). "The study of the sacred page," according to the same Constitution, "is, so to speak, the soul of sacred theology" (*DV* 24).

The Constitution on Revelation strongly recommended the use of Scripture by all Catholics. "Easy access to sacred Scripture," it stated, "should be provided for all the Christian faithful" (*DV* 22). The Scriptures were here compared to the Eucharist, since each in its own way offers to the faithful the bread of life (*DV* 21). And in the same paragraph we find the following eloquent sentence: "For in the sacred books, the

Father who is in heaven meets His children with great love and speaks with them; and the force and power of the word of God is so great that it remains the support and energy of the Church, the strength of faith for her children, the food of the soul, and a pure and perennial source of spiritual life."

Besides rehabilitating the Bible, the council sought to renew the ministry of preaching. It called on Catholic preachers to provide the nourishment of the Scriptures to the People of God (*DV* 23) and warned that, as Augustine had said, "those who do not listen to the word of God inwardly will be empty preachers of the word of God outwardly" (*DV* 25). Thus priests as well as lay people were exhorted to read the Scriptures prayerfully.

Since the council, such directives have produced excellent fruits. Catholics have learned more about the Bible; many of them attend study and prayer groups that concentrate on the Scriptures. But in this respect, as in others, further progress remains necessary. There is as yet no danger that Catholics, in their enthusiasm for the word, will forsake ritual and sacrament or that, in their devotion to the gospel, they will neglect the law of Christ and the church. The more relaxed attitude toward church law at the present time, while regrettable in some respects, can be viewed as a gain insofar as it helps to overcome an almost pharisaical scrupulosity to which Catholics were subject in the years before Vatican II. Ideally, of course, contrasting elements such as law and gospel, word and sacrament, should not be played off against each other but should rather be mutually reinforcing. The effort to achieve the right balance should be high on the agenda of Catholics today.

Collegiality

It is almost a platitude to assert that the Catholic church from the Middle Ages until Vatican II was pyramidal in structure. Truth and holiness were conceived as emanating from the pope as commander-in-chief at the top, and the bishops were depicted as subordinate officers carrying out the orders of the pope. In our own day many conservative Catholics lean toward this military analogy of the church.

Vatican II did not deny the primacy of the pope as it had been defined a century earlier by Vatican I, but it did put the papacy into a significantly new context. The college of bishops, together with the pope as its head, was seen as having the fullness of power in the church. The individual bishops were portrayed not as mere lieutenants of the pope but as pastors in their own right. They were in fact called "vicars of Christ" (*LG* 28)—an ancient title that had been given to bishops in the ancient church but that, since about the eighth century, had come to be reserved for the pope.

The principle of collegiality runs through the documents of Vatican II like a golden thread. Just as the pope is surrounded by a college of bishops, so each bishop serves as head of a presbyteral college, called presbytery, and governs his diocese in consultation with presbyters, religious, and laity. Thus the principle of collegiality, understood in a wide sense, may be viewed as pervading all levels of the church. Pastors, according to the Constitution on the Church, "know that they themselves were not meant by Christ to shoulder alone the entire saving mission of the Church toward the world. On the contrary, they understand that it is their noble duty so to shepherd the faithful and recognize their services and charismatic gifts that all according to their proper roles may cooperate in this common undertaking with one heart" (*LG* 30).

Since the council many new institutions have been erected to implement collegiality on various levels; for example, the worldwide synod of bishops, national and regional episcopal conferences, national and diocesan pastoral councils, parish councils, priests' senates, and the like. If in some cases too many questions have been subjected to prolonged discussion and debate, it has been necessary to go through this stage to arrive at the proper mean. Parliamentarianism or democracy, if carried too far, is likely to provoke a reaction in the opposite direction, toward a revival of the preconciliar form of authoritarianism, which seemed relatively efficient and rapid. Here the council still calls upon us to devise mechanisms of decision making that respect both the traditional principle of pastoral authority and the nature of the church as a Spirit-filled community. Neither an army nor a New England town meeting is a suitable paradigm.

Religious Freedom

Up to the very time when the council opened, it was far from certain whether the Catholic church could subscribe to the principle of religious freedom that had by then prevailed in most Protestant bodies and won approval in the Assembly of the World Council of Churches at New Delhi in 1961. More specifically, it was being asked whether the church could respect the right and duty of each person to follow his or her conscience with regard to the acceptance or nonacceptance of religious belief. For centuries the Christian churches, Protestant as well as Catholic, had striven to gain control of the apparatus of civil power so as to obtain a privileged status. In the 1950s, when John Courtney Murray began to defend the idea of a religiously neutral state, his orthodoxy was questioned by other American theologians and even by some Roman authorities. Over the protests of his opponents, however, he was invited to Vatican II (not indeed to the first session but from the second session on) and he, as much as any individual, was responsible for the Declaration on Religious Freedom. This Declaration clearly taught that there is no need for the state to profess the true religion or give it a legally privileged status. It approved of civil tolerance for all faiths and rejected, on theological grounds, any coercion in the sphere of belief.

For most Americans the principle of religious freedom offers no difficulties. We almost take it for granted. Our tendency is rather to fall into the opposite extreme, religious indifferentism. We have to remind ourselves that the Declaration itself asserted the unique status of the Catholic faith and the obligation of all believers to profess and defend that faith. Those who sincerely believe and love the truth received from Christ will strive, as did Christ and the apostles, to bear witness to it by their words and deeds and to share their faith with others.

The Active Role of the Laity

In the Catholic church, at least in modern times, priests and religious have borne almost total responsibility for the mission of the church. The apostolic spirit of the clergy and religious orders has been admirable but, generally speaking, the laity have been rather passive. Seeking to remedy this situation, the movement known as Catholic Action, in the period between the two world wars, sought to involve elite members of the laity in the apostolate of the hierarchy. Not satisfied with this, some progressive theologians during the decade before Vatican II held that the laity, besides associating themselves with the apostolate of the hierarchy, should exercise an active apostolate in their own right as baptized believers. The council, endorsing this development, exhorted lay persons to advance the kingdom of God by engaging in temporal affairs and by discharging their familial and vocational obligations in a manner faithful to Christ.

Since the council some have maintained that the clergy have as their proper sphere of operation the inner affairs of the church, whereas lay persons should regard secular matters as their area of competence. The council, however, does not authorize such a sharp division of labor. The Decree on the Apostolate of the Laity, *Apostolicam actuositatem*, exhorts lay persons "to exercise their apostolate both in the Church and in the world, in both the spiritual and the temporal orders" (*AA* 5). In other documents the council provides for active participation of the laity in divine worship, in pastoral councils, and in the sphere of theology. In this last area Vatican II calls upon the laity to speak freely and openly. "In order that such persons may fulfill their proper function," says the Pastoral Constitution, "let it be recognized that all the faithful, clerical and lay, possess a lawful freedom of inquiry and of thought, and the freedom to express their minds humbly and courageously about those matters in which they enjoy competence" (GS 62).

Since the council we have seen in the church a great increase of lay ministries, not only the canonically erected ministries of reader and acolyte, but also ministries of teaching, music, social action, counseling, and even the distribution of Holy Communion. There has been a great and welcome influx of laymen and laywomen into theology. These new developments, predictably, have raised difficult questions about the specific role of clergy and religious and the responsibilities and powers of the laity. Even if progress in these areas at times has been slow, we may be thankful that much has been accomplished in a relatively short time. In a period of diminishing vocations to the clerical and religious life it is urgent that lay persons assume greater responsibility than ever for the faith and life of the church.

Regional and Local Variety

From the late Middle Ages until Vatican II the characteristic emphasis of Catholicism had been on the universal church, commonly depicted as an almost monolithic society. Vatican II, by contrast, emphasized the local churches, each of them under direction of a bishop who is called a "vicar of Christ." Many of the council texts portray the universal church as a communion, or collegial union, of particular churches. "In and from such individual churches," says the Constitution on the Church, "the one and only Catholic Church takes its rise" (LG 23). The local bishop, on the ground of his ordination and appointment, is given authority to be a true pastor of his own community, making responsible decisions rather than simply carrying out Roman directives.

Vatican II made provision also for regional groupings. Speaking of the differences between Eastern and Western Christianity, the council said, "Far from being an obstacle to the Church's unity, such diversity of customs and observances only adds to its splendor and contributes greatly to carrying out its mission" (*UR* 16). Vatican II accordingly recognized a legitimate variety among regional churches, even in the formulation of doctrine. Elsewhere it declared, "The variety of local churches with one common aspiration is particularly splendid evidence of the catholicity of the undivided Church" (*LG* 23). "The accommodated preaching of the revealed word," says the Pastoral Constitution, "ought to remain the law of all evangelization" (*GS* 44). Each nation, we are told, must develop the ability to express Christ's message in its own way and must foster a living exchange between the church and the various human cultures (ibid.).

The differences between the Catholicism of different regions are much more evident today than twenty years ago, when the customs and liturgy of the Roman church, with its Latin language, were universally enforced. This diversification has not yet run its course. John Paul II, addressing the Zairean hierarchy in May of 1980, spoke in favor of Africanization.[2]

Americanization has been and is taking place in our own Catholicism. Because of our distinctive cultural and political tradition, we must expect certain distinctive ways of thinking and acting in the church. We have different views than Europeans on how the church ought to relate to politics and economics. We have different views regarding human rights and due process growing out of our common law tradition. Probably too, we are more prepared than many other countries to see women rise to positions of leadership in the church, as they have in political and economic life.

While seeking a sound inculturation, we must avoid thinking that our own national traditions are above criticism or that Americans are a superior people who have nothing to learn from other nationalities. Even where legitimate differences exist, we must take care that they do not disrupt our communion with the rest of the Catholic church. In this regard we should respect the authority of the Holy See, which has the responsibility before God both to "protect legitimate differences" and to make sure that "such differences do not hinder unity but rather contribute to it" (*LG* 13).

Ecumenism

Since the Reformation, Catholics have commonly adopted hostile and defensive attitudes toward other Christian churches and especially toward Protestantism. Such hostility has left traces in official documents of the Holy See, notably between Pius IX and Pius XI. In this regard Pope John XXIII and Vatican II effected a quiet revolution. The council in its Decree on Ecumenism expressed reverence for the heritage of other Christian churches, called attention to their salvific importance for their own members, and acknowledged that they possess true elements of the Church of Christ. As a result, anathema has yielded to dialogue. In the ecumenical dialogues since the council, great progress has been achieved in overcoming major differences that have divided the churches for centuries. While formal reunion between the Catholic church and other communions remains only a distant prospect, Christians of different confessional groups have achieved a far greater measure of mutual understanding, respect, and solidarity.

The proper implementation of ecumenism, as of the other principles we are here considering, requires realism and good judgment. On the one hand, we must overcome our habitual attitudes of hatred and suspicion and be open to appreciate all the sound values in other forms of Christianity, both Eastern and Western. On the other hand, we cannot act as though all the ecumenical problems had already been solved. Instead of simply wishing away the remaining disagreements, we must work patiently over a long period to achieve, through prayer and dialogue, a consensus based on truth.

Dialogue with Other Religions

Vatican II was not slow in perceiving that the changed attitude of Catholics toward other Christian churches called for a corresponding shift in their attitude toward the other religions and their adherents. The council accordingly drew up a Declaration on Non-Christian Religions, which contained a major section on Jewish-Christian relationships. Since the council important dialogues have taken place between Catholics and Jews, both in this country and abroad.

The principle of interreligious dialogue, like the other principles, challenges us to develop mature and responsible attitudes. Some commentators have introduced an antithesis between mission and dialogue, as if the importance of the one must undercut that of the other. The council, however, kept mission and dialogue in dynamic tension. While recognizing in its Declaration on Non-Christian Religions, *Nostra aetate*, elements of truth and goodness in all the great religions, and hence the desirability of respectful dialogue (*NA* 2), the council in its Decree on Missionary Activity, *Ad gentes*, insisted on the God-given uniqueness of the Church of Christ and consequently on the abiding necessity of missionary labor so that Christ may be acknowledged among all peoples as universal Lord and Savior (*AG* 6–7).

For Americans the most obvious application of the Declaration on Non-Christian Religions has to do with Judaism. In parts of the country many Catholics still hold a latent attitude of hostility, deeply rooted in ethnic and cultural factors. We need to make a special effort to rise above these negative attitudes, which are utterly contrary to the gospel precept of love. As mentioned above, the church collectively has much to repent of in its historic dealings with the Jewish people. Let us not add to these crimes.

The Social Mission of the Church

Since the Reformation the Catholic church has tended to regard its mission as an exclusively religious one, aimed at preparing individuals through faith, worship, and right behavior to attain eternal life. Gradually, with the social encyclicals of popes such as Leo XIII and Pius XI, the church began to assume responsibility to teach the principles of a just social order, but this order was viewed in terms of conformity to the natural law rather than as an implementation of the gospel.

With John XXIII and Vatican II, the emphasis shifted. The apostolate of peace and social justice came to be seen as a requirement of the church's mission to carry on the work of Christ, who had compassion on the poor and the oppressed. This changed attitude was eloquently expressed in Vatican II's Message to Humanity, released nine days after the opening of the council in 1962. It was more fully elaborated in the Pastoral Constitution on the Church in the Modern World, which described the church as endowed with "a function, a light, and an energy that can serve to structure and consolidate the human community" (GS 42). Since the council this trend has gained momentum. It was reflected in the encyclical of Paul VI, *Populorum progressio* (1967), and even more clearly in the synod document, *Justice in the World* (1971), which depicted the struggle for justice and the transformation of society as constitutive dimensions of evangelization. Seeking to carry out the council's mandate to discern the signs of the times in the light of the gospel (GS 4), popes and episcopal conferences have given increasingly concrete directives concerning matters of public policy. The theme of the church's special solidarity with the poor, already broached at Vatican II (GS 1), has given rise in Latin America to the idea of a "preferential option" for the poor. The theology of poverty and development is further explored by John Paul II in his 1987 encyclical *Sollicitudo rei socialis*.

This tenth principle is no easier to implement than the other nine. It would be irresponsible for the church to avoid all comment on the moral and religious aspects of public policy issues, for the world legitimately looks to religious leaders for advice in reshaping society according to what Bishop James Malone has called "a God-centered value system."[3] On the other hand, ecclesiastical authorities must respect the freedom of individuals and groups within the church to reach conscientious decisions about policies on which intelligent and committed Catholics can disagree. The turbulent debates surrounding the collective pastorals of the American bishops on peace and on the economy make it evident that, while real progress is being made, the right approach to sociopolitical issues is only gradually being found through a process of trial and error.

A Point of Departure

In setting forth these ten principles I have not tried to say anything new or original. On the contrary, my aim has been to articulate what I hope is obvious to anyone seeking an unprejudiced interpretation of the council. The principles are intended not as a point of arrival but as a point of departure; they may serve as premises, not as conclusions.

Because the principles are general and abstract, they leave many open questions, some of which will be addressed in subsequent chapters. These questions can become bitter and divisive, but this need not be the case, provided that the documents are read from within the broad consensus I have described. If the principles outlined here are accepted and internalized by all parties to the discussion, a certain variety of opinion on other points of interpretation and application can be stimulating and instructive. But if the basic principles explained in this chapter are rejected, consensus can hardly be achieved on the more controversial questions to which we shall now turn.

3. The Emerging World Church and the Pluralism of Cultures

Emergence of the World Church

Speaking at the Weston School of Theology in 1979, theologian Karl Rahner asserted that the main achievement of Vatican II was to have been the first official self-actualization of Catholicism as a world church.[1] After propounding this thesis Rahner himself enlarged upon it in other writings, as have other authors such as Walbert Bühlmann in *The Church of the Future*.[2] The emergence of the world church, as explained by these authors, marks the end of the period when Catholicism as a whole could be equated with its expression in the forms of Greco-Roman, Mediterranean, or European culture. We are witnessing the birth of a new multicultural Catholicism in which all the regional churches may be expected to interact, mutually criticizing and enriching one another.

Both Rahner and Bühlmann recognize that the selection of Vatican II as the moment of emergence of the world church is somewhat arbitrary. The council obviously built on the prior labors of farsighted popes and missionaries, especially since World War I. The actualization of the world church at Vatican II was, moreover, only rudimentary. The emergence occurred as much in the lived experience of the council as in its formal teaching. Even though the indigenous hierarchies of Asia and Africa played a relatively minor role in comparison with their European counterparts, the Catholic church at Vatican II exhibited greater geographic and ethnic inclusiveness than ever before in its history.

The novelty of the present situation can be illustrated by contrast with the period from 1500 to 1900, the great epoch of missionary expansion. In that period Christianity, though it was disseminated to all parts of the globe, remained an essentially European phenomenon, exported in European form. Christians of other continents took European names, used European languages in their worship, studied the religious history of the West, and learned their theology from European textbooks.

We cannot say that this period has come to an end, but it is surely on the wane. Vatican II took some cautious steps in the direction of de-Europeanization. It admitted the vernacular into the liturgy, provided for the establishment of the international Synod of Bishops, gave new status to regional and national bishops' conferences, and endorsed the principle of missionary accommodation. Since the council the trend has been carried further by the virtual abolition of the Latin liturgy, the increased vitality of the church in the Third World, and the global travels of Paul VI and John Paul II. The churches and hierarchies of the various continents are acquiring a new sense of their own distinctive identity. They do not simply learn from Europe. They now feel a responsibility to shape the future of the church in their own parts of the world and to contribute insights based on their own experience.

A great number of factors have conspired to bring about this epochal shift. One obvious ingredient was the demise of European colonialism. In organizations such as the United Nations the new national states of the Third World hold a commanding majority and are asserting themselves with commensurate vigor. A second factor is the statistical growth of Christianity in the Third World. Bühlmann points out that South America today contains more Catholics than Europe and that more Catholics live in the southern hemisphere than in the northern. This numerical preponderance of the "Third Church," as Bühlmann calls it, is constantly increasing.[3] A third element is the decline of the classical culture that provided the intellectual apparatus for European Catholicism and its displacement by the new scientific and technological mentality. Connected with this development is yet a fourth: the collapse of the Christian culture that permeated the public life of Europe until relatively recent years. Today, for the first time since antiquity, Christians in most European countries find themselves in what Rahner describes as a "diaspora situation." Generally speaking, they are a minority surrounded by a secular culture that the church can no longer control.

Although our authors are by no means pessimistic, they are conscious of the perils of the present juncture. Only once before, Rahner asserts, has Christianity been forced to undergo such an abrupt cultural shift. That was in the first century, when Gentile Christianity separated itself culturally from the Jewish mother church. For a brief period the Jewish and Hellenistic forms of Christianity existed side by side. Their coexistence occasioned a sharp conflict and nearly led to schism. Division was staved off by frail compromises such as the decrees of the so-called Apostolic Council of Jerusalem, which made certain laws obligatory for Jewish Christians but not for Christians of Gentile extraction. Whether this settlement was ever implemented, and how long it could have been enforced, are moot questions. The crisis was eventually solved by the virtual extinction of the Jewish Christian community after the destruction of Jerusalem. The church then became once again virtually monocultural, and such it has remained, in many respects, until the present day.

The first-century crisis shows how cultural shifts can involve matters of life and death for the church. The current crisis is more complex than that of the first century, for it involves not two but many cultures. It is by no means easy to see how the church can adjust to the new technological culture of the West and at the same time implant itself in the ancient, traditional cultures of Asia and Africa. Can a church that simultaneously moves in these contrary directions keep enough internal homogeneity to remain a single social body? Can the church adopt new symbols, languages, structures, and behavioral patterns on a massive scale without losing continuity with its own origins and its own past? If Rahner and Bühlmann are even approximately correct, the emergence of the world church sets the main agenda for Catholicism in the decades to come. The problems accompanying this transition cannot be handled adequately without a comprehensive pastoral strategy, and this will no doubt involve the formation of new structures and methodologies.[4]

The Problem of Inculturation

Before turning to these practical matters it would be well to reflect on what is theologically at stake. The church is being called to insert itself into the contemporary cultures of six continents (the two Americas, Europe, Asia, Africa, and Oceania). This insertion is called, in recent theological literature, *inculturation*—a term that made its first appearance in official Catholic literature in the public message issued by the international Synod of Bishops in 1977. Since then John Paul II has frequently used the term, notably in two of his apostolic exhortations, *Catechesi tradendae* (1979) and *Familiaris consortio* (1981), and in his Encyclical on Saints Cyril and Methodius, *Slavorum apostoli* (1985).

Inculturation has been defined as "the process of a deep, sympathetic adaptation to and appropriation of a local cultural setting in which the Church finds itself in a way that does not compromise its basic faith in Christ."[5] As this definition suggests, inculturation raises a theological problem: under what conditions can the church appropriate a particular human culture without impairing its fidelity to Christ and the gospel? Since every culture carries with it a set of meanings, attitudes, and behavioral patterns, the acceptance of a new culture would seem to bring with it a modification of the church's established meanings, attitudes, and behavioral norms. Quite evidently, we are here confronted with a new phase of the age-old problem of Christianity and culture, and our understanding of the world church will depend in large measure on how we understand the relationship between Christianity and culture in general.

In his classic study, *Christ and Culture*, H. Richard Niebuhr constructed a typology that may be adapted to the problem before us.[6] For the sake of simplicity, I shall here reduce Niebuhr's five types to three: a confrontation model, a synthesis model, and a transformation model.

By the confrontation model I mean the kind of opposition between Christianity and culture that has sometimes been advocated in modern Protestant theology, whether sectarian or dialectical. In some of his early work Karl Barth, reacting against the "culture Christianity" of Schleiermacher and Ritschl, seemed to be saying that Christianity and culture must always be in conflict.[7] This theory harmonizes with Barth's actualistic ecclesiology in which the church is seen as continually being formed anew by the Word of God. In the footsteps of Paul Tillich one may object that no Christian preacher, even though he be a Karl Barth, can proclaim the gospel without at least provisionally accepting the language and other cultural forms in which one is framing the message.[8] Even a critique of culture, it would seem, must be mounted in a culture. However that may be, the confrontation model has never found a comfortable lodging in the Catholic tradition, and it would scarcely be conducive to the kind of world church that Rahner and others are proposing. Barth's observations, however, remain a salutary warning against an uncritical identification of the gospel with a given cultural expression.

In the synthesis model, by contrast, culture is regarded as good in its own order and as perfective of the human. The classical culture of Greece and Rome, purified by revelation and grace, has frequently been seen as providing Christianity with a suitable cultural base. But further cultural developments have been admitted. Orthodox Christianity tended to identify Christianity with Byzantinism or with "Holy Russia."

In the late nineteenth and early twentieth centuries, Protestant theologians of Europe and North America looked upon individualism, personal freedom, and the capitalist system as the fruits of the gospel when planted in favorable soil. In the Catholicism of the same period, Christian culture was identified rather with the civilization of the Middle Ages. The Thomistic revival, guild socialism, pre-Raphaelite painting, and Gregorian chant were so many facets of a thoroughgoing program of restoration. Many agreed with Hilaire Belloc when he wrote, "Europe will return to the Faith, or she will perish. The Faith is Europe. And Europe is the Faith."[9] By the faith, of course, Belloc meant Roman Catholicism as it had existed before the Reformation.

Christian missionaries from Europe and the United States, working in all parts of the world, were content, even proud, to disseminate Western civilization together with the gospel. They believed that in so doing they were performing a human as well as an apostolic service.

Since World War II this Eurocentric Christianity has been in general disrepute. The synthesis had never been very convincing even in Europe, where Orthodox, Protestant, and Catholic Christians disagreed about what kind of culture should be paired with Christian faith. In Asia and Africa the identification of Christianity with European culture has been increasingly perceived as a form of cultural imperialism and has provoked hostile reactions. Even in the West many Christians today regard the synthesis model, in all the forms here mentioned, as a misguided effort to link Christianity with a dying culture.

We come, therefore, to the transformation model, which appears to be clearly favored by Vatican Council II and by papal documents issued since the council. This model strikes a kind of balance between the previous two. With the confrontation model it asserts that Christianity imposes demands on every cultural heritage, calling for continual renewal and reform. With the synthesis model it holds that Christianity must embody itself in appropriate cultural forms. The essentials of the transformationist position may be set forth in the following five points:

1. In a certain sense, Christianity is supracultural. The living presence of the Holy Spirit, which is constitutive of the church, is not reducible to any culture, however sacred. Thus Paul VI could correctly state, "The gospel, and therefore evangelization, cannot be put in the same category with any human culture. They are above all cultures."[10]

2. Christianity has always been, and must be, culturally embodied. Human culture gives the church a language, artistic forms, and conceptual structures so that it can communicate itself to individuals and societies. As John Paul II has put it in the letter by which he established the Pontifical Council for Culture, "The synthesis between faith and culture is not only a demand of culture but also of faith . . . A faith that does not become culture is a faith not fully received, not entirely pondered, not faithfully lived."[11]

   Expanding somewhat on this second point we may say that, sociologically speaking, Christianity has certain features of a culture. Like a culture, it is a system of meanings, historically transmitted, embodied in symbols, and instilled into new members of the group so that they are inclined to think, judge, and act in characteristic ways.[12]

3. Culture is broader than Christianity or any religion, for it includes matters of civility, social customs, artistic and literary conventions, and many other ingredients that, at least in the modern West, are separate from religion. In a secularized society such as our own Christianity has the sociological status of a subculture.[13]

4. Christianity is not exclusively linked to any one culture. According to the Gospels, Jesus himself challenged the cultural and racial exclusiveness of the Jewish religious

authorities. Paul advanced the process of cultural wean-
ing by insisting that circumcision should not be obligatory
for pagan converts to Christianity. Vatican II encapsu-
lates this theme for the contemporary church: "The Church,
sent to all people of every time and place, is not bound
exclusively and indissolubly to any race or nation, nor to
any particular way of life or any customary pattern of
living, ancient or modern. Faithful to its own tradition
and at the same time conscious of its universal mission,
it can enter into communion with various cultural modes,
to its own enrichment and theirs too" (*GS* 58).

5. The evangelization of cultures—to borrow a term from
Paul VI—pertains to the mission of the church. It cannot
simply accept cultures as they stand but must, as Paul
VI insisted, regenerate and inwardly renew them (*EN* 20).
The Bishops' Synod of 1977 stated that Christianity must
not only find roots in human cultures but must transform
them.[14]

Autonomy or Reciprocity of Cultures?

Using a finer sieve, one may divide proponents of this transformationist position into two subtypes or, perhaps better, two
tendencies, since the division between the two is not always
clear. The first type stresses cultural autonomy; the second,
the reciprocity of cultures.

The autonomist position goes back in Protestant theology to
Ernst Troeltsch, who proposed a polymorphic doctrine of truth
and espoused a radical cultural relativism.[15] The specific ker-
nel of all genuine religion, he believed, is unique and divine,
but the particular form of a religion is determined by the type
of culture in which it inheres. Christianity in the West, according to this view, is inseparably bound up with the ancient and
modern civilization of Europe. The Christianity of the Rus-
sians and other non-Western peoples (Jacobites, Nestorians,

Armenians, and Abyssinians) is so different as to be another religion. The great religions of Asia, for Troeltsch, corresponded to other types of culture, in which contact with the divine had to be differently experienced. It would be quite impossible for these diverse religions to be synthesized or for one to be converted into another. All religions are under obligation to increase in depth and purity by their own inner impulse. In this process contact with Christianity may be beneficial to other religions, but Christians should not attempt to convert Hindus and Buddhists to their own religion.

In contemporary Catholicism certain tenets of transcendental theology, especially as expounded by Bernard Lonergan, have been used to justify a sort of cultural relativism. Lonergan rejects the normative view of culture, which he identifies as classicist, and favors what he describes as the modern, empirical concept of culture. Christian classicism, canonizing a particular form of culture, preached that culture along with the gospel, but the classicist view is no longer acceptable.

To preach the Gospel to all nations is to preach it to every class in every culture in which it has not been known. To make it known there, there must be found in the local language the potentialities for expressing the Gospel message, and it is by developing these potentialities and not by imposing an alien culture that the mission will succeed.[16]

Classicist orthodoxy, which identified Christianity with a single cultural expression, according to Lonergan, "was never more than the shabby shell of Catholicism. The real root and ground of unity is being in love with God—the fact that God's love has flooded our inmost hearts through the Holy Spirit he has given us (Rom 5:5)."[17] On the ground that the experience of divine love is not dependent on the prior preaching of the gospel, Lonergan can claim that his theory provides the framework for a fruitful encounter between all religions with a basis in religious experience.[18] Lonergan's doctrine of the outer word of God may contain resources for some give and take among cultures touched by the gospel, but the transformation of cultures by the gospel does not seem to be envisaged.

A number of Indian Catholic theologians, most notably Raimundo Panikkar, have tried to protect the indigenous religions and cultures from the intrusions of a Christianity that has assumed Western cultural forms. For Panikkar Jesus is only one, albeit the most important, of many epiphanies of the Christ. The Christian must find Christ already present in the epiphanies recognized by Hinduism and help make that presence explicit. Christianity in India should consequently be "not . . . an imported, fully fledged and highly developed religion, but Hinduism itself *converted*—or Islam, or Buddhism, whatever it may be."[19]

In theological works of this tendency it is common to read that the main effort of Christian preachers should be not to convert Indians to Christianity but to bring them closer to God through their own religions.[20] Some suggest that Indian Christian communities should treat the Hindu Scriptures as being for them, at least in an analogous way, an Old Testament, pointing the way to Christ much as did the Hebrew Bible for the early Jewish Christians. These nonbiblical Scriptures may therefore find a place in Christian liturgical worship, and specifically in the Eucharist.[21]

This polymorphic or relativist version of transformationism expresses many sound insights that we shall have to consider. The danger, however, is that in emphasizing the barriers between cultures the theory could promote a certain alienation among Christians of different races and nations. When the Bible, dogmas, sacraments, and ecclesiastical structures are branded as culture-bound, the sources of continuity and communion in the church are weakened. The idea of a visible world church is undercut, and its place is taken by an invisible fellowship of an elite who have undergone intellectual, moral, and religious conversion within their own cultures and religions.

I turn, therefore, to the second type of transformationism, which accents reciprocity. In formulating this position, which is my own, I am indebted to Ary Roest Crollius,[22] who has in turn borrowed some ideas from David Tracy.[23] Both Tracy and Roest Crollius contrast three attitudes: cultural univocity, cultural equivocity, and cultural analogy. By univocity they mean approximately what I have described as synthesis and what Lonergan describes as classicism. Their equivocity corresponds to the kind of cultural relativism or polymorphism I have attributed to Troeltsch and Panikkar. Their third attitude, cultural analogy, would recognize the originality of each culture, the inadequacy of each, and the consequent need for mutual criticism and openness. This third attitude, which I prefer to call cultural reciprocity, seems to me most consonant with recent papal teachings and most acceptable on theological grounds.

The reciprocity theory differs in several major respects from the polymorphic. It does not see the gospel simply as stimulating interior impulses in other religions and cultures but holds that the Christian message, in articulated form, introduces a new element into the situation. As John Paul II points out, the gospel message does not spring spontaneously from any cultural soil; it must always be transmitted by apostolic dialogue.[24]

The reciprocity theory, moreover, is not content with a merely empirical, nonnormative concept of culture. It discriminates among cultures in the light of their harmony or lack of harmony with the divinely established order. There is thus a qualitative difference among cultures. John Paul II holds that inculturation must be subject to the two principles of compatibility with the gospel and communion with the universal church.[25] These two principles, I believe, may be considered normative in the evaluation of cultures.

Most importantly, the theory of reciprocity stresses that cultures do not simply exist side by side. They are not like sealed containers but more like houses with doors and windows. They can mutually criticize and enrich one another through dialogue. Rejecting the synthesis and autonomist models, Roest Crollius remarks, "Neither the mere conservation of traditional cultural values nor the seclusion of cultural *apartheid* contains a promise of life."[26] For our present purposes, the reciprocity theory has the advantage of showing how multiple inculturation may be of benefit to the universal church.

As Paul VI insisted in opposition to certain contemporary trends, the universal church is more than a federation of particular churches. Autonomous local churches, as he warned, can easily fall prey to local separatist forces (*EN* 62). John Paul II, in his encyclical on Cyril and Methodius, made a similar point. Every local church, with its particular culture and traditions, must, he insisted, "remain open and alert to the other churches and traditions and, at the same time, to universal and catholic communion; were it to remain closed in on itself, it too would run the risk of becoming impoverished."[27]

It is essential, in my judgment, for the church to retain its capacity, so astonishing to the ancient world, of bringing Jews and Gentiles, Greeks and barbarians, into a single people. In Christian antiquity the sense of worldwide fellowship was assiduously cultivated by adherence to a single rule of faith, concelebration of the liturgy, Eucharistic communion, letters of peace, mutual hospitality, and charitable assistance.[28] The centrifugal tendencies of regional churches in our own day must be offset by unitive practices.

If the church is, even analogously, a single people, it must have something like a common culture, for, as Christopher Dawson says, "The society without culture is a formless society—a crowd or collection of individuals brought together by the needs of the moment."[29] The Catholic church as a whole must have a system of meanings, historically transmitted, embodied in symbols, and instilled into its members so that they are inclined to think, judge, and act in characteristic ways. In order to be a Christian, therefore, it is not sufficient to be inculturated into a basic community, a parish, or a diocese. One must be socialized into the universal church, with its shared meanings, common symbols, and normative behavior patterns. The worldwide unity of the church cannot be merely ethereal and abstract; it must be expressed in tangible signs and upheld by overarching structures of unity. Otherwise, as the Protestant moral theologian James Gustafson explains, the church could not "remain an historically and socially identifiable community through time and across cultural boundaries."[30]

Another Protestant, the sociologist of religion Robert N. Bellah, has emphasized the contemporary urgency of maintaining the structures of unity. The common good in the United States, he holds, is threatened by an insidious combination of radical individualism and managerial manipulation.[31] Only a church with strong sacramental and hierarchical structures, resistant to individualism and sectarianism, can effectively oppose this threat. Catholicism has traditionally exhibited these structures and characteristics. It can make a vital contribution provided that it does not yield to the present tendency to fragment into small, egalitarian base communities.

Historical Concreteness

The point where the most serious tensions arise between the two versions of the transformationist model is the issue of historical concreteness. Advocates of cultural autonomy object, not without reason, that the traditional symbols and structures of unity, such as the Bible, the creeds, sacraments, episcopacy, and papacy, are shot through with the particularities of Semitic and Western culture and are therefore alienating to non-Westerners. In reply some have pointed out that the transformative power of Christianity comes from culturally transcendent principles such as faith, love, reason, and justice.[32] But to say no more than this would be to overlook what is most central and specific to Christianity.

The source and center is not some abstract metaphysical principle or virtue but a concrete universal, Jesus of Nazareth. Christianity, as a historical religion, cannot escape from what has been called "the scandal of particularity."[33] Grounded in the once-for-all events of biblical history and in the personal life of its Founder, the church has gradually progressed in self-understanding through irrevocable decisions made at specially graced moments of its history. Salvific truth owes much of its disclosive and transformative power to its embodiment in the concreteness of human history.

It may seem unfitting for God to have revealed himself through the symbols and culture of a militaristic, patriarchal, ethnocentric society such as that of ancient Israel. If God had wanted the best, we may admit, he would have spoken rather through the philosophers, statesmen, poets, and artists of Greece and Rome. But even in the cultural order he evidently preferred to choose the weak and foolish things of the world, lest any flesh should glory in his sight (1 Cor 1:29).

The particularities of the biblical culture are not, and need not, become ours. We do not have to wear beards if or because Jesus wore one, nor are we obliged to imitate the marriage customs and menus of the biblical peoples. But if we wish to nourish ourselves from the wellsprings of the faith, we must go back to the biblical events and symbols, seen in their own context. Just as the life of a nation is sustained by the memory of the founding events, as enshrined in sagas and rituals, so the corporate life of the people of God is shaped by ancient texts and by ceremonies that actualize what those texts record. Thanks to its native power of transcendence, the human mind is never locked into a single culture but is capable of drawing inspiration from times and cultures remote from its own. Far from being alienating, these voyages of the spirit are liberating.

For the sake of the emerging world church we must resist the conventional view that particularity is divisive and that inclusiveness must be abstract. To escape the dilemma between segregated concreteness and featureless generality we must learn to appreciate concrete universality and inclusive particularity. Only in this way will it be possible for the church of the future, with all its cultural differences, to affirm its own origins and its own past history, culturally conditioned though both of these may have been. Recognizing that foundations are only foundations, we can move forward to build the future. The biblical and ecclesiastical paradigms can inspire us to new imaginative achievements, faithful to what has been given but not slavishly repeating it. New symbols, rites, words, and concepts must be found to actualize the biblical and traditional patrimony in new circumstances. The foundational symbols, however, will always be needed to maintain the sense of continuity and to provide standards of authenticity.

Structures of Unity

Since the principles grounding the world church call for unity and variety, continuity and change, the applications will frequently be controversial. Some local churches will consider that their pastoral situation requires departures from what has long been accepted as universal Catholic tradition, whether in liturgy, in doctrine, in ministry, or in moral conduct. Impasses such as occurred between Jerusalem and Antioch in apostolic times will erupt again. Such disputes can rarely be settled by sheer deductive argument from authoritative texts. Solutions must be found through discernment in communities committed to the gospel and protected from partisan politics and external manipulation. New structures and forums for discernment may have to be instituted for the world church. Vatican II took steps in this direction by calling for the internationalization of the Roman curia, for regional episcopal conferences, and for the international Synod of Bishops.

These and other structures can be used profitably to assure a fair hearing for all parties, to prevent hasty judgments based on prejudice or passion, and to afford access to guidance from the Holy Spirit. Consensus is always to be sought. It must be recognized, however, that in many disputes no conceivable solution can do justice to all the values cherished by all the parties. Realism may require the acceptance of compromises not fully satisfying to any.

If the Catholic church is to continue in its role as a great international force for unity and truth, justice and peace, it is important to preserve solidarity among the regional churches. Dialogue is needed both because each particular church may have special insights of value to the others and because each, being immersed in a particular culture, has its own characteristic blind spots. Each local or regional church is accountable to its sister churches and to the church of Rome, which presides over the whole assembly of charity. As noted in *Lumen gentium*, the Petrine see has a dual responsibility: to protect legitimate differences and to see that these differences do not hinder unity (*LG* 13). Far from becoming less important, the papacy takes on greater responsibilities than ever as the new world church becomes a reality. The papacy has been effectively used as a symbol and agent of unity by the recent popes, including John Paul II. The new structures of collegiality, such as the Synod of Bishops, are still in the early stages of development.

The emergence of the world church as depicted by Rahner need not be viewed as a blow to Catholic unity. Diversity is surely needed for Catholicism to become vitally implanted in the six continents, but such diversity cannot flourish except within a larger unity and on the solid basis of tradition. Various though the ministries, rubrics, devotional practices, spiritualities, and theological interpretations may be, they will not displace the shared symbols and structures of unity and continuity. Within this framework the inner differences can be enriching. Just as a living body has greater unity by reason of the functional interrelationship of its different parts, so the world church can be more intimately knit together if each of the local churches develops its own distinctive character. Deeply integrated into the life of its own people, each regional community can make its specific contribution to the life of the whole, while receiving input and correction from other communities.[34]

By way of summation, let me paraphrase what Wolfhart

Pannenberg has said in a recent essay on the abiding value of the ancient creeds.[35] Some concern for cultural distinctiveness and for the inculturation of the gospel into a plurality of human contexts, he asserts, is entirely legitimate. But cultural autonomy should not be absolutized at the expense of Christian unity. In the early centuries, he recalls, the Greeks and Romans had to accept Christianity in the contingent forms it had acquired on Palestinian soil. They resisted the temptation to banish the Old Testament as something alien to Hellenistic culture. As the Celtic, Germanic, and Slavonic peoples of northern Europe accepted the new faith, they allowed their cultures to be enriched by the Jewish and Hellenistic features of classical Christianity. This process of assimilation has not come to an end. New cultural elements can always enter into the Christian synthesis, but the church's continuity with its origins must always be preserved. Generally speaking, such fidelity does not impede adaptation. On the contrary, those who have learned to respect the common heritage are best equipped to appreciate the diverse contributions of the younger churches as enriching the body of the *una sancta.*

The problem of unity and diversity in the world church brings us, inevitably, to the point of reflecting more deeply on what it means for the church to be truly Catholic. This will be the subject of the next chapter.

4. The Meaning of Catholicism: Adventures of an Idea

The term *Catholic* is frequently used as the proper name of the organized body of Christians that looks to the bishop of Rome as the successor of Peter and as visible head. The term is also used, more often with a small *c,* to designate a property of the true Church, namely its universality or "catholicity." In the present chapter we shall be discussing *Catholic* in yet a third sense: the adjectival form of *Catholicism* considered as a particular type or style of Christianity. The varying hues taken on by the concept of Catholicism in its journey down through the centuries forms one of the more fascinating and instructive chapters of the history of ideas.

I shall open the present survey at the beginning of the nineteenth century, when philosophers and theologians in Germany started to look for an underlying essence of Catholicism beneath the manifold appearances. In the first part of the chapter I shall discuss the views of Catholicism proposed by Protestants or, more precisely, by members of churches stemming from the Reformation, including Lutheran, Reformed, and Anglican. In the second part I shall summarize some ideas of Catholicism elaborated from the Roman Catholic side prior to Vatican Council II. Then in a final part I shall attempt, with the assistance of the teaching of Vatican II, to draw some conclusions about the nature of Catholicism.

Protestant and Anglican Perspectives

German Idealism

Taking the Protestant views chronologically, one may suitably begin with the philosopher Georg W. F. Hegel.[1] For him

Catholicism was characterized by an external or objectifying view of the divine presence in history. Catholics, according to Hegel, depict Jesus as objectively present in the sacraments, and especially in the Eucharist, which is adored as if Christ were still present in palpable form on earth. Hegel adds that Catholics divinize the church as an institution and accept its teachings as coming from God. In Catholicism, Hegel believes, the holy is identified with a particular institutional embodiment. As a consequence Catholics set the sacred over against the secular, church against state, and clergy against laity. While Hegel respected the power of Catholicism to preserve the objective content of the Christian message, he deplored the dualism and alienation that he regarded as intrinsic to Catholicism. Protestantism, he believed, was better able to achieve a personal, subjective appropriation of Christian revelation, even though in its existing forms Protestantism ran the risk of dissipating the doctrinal content of Christianity.

Hegel's views of Catholicism were followed to a great extent by his contemporary, Ferdinand Christian Baur, who accused Catholics of crudely identifying the ideal essence of the church with its historical manifestations.[2] According to Baur, therefore, the Catholic church was incapable of historical consciousness. It conceived of itself as perpetually the same rather than as undergoing real historical changes, and thus it attached transcendent value to its own dogmas and structures. Yet it surpassed Protestantism, he believed, in its capacity to find absolute truth in the Christian dogmas. Baur looked forward to a future synthesis that would incorporate the best features of both Protestantism and Catholicism.

A still more benign view of Catholicism was taken by another early nineteenth-century German Protestant theologian, Friedrich Schleiermacher. In his classic work, *The Christian Faith*, Schleiermacher presented Christianity as a single faith institutionalized in two concurrent forms, neither of which could claim total adequacy. The basic difference between the churches, he believed, is that for Catholics the individual's relationship to God is made dependent on a relationship to the church, whereas in Protestantism the order of relationship is reversed.[3] The opposition between Catholicism and Protestantism, however, is merely relative and is destined to be overcome. In his own theology Schleiermacher so emphasized the social nature of the Christian religion that in some respects he seemed to lean toward Catholicism as he defined it, but on many particular points he argued against the Roman Catholic dogmatic formulations.

The ideas of Hegel and Schleiermacher, combined with others derived from Friedrich Schelling and Philipp Marheineke, were introduced into the United States by the German Reformed theologian Philip Schaff. Shortly after his arrival in this country in 1844, he delivered a controversial inaugural lecture at Reading, Pennsylvania, in which he contended that Catholicism embodies the principle of authority and law, whereas the principle of Protestantism is that of free justification through the gift of faith. Either principle taken by itself, he declared, in one-sided and incomplete. "The true standpoint, all-necessary for the wants of the time, is that of Protestant Catholicism, or genuine historical progress."[4] He hoped that in the new nation of his adoption the reconciliation of the two branches of Christianity might be effected, inaugurating the final epoch of church history.

Liberalism

In the late nineteenth and early twentieth centuries the intellectual climate in Germany shifted from idealism to liberalism, which gave clear preference to Protestantism as the superior form of Christianity. Unlike the idealists, who looked upon Catholicism as the more primitive stage, the liberals saw Catholicism as a lapse from an initial state of ecclesial grace. Theologians such as Albrecht Ritschl, Adolf von Harnack, Rudolph Sohm, and Ernst Troeltsch all reflected deeply on the origins of Catholicism. They agreed that primitive Christianity, in its pre-Catholic phase, was practically oriented, experiential, free, and spontaneous. Catholicism they saw as a later development arising from Greek and Latin cultural influences, which transformed Christianity into a religion of dogma and law, priesthood and ritualism. Sohm in particular accused Catholicism of attributing divine authority to the human institution, and even Troeltsch, who was much more cautious, reproached Catholicism for materializing and externalizing the Christian religion and binding the original spiritual and inward idea indissolubly to a clerical and sacramental organization.[5]

Protestantism, for the liberals, was a return to the simplicity and purity of the original gospel. Harnack found this in the teaching of Jesus, which was allegedly centered on the fatherhood of God, the infinite value of the human soul, the higher righteousness, and the commandment of love.[6] The French theologian Auguste Sabatier showed in detail how Catholicism had degenerated by embracing, in historical succession, the dogmas of "Church, tradition, supernatural priesthood, episcopate, and papacy."[7] The infallibility dogma of 1870 was for Sabatier the logical consummation of this departure from the pure religion of the spirit, a religion without external authority of any kind.

Anglicanism and High-Church Lutheranism

In England the situation was more complex. In 1833 the Oxford movement was launched with the explicit intention of proving that the Church of England was not Protestant but Catholic. According to Tractarians such as John Keble and Edward Pusey, Protestantism was an inclined plane that could lead only to rationalism and unbelief. Catholicism, with its principles of dogma, priesthood, and sacramentality, was needed to resist the onslaughts of secularity and free thought. Catholicism, these Anglicans maintained, exists in three distinct forms: Greek, Roman, and Anglican. The Roman form was clouded by errors and corruptions, but it retained the essential patrimony of the ancient church.[8]

Since the Tractarian movement the Catholic party in the Anglican movement has passed through several distinct phases.[9] In the wake of World War I the Lux Mundi movement, under the leadership of Charles Gore, promoted a liberal and critical version of Catholicism. In 1933, on the centenary of the Oxford movement, Norman P. Williams and others maintained that the Church of England had never been anything but Catholic. Williams developed the concept of a "northern Catholicism" that would group the Church of England with churches such as those of Scandinavia and peacefully coexist with other forms of Catholicism, namely the eastern and the southern.[10] A more conservative type of Catholicism was revived after World War II. In a report entitled "Catholicity," commissioned by the Archbishop of Canterbury in 1945, a group of Anglo-Catholics under the chairmanship of Arthur Michael Ramsey identified Catholicism with "the undivided wholeness of the primitive Tradition" and called for "constancy in Scriptures, Creeds, Sacraments, and Apostolic Succession."[11]

Inspired in part by Anglo-Catholicism, high church movements arose within Lutheranism in Scandinavia and Germany. Some Lutherans sought to shed the Protestant label. Nathan Söderblom, Wilhelm Stählin, and Friedrich Heiler, among others, called for "evangelical Catholicism," or at least "evangelical catholicity." In a lengthy work entitled *Catholicism: Its Idea and Appearance*,[12] Heiler praised Catholicism for its adherence to the full patrimony of the faith, for its ability to incorporate all that is humanly and naturally good, and for its capacity to transcend the differences between disparate cultural and ethnic groups. But the weakness of Catholicism, he held, was its openness to innumerable contrasting elements, many of them not specifically Christian. Catholicism, in his view, could not be authentically Christian unless its universalism were balanced by evangelical concentration, and this balance he found wanting in the Roman church.

Heiler spoke for many in asserting that the Roman church, by its absolutistic claims and despotic behavior, had deserted

Catholicism and turned itself into a sect. But this was not the opinion of all high-church Lutherans. In the 1950s a small group, including Hans Asmussen and Max Lackmann, contended that there could be no true Catholicism without union with Rome as the visible center of the universal church. The papacy, they argued, could properly be criticized but not discarded. The intention of the Reformers, as they interpreted it, was not to form a new church but to reform the existing church. That intention could not be fulfilled until evangelical Christians, with their Reformation principles, became integrated into the Roman Catholic church.[13]

Recent Protestant Views

Karl Barth, perhaps the most influential Protestant systematician of the twentieth century, reflected profoundly on the Protestant-Catholic relationship from a Reformed Christian standpoint.[14] He held that the substance of the church, though distorted in Roman Catholicism, is better preserved there than in liberal Protestantism. Catholicism upholds the divinity of Christ and his presence and activity in the sacraments and in the teaching of the church. But it neglects the Word of God and consequently fails to take sufficient account of the sinfulness of the church and its need for mercy. Catholicism exaggerates the value of human effort, the continuity between nature and grace, the holiness of creatures, and especially the holiness of the church. God's word in Scripture is used as a source for proving the doctrines of the church but not for controlling and correcting the church. In Catholicism, moreover, catholicity is presented in sheerly quantitative terms and is thus misunderstood.

Concerns such as Barth's asserted themselves at the First Assembly of the World Council of Churches at Amsterdam in 1948. According to the Assembly Report the "deepest difference" among the member churches lay between two contrasting ways of understanding the church. The "catholic" view attached primary importance to the visible continuity of the church and to apostolic succession in the episcopate. The "protestant" view, on the contrary, stressed the initiative of the Word of God and the response of faith; it accepted the doctrine of justification by faith alone. This fundamental cleavage, according to the Assembly Report, constituted "a hard core disagreement between total ways of apprehending the church of Christ."[15]

Paul Tillich, who rivals Barth for eminence in the field of Protestant systematics, held a similar point of view on the merits and defects of Catholicism.[16] Drawing on the thought of nineteenth-century idealist philosophers, notably Schelling and Hegel, he portrayed Christianity as involving a perpetual tension between two dialectically opposed elements, the priestly and the prophetic. The Catholic church, thanks to its sacerdotalism, best preserves what Tillich called the Catholic substance. But the Protestant churches, more prophetically oriented, were in his judgment better equipped to combat an unhealthy divinization of the sacraments and institutional structures, to which Catholics accorded a sacred status. By his insistence on the "Protestant principle" as a rejection of all absolute claims made on behalf of finite realities, Tillich sought to combat the tendency to regard human persons and institutions as unambiguous embodiments of the divine.

Tillich's dialectic between the Catholic substance and the Protestant principle has been taken up by many other theologians of the Lutheran and Reformed traditions. Jaroslav Pelikan, for example, argues that the Lutheran Reformers combined a Catholic respect for tradition, liturgy, and dogma with a Protestant aversion to authoritarianism. Pelikan himself espouses the kind of "evangelical catholicity" he attributes to Luther. The essentials of Catholic Christianity, he believes, can be retained without union with the Church of Rome.[17]

Langdon Gilkey, an American Baptist theologian influenced by Tillich, gives the Catholic church high credit for its ability to maintain community among its members and continuity with the ancient tradition. He praises in Catholicism its ability to use sacramental symbolism involving the whole person. Finally, he respects the way in which Catholicism has combined faith with sober rational reflection. But he sees Catholicism as threatened by modern secularity. He therefore calls for a new secularized form of Catholicism, purified from its traditional sacralism and supernaturalism. Protestantism, he believes, has had greater experience in the effort to integrate modernity with the Christian tradition. Gilkey's book on Catholicism, though published in 1975, shows traces of the confident secularity of the 1960s.[18]

Summary

It is not easy to construct a composite picture from the authors thus far surveyed. On some points there seems to be rather general agreement. Catholicism is the religion of authority and law, of dogma, priesthood, and sacrament. To this many theologians add the features of tradition and apostolic succession. The merit of Catholicism is found in its ability to command unquestioning loyalty from its adherents and thus to protect the substance of the faith against erosion. Some praise the international and supratemporal character of Catholicism and its consequent ability to establish communion among believers separated in space and time. Among the defects of Catholicism, Protestant authors mention its lack of immediacy to Christ, its preoccupation with externals, its authoritarianism, its supernaturalistic dualism, its tendency to self-deification, and its deafness to the challenge of the gospel.

Regarding a number of points there is disagreement. The idealists and liberals, as already noted, differ about whether Catholic or Protestant Christianity is the more primitive. Depending on their point of view, Protestant critics judge Catholicism to be either too static (Hegel, Baur) or too fluid (Harnack, Heiler). There are sharp differences of opinion about the relationship between Protestantism and Catholicism. Both the liberals on the left and the Tractarians on the right hold that it is necessary to choose between Protestantism and Catholicism, though they disagree about which of the two ought to be chosen. Mediating theologians hold that either without the other is incomplete and that a kind of Protestant Catholicism, or evangelical catholicity, is to be cultivated. Some mediating theologians, while seeing value in both Catholic and Protestant Christianity, hold that the two cannot be harmoniously synthesized. Rather, they must be held in tension as polar opposites.

Finally, our authors disagree about how Catholicism is related to Rome. Some hold that Rome represents one of several forms of Catholicism, perhaps the one best suited to the "southern" mentality. Others, looking on Roman Catholicism as sectarian distortion, question whether the terms *Roman* and *Catholic* are really compatible. Still others see Romanism as the most intense and consistent realization of Catholicism. This last group embraces some who deplore Catholicism (Sabatier) and others who approve of it (Lackmann).

Catholic Perspectives

German Idealism

Roman Catholics in Germany, who began to reflect on the essence of Catholicism about the beginning of the nineteenth century, were, like their Protestant colleagues of the day, strongly influenced by the Romantic movement in art and literature as well as by the philosophical speculations of Hegel and Schelling. They extolled the organic vitality and poetic splendors of Catholicism as remedies for the individualism and rationalism of the Enlightenment.

Johann Sebastian Drey, the founder of the Catholic Tübingen school, held that the essence of Catholicism consists in the subordination of the individual to the church as a whole, with its living tradition and its institutional authority. Catholicism is the Christian system that best retains the original impulse of Christianity thanks to its sacramental rites, its ethos of mutual love, and its divinely instituted hierarchy.[19]

In response to the contention of Schleiermacher and others

that Christianity must appear under a double form, Drey argued that such duality might be accepted but that Protestantism could not claim to be the second form, for its principle of private judgment was destructive of all churchly reality. The second form of religion for Drey was mysticism, which respects the structures of the church but prevents them from degenerating into lifeless mechanisms. Mysticism guards against the absolutization of external forms by emphasizing the primacy of interior religion.[20] Whenever the church is in good health, Drey maintained, mystical religion is a vital force. Protestantism itself originated in a kind of eccentric, exaggerated mysticism, but it went awry by doing away with the external forms that are the necessary vehicles of interior grace. By dissolving the connecting links between the modern Christian and the gospel, Protestantism compelled the contemporary believer to reconstruct Christianity according to arbitrary principles taken from philosophical speculation rather than from the living heritage of faith.

Drey's disciple, Johann Adam Möhler, carried the thought of his master one step further. Catholicism, he declared, is the form of Christianity that fully accepts the Incarnation, which is, as Drey had recognized, the fundamental Christian mystery. "The visible Church," wrote Möhler in a famous passage, " . . . is the Son of God himself, everlastingly manifesting himself among men in a human form, perpetually renovated, and eternally young—the permanent incarnation of the same, as in Holy Writ, even the faithful are called the body of Christ."[21] Thus the church, he concluded, is not merely human. It is at once human and divine.

For Möhler, as for Drey, Protestantism was an unauthentic form of Christianity. Luther and Calvin, he held, made a fatal separation between the invisible church of the saints and the visible church of history, looking upon the former alone as holy and upon the latter as a merely human, adventitious association. As a result of this fatal flaw, Protestantism gradually lost the sacramental and dogmatic heritage handed down from antiquity.

Möhler's Protestant colleague on the faculty of Tübingen, Ferdinand Christian Baur, wrote a book-length reply to Möhler,[22] but in this response he defended not the Protestantism of Luther and the Reformation but a dialectically progressive religion that owed more to philosophical speculation than to Christian revelation. Baur's work was not well received by his fellow Protestants, and Möhler was able to reply to it confidently.

Newman

About the time that Drey and Möhler were at the height of their careers, John Henry Newman was beginning to say many of the same things quite independently in England. In the 1830s he was associated with John Keble and Edward Pusey in the high-church Tractarian movement. He tried to convince his fellow Anglicans that the Thirty-Nine Articles should be interpreted in a Catholic sense, as affirming the dogmatic and sacramental heritage of ancient Christianity, rather than in a Protestant sense. His interpretation, however, was widely rejected by his coreligionists. Increasingly, as he studied the patristic age, he became convinced that the English church, in its present condition, lacked the mark of catholicity. It was an isolated national church out of communion with the main body of the Church Catholic, in a situation analogous to that of ancient heresies such as Donatism and Monophysitism.

Newman's view of Catholicism may be gathered best from his *Essay on the Development of Christian Doctrine*, composed on the eve of his conversion. Here he depicts Christianity as an idea that, like other living ideas, can be assimilated only through prolonged experience and meditation. Centuries were required, according to Newman, to disclose what was concretely implied in the Incarnation, which Newman, like Drey and Möhler, took to be the central Christian doctrine.[23] Catholicism, the sole authentic form of Christianity, was perpetually living and therefore developing. Its sacramental rites, hierarchical structures, and dogmatic formulations took on continually new forms in response to changing situations. True to its incarnational character, the Catholic church should seek not to stand apart from the world and its history but rather to appropriate all the sound values of human cultures, including those of the pagan religions.

Protestantism, with its appeal to Scripture alone, impressed Newman as an impoverished form of Christianity. Even the Church of England, though it accepted the dogmas, sacraments, and hierarchal forms of the patristic church, seemed to Newman to be stunted, since it had no living principle of development. Only the Roman Catholic church, with its infallible teaching office, seemed capable of keeping pace with the times while simultaneously holding in check what Newman referred to as "the suicidal excesses" of freedom of thought.[24]

All in all, Newman's organic, developmental model of Catholicism closely resembles that of the Catholic Tübingen theologians, Drey and Möhler, although he seems not to have been significantly influenced by these authors.

The Modernists

The next group of Catholic theologians who seriously grappled with the idea of Catholicism were the modernists at the turn of the century. Alfred Loisy, the leading French modernist, was an intense admirer of Newman. He made use of Newman's organic, developmental ecclesiology in order to refute liberal Protestants such as Harnack and Sabatier, whom he accused of religious individualism and of a static, nonhistorical conception of Christianity. Harnack's efforts to reconstruct the religion of Jesus were in Loisy's estimation a pitiful effort to repristinate the remote past. "To reproach Catholicism for all its developments," wrote Loisy, "is to reproach it for remaining alive."[25]

The leader of the English modernists, George Tyrrell, as a convert to Roman Catholicism, despised Protestant liberalism and, like Loisy, tended to ridicule it. He celebrated Catholicism as the religion that stands closest to the oldest, deepest stream of collective human experience, capable of assimilating the fruits of pagan religiosity and of satisfying the mystic need of conscious communion with the suprasensible world.[26] "Catholicism," he wrote, "is more nearly a microcosm of the world of religions than any other known form,"[27] for in it we find nearly every type of religious expression, from the lowest to the highest, straining towards unification and coherence. By comparison, Protestantism in its various forms seemed to Tyrrell to be an artificial, incomplete form of religion, one that had been impoverished by separation from the natural religious process.

Loisy and Tyrrell, of course, both had their difficulties with Rome, and on occasion they bitterly denounced the church authorities. Rome, they believed, was too restrictive and was misguided in its efforts to withstand modernization. In principle, however, they conceded that centralized authority in the church was a necessity. Tyrrell, at least, continued to hope for a better day when Rome's current excesses would be corrected.

Another English Catholic modernist, who always remained in good standing in the church, was the Baron Friedrich von Hügel. Like his friend Tyrrell, he wrote extensively of the excellence of Catholicism, which he regarded as the fullest and richest form of religion, distinguished from all others by its balance and inclusiveness.[28] In a major study of St. Catherine of Genoa, von Hügel contended that Catholic Christianity holds in balance the three elements of religion—the institutional, the intellectual, and the mystical. Mysticism itself, he maintained, cannot flourish except in tension with the historical and institutional embodiments of the Spirit. A distinguishing mark of Catholicism, in his view, was its perception that faith and spiritual experience must always begin with the senses.[29]

For the modernists, then, Catholicism was a religion of irreducible complexity, rooted in the depths of the human psyche, and able to appeal to the whole person—body and soul, mind and emotions. The German Lutheran, Heiler, was strongly influenced by the modernists. He praised the universalism and inclusiveness of Catholic Christianity but, as mentioned above, he wished to see it subordinated to the simple message of the gospel.

In his justly famed work, *The Spirit of Catholicism*, the German Catholic theologian Karl Adam responded to Heiler in 1924.[30] Heiler, he conceded, had said many true things but had missed the essence of Catholicism, which is discernible only to those who live within the community of faith. Seen from within, Catholicism may be called the religion of affirmation rather than of denial, of wholeness rather than of selectivity. The church, in its inmost reality, is a communion of persons in the life that was brought into the world through Jesus Christ. The life of grace, moreover, is expressed and communicated through tangible institutions, such as hierarchy, dogmas, and sacraments, which are not to be written off as merely human contrivances, still less as unchristian distortions. Adam thus rejected the charge made by Harnack and others that Catholicism set divine value on merely human institutions.

The "New Theology"

The next major contribution came with the so-called "new theology" that arose in France on the eve of World War II. The French Dominican Yves Congar launched a new epoch in the theology of catholicity by his ecumenical study, *Divided Christendom*, published in French in 1937. In this and many subsequent works Congar broke with the static, quantitative understanding of catholicity that had long been current in Catholic apologetics and opted for a dynamic, qualitative understanding. By catholicity he meant the plenitude of truth, redemptive power, and spiritual vitality that Christ communicates to the church through the Holy Spirit. The catholicity of the church, Congar stated, "is the dynamic universality of her unity, the capacity of her principles of unity to assimilate, fulfill and raise to God in oneness with Him all men and every man and every human value."[31]

The Catholic church, according to Congar, can properly claim to be catholic, for it possesses the full deposit of faith, sacraments, and ministry. Non-Roman Christianity is deficient in catholicity, at least insofar as, lacking union with Rome, it is separated from the center of visible unity and apostolic authority. Congar, however, did not deny that the division of Christians into separate communions and confessions deprives even the Catholic church of certain human values and experiences which, if incorporated into it, would greatly enhance one aspect of its catholicity, the fullness of its Christian life. While identifying catholicity primarily with plenitude, Congar expressed reserve about the widely current view that, whereas Catholicism seeks plenitude, Protestantism is more conspicuous for purity. Catholicity, he remarked, is inseparable from the other classical "marks" of the church, and hence from holiness, which implies purity. The Council of Trent, for this reason, expressed its concern for the purity of the gospel.[32] The contrast between Catholicism and Protestantism, for Congar, is rooted especially in their divergent conceptions of apostolicity.

In the very year that Congar published his *Divided Christendom* the French Jesuit Henri de Lubac completed the first edition of his *Catholicism*, a work drawing extensively on Augustine and other patristic writers. Protestantism, de Lubac objected, unduly separates the human organization of the church from the invisible body of Christ. Anticipating the Second Vatican Council, de Lubac depicted the church as the sacrament of Christ—that is, the sign that renders him really and actively present in every place and time where the church is present.

The church, being catholic, is truly universal. It is at home everywhere, and everyone should be able to feel at home in it. In de Lubac's words:

Nothing authentically human, whatever its origin, can be alien to her. . . . To see in Catholicism one religion among others, one system among others, even if it be added that it is the only true religion, the only system that worked, is to mistake its very nature, or at least to stop at the threshold. Catholicism is religion itself. It is therefore the very opposite of a "closed society."[33]

This survey would be incomplete without mention of one more living author, Hans Urs von Balthasar, who studied under de Lubac from 1933 to 1937, and who in 1943 translated *Catholicism* into German. Influenced both by de Lubac and by the German Jesuit Erich Przywara, von Balthasar advocates a tension-filled "Catholicism of fullness." The concept of *pleroma*, he points out, was a major theme of the New Testament and one that continued to appear in the writings of the fathers. Catholicism is the fullness of the incarnate love of God, which in Jesus Christ divests itself of all possessiveness and thereby opens itself to every positive and authentic human value. To be Catholic, for the church, means to receive the fullness of God paradoxically present under the forms of poverty and nakedness, the signs of total and selfless giving.[34]

Catholic Christianity, according to von Balthasar, could not exist at all unless it were realized in an exemplary way at two salient points—as life and as institution. It became life when, through Mary's loving and believing acceptance of God's plan, the divine Word took on human flesh. The Incarnation itself already implies, in nucleus, the existence of the holy immaculate church. Second, von Balthasar asserts, the continued existence of the church requires an organ of unity that can keep the community as a whole faithful to the gospel. This organ is the apostolic college with the see of Peter at its center. The holiness of Mary and the authority of Peter are complementary aspects of the same mystery, and in John, the disciple of love, the two are reciprocally mediated and conjoined.

The Catholic church, von Balthasar admits, is always menaced by sin and always in need of reform. But unless it possessed the gifts of holiness and truth, it would have within it no principle by which to effect reform. Personal holiness should never be played off against the visible structures of the church.

According to von Balthasar, these structures are the condition of possibility of personal union with Christ. Christ's presence is institutionally mediated by hierarchical office, tradition, sacrament, and canon law. The empirical church, immersed in the ambiguities of history, is the only real church. We cannot turn from it to any separate, invisible, purely spiritual church. The church that we see about us, with all its defects, is itself the church of the saints.

Summary

The Roman Catholic theologians included in the present survey, in contradistinction to many of the Protestants, tend to define Catholicism more in terms of its organic vitality than in terms of its institutional features. Its life, they declare, is rooted in the Incarnation. Christ's life is communicated to the faithful through the gift of the Holy Spirit. As an analogous continuation of the Incarnation, the church may be called the body of Christ or the sacrament of our encounter with Christ. The superabundant richness of the divine life demands a multiplicity of historical expressions. Catholicism is therefore marked by a tension-filled unity in variety. The Catholic idea, moreover, demands time for its assimilation. Hence the church is seen as developing through the centuries in an essentially continuous way, thanks to the abiding gift of the Spirit as its divine principle of life.

On several points the Catholic authors do not seem to agree. For instance, there are two views on the question whether Catholicism demands a counterbalance to prevent it from becoming one-sided. Drey speaks of an equilibrium between Catholicism and mysticism, but von Hügel holds that the mystical is itself a dimension of Catholicism. The majority of Catholic authors take a preponderantly positive attitude toward the non-Christian religions, but some, such as von Balthasar, look on these other religions with suspicion as merely human and partly distorted efforts to attain the divine.

Those who discuss the relationship of Catholicism to Rome

generally agree that there can be no authentic Catholicism except in union with the bishop of Rome. A few tend to speak as though Rome were the source and origin of all authority and unity in the church, but most of the authors we have examined look on Rome rather as the center and touchstone of unity and authenticity in the Catholic communion.

Just as the Protestant authors we have examined are prone to emphasize the deficiencies of Catholicism, so the Catholics tend to depict Protestantism in rather unflattering colors. Many, holding that Protestantism is founded on a partial rejection of the divinely given Christian substance, conclude that it is necessarily incomplete and one-sided. A recurrent charge is that Protestantism, failing to appreciate the logic of the Incarnation, separates the visible church from the invisible community of grace. Some Catholic authors add that Protestantism, lacking an organic principle of continuity and authority, confronts its members with the necessity of choosing between an archaistic repristination of the religion of Jesus and an arbitrary modernization based on the fashions of the moment.

A Contemporary Synthesis

With the help of the authors we have surveyed and that of Vatican II we may now be in a position to draw some conclusions about the essence of Catholicism as seen from a Roman Catholic perspective.

Catholicism and Christianity

Theologically speaking, it would be a mistake to see any essence or idea of Catholicism that differs from that of Christianity itself. As Newman insisted, the idea of Christianity, rightly understood, is itself Catholic. Vatican II, in its Constitution on the Church, stated that the church of Christ, "constituted and organized in the world as a society, subsists in the Catholic Church . . . " (*LG* 8). This statement, in my judgment, implies that Catholicism has identically the same essence as the Church of Christ, "which in the creed we avow to be one, holy, catholic, and apostolic" (*LG* 8). Wherever these essential properties of Christianity are integrally present, there is the Catholic church. Catholicism, consequently, is not just one of several legitimate Christian types, nor does it need to be offset, for its own protection, by some countervailing type of Christianity.[35]

The Church of Christ, however, is not exclusively identical with its Roman Catholic realization. Other Christian churches and communities may strikingly embody certain aspects of the Church of Christ. By comparison with these other communities, Catholicism may be said to have certain distinctive attributes. This can be appreciated better if we consider how the four attributes mentioned in the creed (one, holy, catholic, and apostolic) are characteristically understood from the Catholic and Protestant points of view.

Catholicism and Unity

With regard to *unity*, Catholicism from the Counter-Reformation down to the most recent times has particularly stressed a visible unity that transcends all divisions of class, language, culture, and nationality. In the sixteenth century the churches that broke away from Rome became organized on a national or territorial basis and were governed in many cases by the political authorities. The Catholic church, for its part, insisted on a religious unity that cut across all political frontiers. In Counter-Reformation Catholicism very little scope was given to individual differences among local and regional churches, which were viewed as mere parts or districts of the universal Church. Catholicism gave its members a powerful sense of belonging to a single religious community, but the doctrines and precepts of religion were proposed in an abstract style rather unrelated to the circumstances in which the faithful lived. The result was an unhealthy dualism between religion and day-to-day existence. Vatican II, seeking to remedy this situation, resuscitated the doctrine of the local and regional church and began to insist on what has since come to be called inculturation. Catholic unity was described by the council as one in which "each individual part of the Church contributes through its special gifts to the good of the other parts and of the whole Church" (LG 13).

Meanwhile, the Protestant and Anglican churches, which had suffered from a lack of worldwide communion, began to emerge from their national and linguistic isolation. In the twentieth century there has been a new emphasis on "world confessional families" and on membership in worldwide ecumenical organizations. Thus the search for a variegated unity that overcomes the divisions among particular geographically defined groups without eliminating healthy distinctions is increasingly shared by Catholics and Protestants alike.

Catholicism and Holiness

The second major difference consists in the understanding of *holiness*. Protestantism in its classical and orthodox forms, which continue to be influential, holds that believers are holy through faith, which lays hold of the incomparable merits of Jesus Christ, but that they remain sinful in themselves and hence incapable, even with the help of grace, of moving themselves toward God, before whom they must stand as passive recipients. Catholicism, by contrast, takes a more optimistic view of human nature as essentially sound and as capable of being healed and transformed by the power of grace. It accordingly sees the church as intrinsically holy, in spite of the lapses of its members. Pius XII expressed this position in the rhetoric of his day:

The living Mother is spotless in the sacraments, by which she gives birth to her children and nourishes them; she is spotless in the faith which she has always preserved inviolate; in her sacred laws imposed upon all, in the evangelical counsels which she recommends, in those heavenly gifts and extraordinary graces through which, with inexhaustible fecundity, she generates hosts of martyrs, virgins, and confessors. But it cannot be laid to her charge if some members fall weak or wounded. . . . [36]

In spite of the somewhat triumphalistic disclaimer of the church's responsibility for the failures of its delinquent members, this passage reflects an authentically Catholic sense of the continuing holiness of the church. Giving thanks for the gifts of the Holy Spirit, the church celebrates the memory of the saints and seeks, by invoking them, to place itself under their influence.

To Protestant sensitivities these attitudes may seem Pelagian or at least semi-Pelagian. In some strains of Catholic theology, we may admit, the goodness and autonomy of nature and the transforming efficacy of grace have been so emphasized that the need of repentance and forgiveness has been minimized. Here again, Vatican II has sought to curb the exaggerations to which the Counter-Reformation gave added impetus. The recent council stated that the church, "holding sinners in its embrace, is at the same time holy and always in need of being purified, and incessantly pursues the path of penance and renewal (*LG* 8; cf. *UR* 6). By recovering this penitential outlook Catholicism has achieved a better balance and has done justice to some Protestant themes without abandoning the doctrine of the abiding holiness of the church.

Catholicism and Catholicity

What must be said about the third mark, *catholicity*, has been anticipated, in some measure, by the preceding remarks on unity. Narrowness and particularism have no place in the true church of Christ. As we have seen, catholicity means more than numerical or geographical inclusiveness. To be qualitatively catholic the church must be receptive to the sound achievements of every race and culture. Catholicism pays respect not to the mind alone, nor only to the will and the emotions, but to all levels and aspects of human existence. Not content with what is naturally sound, it seeks to embody and transmit the full content of Christian revelation and the full heritage of authentic tradition.

We have seen how Tyrrell, Heiler, and Adam, from their differing perspectives, focus on inclusiveness and universality. They are inclined to regard Catholicism as a paradoxical *com-*

plexio oppositorum in which nature and grace, faith and reason, tradition and progress, word and sacrament, spirit and institution, cross and glory are brought into a dynamic synthesis. In contrast to the Catholic "both-and," Protestantism is characterized as standing for an "either-or."

This very inclusiveness has given rise to criticisms from the Protestant side. Some complain, as we have seen, that Catholicism is too complicated and that it lacks focus. This charge deserves careful consideration. It must be admitted that Catholics, in their scrupulous concern for completeness, often fail to see the forest for the trees. They find it difficult to speak of Christ without feeling that they must bring in Mary, the saints, the sacraments, the pope, and a thousand other considerations that are not, by any sane standard, of comparable importance. They are therefore at a disadvantage in the task of evangelization.

Vatican II took cognizance of this difficulty. It spoke, in a somewhat enigmatic sentence, of the "order or 'hierarchy' of truths, [which] vary in their relationship to the foundation of the Christian faith" (*UR* 11). Several modern theologians have pleaded for a development of doctrine by way of simplification rather than by way of further complexity. It is important that every article of belief be seen in relation to the heart and center of the Christian message, which is surely God's work in Jesus Christ. Such concentration, far from being reductionistic, can point up the meaning and importance of the "subordinate" or "derivative" doctrines.

Catholicism and Apostolicity

The final property of the Church of Christ, subsisting in the Catholic church, is its *apostolicity*. Protestants have tended to define apostolicity as adherence to the gospel, as set forth in Holy Scripture. From a Catholic point of view this is necessary but not sufficient. A living apostolic authority belongs permanently to the church. The threefold deposit of apostolic faith, sacraments, and ministry is seen as developing in continuity with what was initially given in apostolic times. The church's binding doctrines are intended to articulate, in an authoritative manner, what is implied by Christianity itself. The sacraments are seen as ways in which the church actualizes its own essence as an efficacious sign of God's grace in Jesus Christ. The apostolic ministry, in turn, is a divinely empowered body of pastors who perpetuate the supervisory functions of the apostles themselves in the public direction of the church. As priestly figures the hierarchy sacramentally represent Christ, the great high priest.

Protestant writers sometimes object that the heavy machinery of ecclesiastical mediation in the Catholic church tends to impede rather than assist the living relationship of the individual believer to Jesus Christ. In their eyes Catholicism has often appeared to be the religion of law, ritual, and dogma, but not the religion of the Spirit. They speak in this connection of heteronomy and alienation. To a great extent these charges are based on the impressions of outsiders who have no inner experience of Catholic prayer and devotional life, but in some segments of Catholicism, especially perhaps in the nineteenth century, there has been an overemphasis on obedience and conformity to ecclesiastical commands and regulations. Twentieth-century Catholicism, especially under the star of Vatican II, is more conscious that the institution is not an end in itself but that it must express and mediate the Spirit. Without diluting the institutional aspect, the council accented the values of personal freedom, inner appropriation, and active participation. This new look has disappointed some Catholics who would prefer an objectivistic, authoritarian form of religion, of the kind that Hegel found in Catholicism, but many others welcome the shift away from the defensiveness and rigidity of the Counter-Reformation.

The question of the relationship between Catholicism and Rome may fittingly be discussed under the heading of apostolicity. In some Catholic ecclesiologies prior to Vatican II the primacy of the pope was so emphasized that *romanitas*, in effect, became a fifth mark of the true church, swallowing up the other four. Complaints were heard, especially from non–Roman Catholics, that catholicity was being explained in such a way that it resided in the pope alone. Some rejected the authority of Rome because they saw no other way of escaping from the excesses of papalism.

Here again, Vatican II has helped to restore the balance. It contextualized the papal primacy by setting it in the framework of episcopal collegiality. In contemporary theology it has become clear that Rome does not and cannot by itself alone possess the fullness of catholicity, and conversely that the other bishops and churches cannot be fully Catholic without being in union with Rome. In the absence of the Roman center the college of bishops and the communion of churches would lack their center of unity and apostolic authority. But without these other bishops and churches, Rome would be like a head without a body, like a center without a circumference.

In the perspectives of some two centuries of Protestant-Catholic discussion the clarifications brought to the concept of Catholicism by Vatican II seem eminently sane. The council was faithful to the traditional self-understanding of the Catholic church, and yet it spoke in a way that took account of certain justified criticisms that have come from the Protestant side.[37]

5. Vatican II and the Recovery of Tradition

Our survey of the idea of Catholicism in the last chapter touched at several points on the subject of tradition, which Catholics generally understand as a factor making for continuity within development. The acceptance of a divinely authoritative tradition is characteristically Catholic, as opposed to Protestant. Yet the concept of tradition, like that of Catholicism, has varied over the centuries. We shall here study it, as we have studied the idea of Catholicism, primarily in the light of Vatican II.

Tradition at Vatican II

Probably no document of Vatican Council II underwent more thorough revision than the Dogmatic Constitution on Divine Revelation. Some of the most dramatic changes in that document concern the theme of tradition. The 1962 schema *De Fontibus Revelationis*, drawn up by the Doctrinal Commission, emphasized the insufficiency of Scripture and the indispensability of an authoritative apostolic tradition to make known the full content of divine revelation. By the time this schema reached the council floor many of the fathers had in hand several substitute texts, including one authored by Karl Rahner with the help of Joseph Ratzinger and another by Yves Congar. Rahner's draft, entitled *De Revelatione Dei et hominis in Jesu Christo facta*, though composed on short notice, was recommended as a basis for the conciliar discussions by the presidents of the episcopal conferences of Austria, Belgium, France, Germany, and Holland.[1] Congar's draft, entitled *De Traditione et Scriptura*, composed in October 1962 with a group of about a dozen bishops, began to circulate in November.[2] Partly because of the favorable impression made by these alternative texts, the official schema met with severe criticism and had to be withdrawn after the negative vote of November 20.

A new schema, prepared by the Mixed Commission during the winter of 1963–64 and circulated in the spring of 1964, gave only scant attention to the theme of tradition, emphasizing above all the inseparability of Scripture and tradition. The council fathers, in their written critiques, expressed considerable dissatisfaction with this schema. "The most lamented deficiency, judged to be a real doctrinal regression, was the lack of an explicit treatment of tradition. To remedy this lack it was requested that a special chapter, or its equivalent, be devoted to tradition, which in the schema appeared as a Cinderella."[3] Without ever being presented on the council floor, the schema was in effect rejected.

On March 7, 1964, the Doctrinal Commission established a new subcommission to rework the schema in accordance with the directives of the pope and the Coordinating Committee, taking into account the written criticisms. Among the prominent *periti* on the new subcommission were Umberto Betti (secretary), Yves Congar, and Karl Rahner. Both Congar and Rahner were requested to prepare drafts on tradition for this subcommission. Betti, taking advantage of these and other drafts, then submitted a proposed text of his own, which was accepted by the subcommission as a basis for its labors. In this way many of the ideas of Rahner and Congar got into the new schema on Divine Revelation presented to the council in September 1964. After further debate in the general sessions of late September and early October, this schema was again significantly revised, until it came to be officially approved for inclusion into the Dogmatic Constitution on Divine Revelation.

The treatment of tradition in *Dei Verbum* has drawn attention for several reasons. Many have remarked on the ecumenical importance of its handling of the relations between Scripture and tradition.[4] Since the sufficiency of Scripture according to

Vatican II has been thoroughly studied by other authors,[5] I shall in these pages dwell rather on the significance of the notion of tradition proposed in *Dei Verbum*. Getting away from an excessively rigid, conceptual, and authoritarian view of tradition, the council emphasized that tradition arises through a real, living self-communication of God in grace and revelation, that it is rooted in the life of the community of faith, and that it adapts itself and develops in changing historical situations.

Admirers of the council have not overlooked the merits of its teaching on tradition. The American church historian, James Hennesey, S.J., applauds Vatican II for having described tradition as "the perpetuation, the constant continuation and making present of everything that the church is and believes."[6] In the council documents Hennesey finds "a ringing affirmation of the role of tradition in a Catholic understanding of Christianity."[7]

Attempting to assess the achievements of Vatican II from a distance of twenty years, Robert Imbelli, an American priest and theology professor, writes with evident enthusiasm:

Were I asked to state briefly the major theological achievement of the Second Vatican Council, I would unhesitatingly reply: the recovery of *tradition*. There are two inseparable aspects of this. On the one hand, there was the rediscovery, thanks to the careful historical labors of the 1940s and '50s, of rich veins of liturgical and ecclesial tradition antedating the 'traditional Catholicism' of the post-Reformation Church. On the other hand, there was the even more radical realization that tradition is as much process as content (*traditio* as well as *tradita*), and that this process is living, creative, and community-based.[8]

The Objectivist Concept of Tradition

The reception given to the council's handling of tradition, however, has not been uniformly enthusiastic. Many critics object that Vatican II, in its eagerness for openness, modernization, and adaptation, eroded the Catholic sense of tradition.

In the decade following the council, traditionalist movements sprang up in many countries of western Europe and North America. Archbishop Marcel Lefebvre, the leader of one such movement, composed in 1974 a Profession of Faith in which he stated,

We formally hold to everything that has been believed and practised in the faith—the customs, worship, teaching of the catechism, formation of priests, and institution of the Church—by the Church as she has always been and codified in the books which appeared prior to the modernist influence of the Council, while waiting for the true light of Tradition to dispel the shadows that darken the sky over Eternal Rome.[9]

The rhetoric of this passage, with its wistful appeal to the church "as she has always been" and to "the sky over Eternal Rome," is typical of contemporary traditionalism. Typical, too, is the identification of tradition with past styles of worship, catechesis, and clerical formation. Traditionalism tends to put all received doctrines and customs on the same level and to speak as though the usages of the nineteenth and early twentieth centuries had existed from the dawn of Christianity. Any effort to reformulate or critically adapt the established usages and teachings is dismissed under the label of modernism.

It is evident, then, that the conflicting evaluations of Vatican II turn upon different concepts of tradition. For Imbelli tradition is not so much content as process—a process that is, in his words, living, creative, and community-based. What Lefebvre dismisses as "modernist influence" can therefore be defended by Imbelli as a rediscovery of an ancient and precious heritage. By characterizing "traditional Catholicism" as a modern product, Imbelli turns back against the traditionalists their own accusation that authentic tradition is being forsaken.

As Imbelli suggests, the traditionalist idea of tradition has been widely prevalent in post-Reformation Catholicism. In opposition to the heralds of innovation and progress, Catholic theologians then tended to depict the contents of Christian revelation as permanently deposited in two distinct sources—the Bible and tradition. Tradition, then, would be a second source of revelation, parallel to Scripture—one that contains certain doctrines and prescriptions not explicitly attested in Holy Scripture. Since tradition in this sense comes from God through the apostles, it was considered equal in dignity to the Bible itself and thus exempt from criticism within the church.

This objectivist, authoritarian concept of tradition, still dominant in contemporary traditionalism, is widely criticized in our day. Let me enumerate five common criticisms, which have a certain element of truth in them, though, as we shall later see, the criticisms themselves must be critically appraised.

First, tradition, by its very nature, is vague, imprecise, and subject to distorting developments. An oral tradition that has been handed down for generations or centuries is notoriously unreliable. To put popular tales about Jesus and his family on a par with historically validated knowledge is to expose oneself to superstition and error. Modern biblical scholars generally admit that the four canonical Gospels are not entirely free from myth and legend, but many affirm that the Gospels give a substantially reliable representation of Jesus, whereas the later apocryphal Gospels, drawing more freely on oral tradition, obscure the true lineaments of Jesus' person and message. Tradition, then, is regarded as undependable.[10]

The inadequacy of tradition as a criterion is still more evident when one takes into account, second, the multiplicity of conflicting traditions competing for credence. We are all confronted by the claims of rival traditions, whether religious or antireligious. To rest one's convictions on tradition is to invoke an argument that can be turned against oneself, for the religions and ideologies one rejects are themselves warranted by tradition. Tradition cannot provide an adequate norm for choosing among traditions. By failing to examine and criticize our own traditions we immure ourselves in an intellectual ghetto and cut ourselves off from the wider human conversation.

A third objection may now be mentioned. As history shows,

every major advance in thought or achievement is followed by a period of inferior imitation and commentary. Jesus himself castigated the Pharisees for allowing human traditions to obscure the word of God as given through Abraham and the Sinai revelation. Reformers of all ages have felt the need to clear away the secondary growth by which the message of the gospel becomes encumbered. To recapture the freshness of the original inspired insights, it is often necessary to bypass the second-rate minds who have tried to explain and interpret them. Martin Heidegger lucidly expressed this danger. "Tradition takes hold of what has come down to us and delivers it over to self-evidence; it blocks our access to those primordial 'sources' from which the categories and concepts handed down to us have been in part quite genuinely drawn."[11]

Still another criticism is made by Immanuel Kant and the champions of the Enlightenment.[12] Thought, they maintain, should be personal and free. By encouraging us to substitute the judgment of others for our own, tradition keeps us in a state of immaturity. The authoritarianism of traditional thinking leads to unauthentic knowledge, in which we hold things to be true or false simply on the ground that others have said so. This procedure is alienating, suffocating, and demeaning of personal dignity.

Finally, it is alleged, tradition binds us to the past and thereby prevents us from responding appropriately to the current situation. Past thinkers, however talented, could not escape being conditioned by the historical and cultural situation in which they lived. Their opinions, consequently, cannot be made normative for our own thinking. In view of the cultural gap that separates us from our ancestors, we are obliged to think for ourselves or else be ignorant. In her book *Between Past and Future* (1961), Hannah Arendt maintained that tradition in religion, philosophy, and politics had simply vanished from the contemporary world. This disappearance, she held, "is neither the result of anyone's deliberate choice nor subject to further decision."[13]

The Modernist Concept of Tradition

These criticisms, directed against the concept of tradition as such, are particularly damaging to what I have described as the traditionalist concept of tradition. In an effort to meet these criticisms, certain twentieth-century thinkers, beginning with the modernists at the dawn of the century, have sought to recast the idea of tradition, so that it is no longer subject to these objections. In light of these efforts, one might be warranted in speaking of a modernist notion of tradition, but this notion, it must be confessed, is a logical construct that would be difficult to verify in the writings of any particular author. Although rarely held in pure form, this modernist conception describes an attitude or outlook that has occasionally surfaced and is still very much in the air we breathe.

For the modernist, tradition is not to be defined in terms of its content, which is variable. Tradition is an activity, a process, whereby new generations are introduced into the previous stages of development and equipped to carry the same process further. Recipients of the tradition are not required to believe or say exactly what their predecessors believed and said, but rather to learn the method by which knowledge is advanced and to pick up the question at the present stage. Far from suffocating personal thought, tradition, as viewed by the modernist, stimulates originality and creativity.

In defense of this progressive view of tradition, some theologians appeal to the history of science. Anyone who wants to become a scientist must become apprenticed, so to speak, to the scientific community and submit to education within that community. Only if you accept the methods of the science can you hope to make new discoveries and get them accredited by your peers. Even in a conflict of opinions, as the philosopher Michael Polanyi points out, intelligent discussion is possible only because the participants are all speaking out of the same tradition. He then continues,

We can see here the wider relationship, upholding and transmitting the premises of science, of which the master-pupil relationship forms one facet. It consists in the whole system of scientific life rooted in a common tradition. Here is the ground on which the premises of science are established; they are embodied in a tradition, the tradition of science.[14]

Philosopher Alfred North Whitehead was struck by the difference of people's attitudes toward advances of knowledge in the fields of science and religion.[15] When a religious belief is proved wrong, he remarked, people regard it as a setback for religion, but when a scientific proposition is disproved, everybody takes it to be a triumph for science. If religion could accept the scientific notion of fluid traditions, Whitehead argued, religion could be as progressive as science and would not continually be put on the defensive against new ideas, as usually seems to be the case.

Alfred Loisy and the modernists of his day may be said to have looked on Catholicism as a fluid tradition of this kind. They believed that the Catholic church took its rise from Jesus and the apostles, but that the modern church was not committed to the particular ideas that Jesus or the apostles had held. Christianity, as they saw it, was a movement that took its departure from Jesus but was in no way bound to repeat what he had thought and said. The task of the living magisterium, they believed, was to keep the Christian consciousness abreast of the times; the magisterium could change, and if necessary reverse, its teaching to keep pace with the dialectic of human and spiritual development.

Attractive though the modernist approach can seem as an answer to current objections, it does not furnish a view of tradition that is satisfactory from the point of view of Christian and Catholic faith. Science is defined not in terms of any particular beliefs but rather in terms of its method. The tradition of science, therefore, is primarily methodological rather than substantive. If religion were a purely human quest, it could be content with methodological traditions of this kind.

But a religion such as Christianity professes to be a divine revelation having a definite content, namely God's gracious manifestation in Jesus Christ of his being and his saving will.

To be a Christian, therefore, means something more than to look upon Jesus and the apostles as the point of departure for a movement that transcends them. Tradition, for the Catholic, is more than a process of adaptation and discovery. It has a content that commands the assent and reverence of its adherents. Although science gets its identity from its method, the opposite is true of religion. The content is the distinctive element that distinguishes one religion from another. Religious tradition, in other words, is primarily substantive. It is inextricably bound up with the ideas and values it transmits.

Blondel and the Tacit Dimension

Are we then caught in a dilemma between the objectivism of the traditionalists and the subjectivism of the modernists, between the static approach of the former and the fluidity of the latter? These questions were faced by the French lay philosopher Maurice Blondel, a contemporary of Loisy. In his *History and Dogma* (1904) Blondel tried to mark out a middle path between the dogmatism of the Scholastics, which he called Procrustean, and the historicism of the modernists, which he called Protean. The dogmatists, he believed, uncritically subjected history to dogma, with the result that history was permitted only to confirm what the dogmatic system required. The historicists, on the other hand, subjected dogma to history and thus fell into historical relativism.

As a means of transcending the antithesis between historicism and dogmatism, Blondel proposed his concept of tradition.[16] The modernists, he believed, neglected the real continuity in the church's teaching, whereas the dogmatists overlooked its flexibility. The common error of both schools was to identify knowledge too closely with conceptual thought and formal declaration. Since the content of Christian faith is mystery, it is never fully reducible to explicit statement; it always remains to some degree unspecifiable. Hence Christianity cannot be transmitted wholly or even primarily by explicit teaching and systematic argument. Tradition, according to Blondel, is able to transmit the lived reality of the past.

Tradition, then, is the bearer of what is tacitly known and thus of what cannot be expressed in clear, unambiguous statements. If its function were to provide only what written texts could say, tradition would be a very inferior source of knowledge about Jesus and the biblical revelation. More important than the question how God's words have been remembered is the question how Jesus has left us the means of legitimately supplementing what he did not say. Tradition, for Blondel, is the church's continuing capacity to interpret, to discern, to penetrate. Far from being a confining or retrograde force, it is a power of development and expansion.

Crucial to the Blondelian system is the idea of tacit knowledge. Although this term may be puzzling, the reality is very familiar to all of us. A prime instance is what we call know-how: I know how to swim, how to ride a bicycle, how to type, and so forth. In none of these instances can I give a clear description that would enable me to transmit the skill verbally. Unless I look at the keyboard I cannot tell you where the letter *K* is, but when actually typing I can without looking hit the right key. In other words, I know more than I can say, even to myself. To actuate my knowledge, I must perform, and in the very performance I can seize my knowledge, as it were, in action.

Already in antiquity Aristotle recognized what we may call the tacit dimension in moral knowledge. To find out in the concrete what is just or prudent or brave or chaste, it is quite useless, Aristotle maintained, to argue deductively. I must ask the person who has the virtue in question. Such a person, by consulting his or her own inclinations, can discern. There are thus two distinct kinds of knowledge: objective knowledge, which is derived by formal inference from looking at objects, and knowledge by instinct or connaturality, which is gained by consulting one's own inclinations or actions. I know how to type because I have acquired the habit or facility; this knowledge is not just in my mind, but in my whole being, including my own body. I can know how to distinguish between courage and foolhardiness if I am a courageous, rather than a foolhardy, person, or if I ask a person whom I know to be courageous. Such a person knows not by theory but by inclination and action.

Similar to this, according to many theologians, is the believer's knowledge of matters of faith. The church and its members know the God of Jesus Christ by a kind of personal familiarity, by dwelling in the faith. Faith-knowledge is, in the first instance, tacit. It is a kind of instinct or second nature that prompts us to worship and to behave as believers do. Only within the practical obedience of love, said Blondel, is the word of God preserved and transmitted in its integrity. "Faithful action is the Ark of the Covenant where the confidences of God are found, the Tabernacle where he perpetuates his presence and his teaching."[17]

The knowledge of faith, though primarily tacit, can to some degree come to expression, just as can the skills of art or the principles of virtue. The church can to some extent educate its new members by handing them documents of the faith, such as the Scriptures, the creeds, and the statements of popes and councils. These statements, however, leave considerable margin for right or wrong interpretation, and thus further training is needed to impart the skill of finding God in the documents. This skill is like that of speaking a new language or singing a new tune. The master cannot say in exact words how to find God in the Bible, but the skill can be imparted by the experience of being affiliated to a community of faith. The novice who has acquired the art knows by a kind of existential affinity rather than by explicit or articulate knowledge. Christian faith is ordinarily acquired by living within the church and participating in its corporate life.

In the light of this digression we may now return to the theme of tradition. Christian tradition is in the first instance the handing on from generation to generation of what is tacitly known by the community. This communication takes place within the community of faith and under the direction of its leaders. Neophytes are inducted into the tradition by guided behavior, under the supervision of those who have mastered the tradition. Prayer, worship, and sacramental life are vital elements in the continuing education by which Christians grow in the tacit awareness we call faith. In order to acquire the tradition one must become as a little child, submitting with docility to the authority of mature believers. Tradition itself is grasped not by objective knowledge—that is to say, by looking at it—but by participatory knowledge—that is, by dwelling in it. Tradition influences us most effectively when we are not expressly conscious of it. By shaping our powers of perception, tradition enables us to perceive in the Christian symbols what the church itself perceives.

I conclude, then, that the essential and primary function of Christian tradition is not to transmit explicit knowledge, which can better be done by written documents, nor simply to provide a method of discovery, but to impart a tacit, lived awareness of the God to whom the Christian Scriptures and symbols point. Christian tradition is marked by a deep reverence for its own content, which it strives to protect against any dilution or distortion. The tradition is not a mere method of investigation and discovery.

Religious Tradition: Conservative and Innovative

Religions, inasmuch as they claim to transmit access to the divine, demand unusually strong commitments and consequently possess unrivaled staying power. It is not by accident that the great world religions—including Hinduism, Buddhism, Judaism, Christianity, and Islam—are older than any existing political, educational, or other secular institutions. In spite of the great strains put upon tradition in the mobile, pluralistic culture of our day, traditional religions show no signs of dying out. In many parts of the world, traditional religion is stronger today than it has been for centuries.

In theory a religion could be individualistic and progressive, as Whitehead wanted religion to be, but in point of fact most religions are predominantly communal and stable. Convinced of possessing either a divine revelation or at least some privileged insights into the divine, religions take strong measures to perpetuate their content. Among these measures are tradition, hierarchy, and Scripture.

Tradition is conservative because, by shaping the apprehensive powers of its own bearers, it enables them to see what the community of faith already sees. The tradition is self-confirming, because the trust that people place in it is rewarded by new powers of vision.

Most religious communities are organized societies dominated by a hierarchy. The tradition is controlled from above by acknowledged leaders who are responsible for maintaining the full heritage of the faith. Popular religiosity exists and may be officially encouraged, but no doctrinal or liturgical innovations are formally accepted without being at least tacitly approved by the hierarchical leadership. In Roman Catholicism the hierarchical element is particularly conspicuous, but approximate equivalents may be found in other branches of Christianity and indeed in practically all religions.

Most of the so-called higher religions (that is, those characteristic of literate cultures) stabilize themselves by adopting certain books as their sacred Scriptures. These canonical writings, composed in the formative stage of the community, are a deposit of early tradition and hence cannot be sharply contrasted with tradition. They serve as norms for later tradition, which develops in partial dependence on them. The church through its living tradition identifies the books that are to comprise its Scriptures and determines, in large measure, how these books are to be interpreted.

This conservative aspect of tradition, however, would be misunderstood unless one took into account another aspect, which we might call innovative, or at least renovative. Tradition, I shall maintain, is not only self-confirming; it is also self-renewing.

In the theory I have propounded (as contrasted with traditionalism) tradition is not an end in itself; it is not perpetuated for its own sake. It is a means to an end. Religious people "dwell in" the tradition in order to achieve personal insight into the reality to which the tradition points. In a scientific tradition the object of interest is the real physical world; in religion, it is God.

This objective provides a touchstone by which traditions can be evaluated and enriched. We can responsibly judge among traditions by applying the goal as a criterion. A tradition is tested, in the first place, by its capacity to provide a happy dwelling place for the human spirit. A tradition that is uninhabitable fails to gather and maintain a community; it simply falls apart. Second, a religious tradition is tested by the ability of the members to find God in it. If it functions properly, it leads to personal experience of the divine. As Friedrich von Hügel put it, there is a mystical element in all religion. Encounters with the divine in worship and contemplation manifest the value of the tradition, which provides the possibility of these encounters, and at the same time show up the limitations in the tradition, because the divine is far greater than all the created means of access to it. Recognizing that human speech and symbolism are inevitably deficient, the mystic is grateful for the help offered by the religious tradition and does not demand that it do the impossible. The tradition is validated to the extent that it enables those who dwell in it to go beyond it and, so to speak, break out.[18]

Jewish and Christian religion deliberately cultivates prophetic and mystical experience as a means of enriching and renewing its tradition. Isaiah and Jeremiah, Paul and John, not to mention Jesus himself, were profoundly indebted to the tradition they inherited. Thanks to it, they entered into personal communion with God and were thereby enabled to energize and reshape their own tradition. Down through the centuries, the Christian tradition has been further enriched by all the holy persons who have experienced and responded to God as made present in the symbols of the tradition. We, their successors, find God not only in the originating symbols that were at the disposal of our forebears, but also in the responses of the saints, who by their living example unfold the riches of the gospel. "The saints," as Hans Urs von Balthasar puts it, "are tradition at its most living."[19]

The relationship between tradition and innovation in religion is thus a dialectical one of mutual priority and dependence. If tradition, as I have suggested, is a matter of dwelling in the already given, innovation may be seen as a process of breaking out. Paradoxically, it is by dwelling in the tradition that we get the force and insight to break out and, so to speak, see for ourselves. But what we see by the help of tradition, we then offer as an enrichment of the tradition. Understood in terms of this dialectic, tradition is not an incessant repetition of the already given. It demands, and in a sense includes, its own opposite, innovation.

Innovation might seem to threaten the substance of the tradition itself. That is a real danger, and therefore the religious community must be continually on guard against disruptive and debilitating change. One of the gravest responsibilities of the hierarchical leadership is to pass judgment on new proposals by estimating their probable impact on the faith of the community. Occasionally a brilliant innovation may be rejected, rightly or wrongly, as antithetical to sound tradition. In such cases, tragic schisms between rival factions are likely to occur. These schisms must sometimes be accepted in order to avoid the still greater tragedy of allowing the tradition to be corrupted.

According to Christian faith, there are limits to innovation. The true content of Christian tradition is nothing other than

Christ, who is the same yesterday, today, and forever (Heb 13:8). If the tradition functions in such a way as to afford a living personal encounter with him, the feedback of the encounter into the tradition will not generally be disruptive but on the contrary clarifying and enriching. Christianity, because it possesses in Christ the ultimate truth, does not stand in need of essential reconstruction, yet it is always open to movement from the implicit to the explicit, from symbolic forms to personal experience, from lived commitment to reflective realization. Recognizing this dynamism, Blondel was able to write, "Nothing can modify Tradition which does not, when put to the test, reveal itself as compatible with it and favorable to its progress."[20] A little later he added, "Careful not to hide its talent safely away, and faithful to the injunction to make it bear fruit, Tradition is less concerned to conserve than to discover: it will only attain the Alpha at the Omega."[21]

This Blondelian understanding of tradition, which I have sought to restate in my own words, promotes the human and religious values that traditionalism tends to impede: personal judgment, direct experience, adaptation, responsible decision, and innovation. Authentic innovations, since they arise out of an experience of the very reality carried by the tradition, do not erode the tradition but rather reinforce and revitalize it.

Vatican II's Debt to Blondel

Blondel's dynamic, personalistic theory of tradition was coolly received by both the modernists and the scholastics of his day. It did, however, come into favor in French Catholicism in the 1940s and 1950s. Thanks in part to *periti* such as Yves Congar, Blondel's approach made its way into the teaching of Vatican II.[22] Blondel's *History and Dogma*, though written sixty years in advance, may almost be read as a commentary on the second chapter of Vatican II's Constitution on Divine Revelation.

Three features of the council's chapter on tradition resonate most notably with Blondel's theory. In the first place, tradition is seen not as an end or object in itself, but as a means whereby the church and its members can enter into a living relationship with God. Through tradition, the council states, the sacred writings "are more profoundly understood and unceasingly made actual" in the church, "and thus God, who spoke of old, uninterruptedly converses with the Bride of his beloved Son; and the Holy Spirit . . . makes the word of Christ dwell abundantly" in the believing community (*DV* 8).

Second, tradition is not seen primarily as a matter of word or propositional truth, but rather as something communicated through action, example, and worship. According to the council the apostles were initiated into the tradition when they received it "from the lips of Christ, from living with him, and from what he did, or what they had learned through the prompting of the Holy Spirit" (*DV* 7). The apostolic tradition (*quod ab Apostolis traditum est*) is not a mere set of doctrines; it "includes everything that contributes to the holiness of life, and the increase of faith of the People of God; and so the Church, in its teaching, life, and worship, perpetuates and hands on to all generations all that the Church itself is, all that it believes" (*DV* 8).

Finally, tradition is seen as progressive and dynamic rather than simply conservative and static. "This tradition which comes from the apostles," says the Constitution, "develops (*proficit*) in the Church with the help of the Holy Spirit" (*DV* 8). The progress is held to occur through the prayer, contemplation, and religious experience of the faithful and through the preaching of the bishops. In this manner, the church, it is affirmed, "constantly moves forward toward the fullness of divine truth until the words of God reach their complete fulfillment in it" (*DV* 8).

The vital, realistic, and forward-looking concept of tradition promoted by Vatican II may impress Archbishop Lefebvre and his fellow traditionalists as a capitulation to modernism. But it is in fact as decisively opposed to modernism as was the teaching of Blondel, who sharply criticized Loisy and the modernists of his day. As Yves Congar points out in response to Lefebvre, tradition is never a matter of slavishly repeating the formulas of the past without regard to the needs and opportunities of the present day. Tradition is a living reality thanks to the abiding presence of the Holy Spirit in the People of God. No Catholic has the right to doubt the involvement of the Holy Spirit in the collegial action of the 2,500 bishops responsible for the decisions of Vatican II.[23]

The few short paragraphs of *Dei Verbum* on the subject of tradition may seem almost insignificant in comparison with the massive total output of the council. Vatican II is chiefly remembered not for its work on tradition but rather for its insistence on flexibility, modernization, and dialogue. These other themes, however, could only be debilitating unless the church had the capacity to preserve its identity in the course of transition. In our kaleidoscopically changing world many Christians are looking for assurance that their faith is not doomed to perish like the religions of ancient Greece and Rome. It is therefore a matter of great urgency for Catholics to appreciate how the Constitution on Divine Revelation found ways of safeguarding the permanence and universality of God's gift in Christ while at the same time allowing for great fluidity in the formulations, customs, and practices by which that gift is communicated.

6. Authority and Conscience: Two Needed Voices

A Pervasive Human Problem

The tension between authority and conscience arises in many areas of life—for example, in the citizen's relationship to political authority, in the scholar's relation to academic authorities, and in the believer's relation to the church. In fact, the problem is likely to emerge anywhere that authority asserts itself and is thought to impose an obligation to assent or obey. Thus a child might feel justified in disobeying its parents or a soldier in refusing to follow the command of an officer. When we hear about conflicts of this kind, our sympathies are torn between respect for the rights of conscience and impatience with those who fail to heed the voice of authority. The liberal spontaneously identifies with the dissident; the conservative spontaneously sides with the guardians of conformity and order.

According to the Catholic ethical tradition, conscience is the ultimate subjective norm of all human action. By conscience I do not here mean a blind feeling or instinct but a personal and considered judgment about what one ought or ought not to do or to have done. By calling conscience the subjective norm, moral theologians intend to distinguish it from the objective norm, which is frequently described as right reason, that is, reason that apprehends the objective order of things, including the will of God as manifested through nature and revelation. A person's conscience can be out of phase with what is objectively right. In such a case the individual will not be guilty for following the voice of conscience but may be guilty for having failed to form that conscience by using the necessary means. Conscience, therefore, is not autonomous. It cannot speak responsibly unless it has been properly educated. When we are in doubt about whether our conscience is correct we have an obligation to seek guidance and instruction.

Without denying the normative value of conscience for the individual, public authority must also defend the rights of persons who might be injured by others seeking to follow the dictates of an erroneous conscience. The fact that a man thinks he ought to commit a murder does not imply the right to carry out such a crime. The state seeks to deter criminal actions, however well intended, and even uses force to restrain criminals from doing what they may feel conscientiously obliged to do. Thus the rights of conscience are far from absolute.

Most societies, of course, try to keep physical compulsion to a minimum. They try to educate members of the community so that each will have a moral judgment that supports the common good. Rather early in life, individuals are subjected to education that will socialize them into the group. The young are trained by parents and teachers in whose selection they have little or no choice. But through such training their freedom is nurtured so that later they can make mature and principled choices. Without social formation we could have only an infantile and stunted freedom. The members of every social group form their personal moral norms with some dependence on the group, its customs, its prevalent axioms, its legal and literary classics, its heroes, and its living teachers. Authority is the voice of those who are presumed to be able to furnish reliable guidance. Just as we turn to lawyers, doctors, and investment counselors in their respective spheres of competence, so we turn to specialists to guide us in making moral decisions. But we remain morally free to disregard the experts and go against their recommendation if we judge responsibly that they have erred. As the general reaction to the Nazi "crimes against humanity" illustrated, obedience is no excuse for doing what offends an upright conscience.

The relationship between authority and personal judgment may be described as dialectical. That is to say, the two are neither identical nor separable. Our personal convictions about what is right and wrong are at least partially shaped by what the community and its leaders have taught us, and on the basis of those convictions we determine whether to follow the community's authorities in a given instance. To the extent that we have been successfully socialized into the community, our free and spontaneous judgments about right and wrong tend to coincide with the rules and expectations of the community.

Cases of conflict are the exception rather than the rule. Yet such cases do arise. In the area of civil life we are familiar with the phenomena of loyal dissent and conscientious objection. An enlightened government with a tradition of civil liberties makes provision for the rights of those who feel bound in conscience not to serve as combatants in a given war or not to undergo blood transfusions. Yet there are limits to what people are permitted to do in the name of conscience. As I have already indicated, they are not permitted to trample on the rights of other persons or to jeopardize the common good.

In the academic world similar conflict situations sometimes occur. The school or university maintains the right to select professors who will impart the ideas and values that it regards as educational. Faculty members, on the other hand, insist on their right to communicate the convictions they have reached on the basis of serious research and reflection. To protect both sets of rights as far as possible, universities have adopted elaborate procedures for hiring, promotion, and dismissals. Sometimes respect for academic freedom compels them to retain faculty members of whose teaching they disapprove—a procedure that the academic world regards as preferable to giving the administration discretionary authority to dismiss otherwise competent professors whose ideas are deemed unacceptable.

Authority in the Church

These introductory remarks about political and educational institutions can greatly help us to understand the subject of this chapter, authority and freedom in the church. The problems

96 / THE RESHAPING OF CATHOLICISM

in each case are similar and yet also profoundly different. The analogies between the church and institutions such as the secular state and the independent university are helpful only to a limited extent, because the church, while it has the features of a human society, is very different in its purpose, origins, and means. Neither the state nor the independent university, at least as conceived in our American tradition, is committed to any substantive set of beliefs about the ultimate nature of reality. The state is a community of people willing to live together under the same laws, even though they may vehemently disagree in their philosophies and theologies. The academy is a community of scholars committed to adhere to certain methods of investigation and communication without necessarily sharing any common convictions about the way things are. The church, however, is by nature a society of faith and witness. It exists only to the extent that it continues to adhere to a specific vision of the world—one centered on Jesus Christ as Lord and Savior. Unlike any secular organization, the church has a deposit of faith that must be maintained intact and transmitted to new members. Thus the church cannot accommodate the same kind of ideological pluralism that is acceptable in the secular state or university.

A second difference flows from the origin of the church. Unlike the secular state, the university, or any other institution on the face of the earth, the church, according to Christian belief, has been established by the action of God in Jesus Christ. The members of the church, including the highest officeholders, are not free to change in a substantive way the beliefs, structures, purposes, and forms of worship of the church. They are trustees, obliged to safeguard the trust committed to them.

Third, the church differs from other societies in the means whereby it discharges its mission. Unlike the secular state and many other organized groups, the church, at least in modern times, does not use physical coercion. It has no prisons and does not execute persons convicted of crimes such as heresy.

It uses only the "sword of the Spirit," which works through love and persuasion and does not impose even spiritual penalties except in the hope of bringing about repentance and reform. The Declaration on Religious Freedom adopted at Vatican Council II, in asserting these principles, cautiously admitted that in the history of the church "there have at times appeared ways of acting which were less in accord with the spirit of the gospel and even opposed to it" (*DH* 12).

The church also has at its disposal special aids not available to other societies. It has received from apostolic times inspired Scriptures and inspired traditions as expressions of its faith and guideposts for future development. Christ, moreover, has promised to remain with the community and its official leaders to the end of time. "Behold, I am with you always, until the end of the age" (Mt 28:20). In the Catholic tradition the hierarchy is considered to be included in the promises originally directed by Christ to the apostles, such as "Whoever hears you hears me" (Lk 10:16) and "As the Father has sent me, I send you" (Jn 20:21). This confidence in the continuing presence of Christ in the church and its hierarchy profoundly affects the attitudes of believing Catholics toward ecclesiastical authority. They are convinced that in submitting to popes and bishops as teachers and rulers, they are submitting to Christ and to God.

When we think of authority in the church, we must surely include Scripture and tradition, popes and bishops, but the system of authorities is in fact much more complex and extensive. As the Second Vatican Council clearly taught, Scripture and tradition were committed not only to the hierarchy, but also to the church as a whole (*DV* 10). All the members of the church share in the priestly, prophetic, and royal offices of Christ and therefore have their own part to play in the mission of the church (*AA* 2). Thanks to a supernatural sense of the faith that characterizes the People of God as a whole (*LG* 12), believers can find reliable guidance in turning to the community of faith. As Cardinal Newman pointed out in his celebrated article *On Consulting the Faithful,* even popes have been accustomed to seek out the opinions of the Christian people before they define mattes of doctrine.[1] Quoting Hilary of Poitiers as a witness, Newman maintained that at times the ears of the faithful have been holier than the hearts of their bishops.[2] Thus, when we think of the authorities available to the Catholic Christian, we should not overlook the consensus of the faithful themselves.

Still another source of authority in Catholicism is that of theologians. The Catholic church has always had a deep respect for learning and intelligence. It has conferred on outstanding theologians the titles of father or doctor of the Church. John Wycliffe in the fourteenth century and Martin Luther in the sixteenth were censured because, among other things, they failed to respect the authority of the theological schools. In the late Middle Ages and in early modern times university faculties of theology exercised a true magisterium, rendering ecclesiastically recognized judgments as to the orthodoxy or heterodoxy of new opinions. Although theological faculties no longer exercise such an independent magisterium, they have continued to collaborate very closely with popes and bishops in making judgments about heresy and in drawing up official doctrinal formulations.

The relationship between the hierarchy and the theologians, at least as it stands in modern times, can be clarified by a distinction between official and personal authority. The popes and bishops, as members of the hierarchy, enjoy authority by virtue of their status or position in the church. Their statements have authority not so much because of their personal wisdom and prudence as because of their sacramental ordination and the office they hold. With theologians the reverse is true. Whatever authority they enjoy accrues to them not primarily because of their position but rather because of their reputation for learning and acumen. Even their scholarly degrees and academic appointments are significant merely as presumptive signs of personal ability.

Once this distinction is understood it becomes apparent why theologians are normally used as consultants by popes and bishops. The authority of office does not simply take the place of personal authority. Rather, it requires for its proper exercise that the officeholder either be a personal authority or make use of others who have personal authority. Otherwise the authority of office will be bought into discredit, to the great detriment of the church. The authority of office is a kind of gift or charism that, if used well, enables the officeholder to draw upon the knowledge and wisdom that is present in the whole community, including the scholars, and bring this to a focus. In so doing the hierarchy is able to formulate the church's faith in an official way and to make judgments about the compatibility of current opinions with that faith.

In its official statements the hierarchical magisterium sometimes imposes a given formulation as an apt expression of the truth of the gospel. Sometimes it condemns a misleading formulation as contrary to that truth. And sometimes it makes judgments of a permissive character—stating not that a given opinion is true but that it may be held and is not to be condemned as heretical. Thus the magisterium serves as an agency for protecting the legitimate freedom of theologians to speculate about the truth without harassment from rival theological schools.

Options for the Hierarchy

When the hierarchy is faced by a conflict of opinions in the church, it does not always succeed in achieving a perfectly adequate response. Broadly speaking, mistakes of two kinds are possible—excessive permissiveness and excessive rigidity. It is hard to know which of the two errors has done more harm.

The first of the two errors was more common at certain earlier periods in history, when communication between Rome and the other countries was difficult. During the Middle Ages, when there was little contact between Rome and Constantinople, the Eastern and Western churches developed different ways of thinking about subjects such as the papacy and the Trinity; the two groups drifted apart until they finally ceased to be able to recognize each other's formulations as orthodox. Then again, on the eve of the Reformation, theological pluralism in northern Europe ran to excess. For example, some nominalist theologians professed an inordinate optimism about human nature, holding that even without grace human beings could perfectly observe the moral law and perform meritorious acts that God would be obliged to reward. Reacting against this, some Augustinians held that human nature had been so corrupted by the Fall that it was impossible for human beings to do anything but sin unless God's grace were to take hold of them, so to speak, by main force. Although doctrinal issues were not the sole cause of the Protestant Reformation, it is possible that the tragic split could have been averted had the excessive pluralism been held in check by a timely exercise of church authority. The price of unity, it may be said, is perpetual doctrinal vigilance.

After the sixteenth century the second deviation became more common. The Roman magisterium did practice vigilance, but in some cases it was inclined to condemn new opinions without sufficient deliberation. A famous example is the Galileo case. More recently, in the first decades of the twentieth century, the Roman Biblical Commission issued a whole series of decrees that proved, with the passage of time, unduly restrictive. For a generation or two Catholic biblical scholars were severely hampered in their dealings with colleagues from other traditions on the basis of new scholarly discoveries. Fortunately, in the pontificate of Pius XII the restrictions were eased, and the result has been an unprecedented flowering of Catholic biblical scholarship.

In retrospect, it seems clear that the reactions of the Roman magisterium to new developments in the physical and historical sciences were excessively defensive. But that was not so clear at the time. When the new theories first arose, the faith of many Catholics was troubled. Perhaps by its conservatism in these matters the hierarchy did in fact shield the faith of many Catholics who would have been shaken by the new advances and gave a needed space of time in which the compatibility of the new science with the old faith could be discerned. Many liberal Protestants, who impetuously embraced the latest hypotheses, watered down their faith or even lost it entirely.

We must recognize, therefore, that there can be such a thing in the church as mutable or reformable teaching. The element of mutability comes from the fact that such teaching seeks to mediate between the abiding truth of the gospel and the sociocultural situation at a given time and place. For example, the condemnations of usury in the Middle Ages were based upon valid moral principles but were linked, more than was recognized at the time, to a precapitalist economy. Once the shift to capitalism had been made, the moral teaching had to be modified. Other changes in doctrine were linked to new astronomical discoveries (such as the overthrow of the Ptolemaic system), new biological theories (such as evolution), new methods in historical criticism, and new developments in politics.

Changes such as those just mentioned have led to important shifts in Catholic doctrine, even within recent memory. Vatican Council II approved of new attitudes toward biblical studies, religious freedom, and ecumenism. Those of us who have lived through these changes have learned how important it is not to confuse reformable doctrine with the content of the faith itself.

Responses to Hierarchical Teaching

At this point we may raise again the question of conscience. In any response to magisterial teaching conscience is of course involved. Two questions must be asked: can we conscientiously assent, and can we conscientiously do other than assent?

The answer will be different according to the kind of teaching involved. In some instances, rather rare, the church invokes its infallible teaching power. Practically speaking, this happens only in matters close to the heart of Christian faith, after much consultation and deliberation, where there has been a virtually unanimous consensus for a long period of time. In such cases the faithful are under strong pressure to assent, for the church has committed itself to such a degree that to reject the definition is in effect to reject the church itself. An outright denial of a recognized dogma or other infallible teaching is tantamount to a renunciation of the Catholic faith and entails a rupture of communion.

On the other hand we must recognize that a given individual may experience considerable anguish in yielding assent even to a dogma. A poorly educated Catholic or one strongly influenced by the secular mentality of the day may feel compelled to say: I do not understand the meaning of this dogma, or if I understand it correctly I do not see how it can be true, but I trust that if it were better explained to me I might be able to find meaning and credibility in it. Such a reaction, though far from ideal, could be a perfectly honest one, compatible with an upright conscience. A person who reacted in this way could still be considered a Catholic Christian.

Most of the difficulty arises in the sphere of noninfallible teaching, which, as we have seen, is reformable. Such teaching is not proposed as the word of God, nor does the church ask its members to submit with the assent of faith. Rather, the church asks for what is called in official documents *obsequium animi religiosum*—a term that, depending on the context, can be suitably translated by "religious submission of mind," "deference," or "respectful readiness to accept."[3] This term actually includes a whole range of responses that vary according to the content of the teaching, its relationship to the gospel, the kind of biblical and traditional support behind it, the degree of assent given to it in the church at large, the person or office from which the teaching comes, the kind of document in which it appears, the constancy of the teaching, and the emphasis given to the teaching in the text or texts. Because the matter is so complex, one cannot make any general statement about what precisely amounts to "religious submission of mind."[4]

Normally, the response of the Catholic to official but noninfallible teaching will be something more than a respectful hearing and something less than a full commitment of faith. Unless one has serious reasons for thinking that the magisterium has erred in the particular case, conscience will prompt one to submit on the basis that the magisterium is generally trustworthy. Some have compared the guidance of the magisterium in such matters to that of a doctor or lawyer, but the differences are important. The doctor or lawyer is not divinely commissioned, and the content of such professional advice would normally have little relation to salvation. Because of the promise of Christ to be with the pastors of the church when they teach in the area of faith and morals, we have special assurances that in following them we are not being led astray.

With respect to noninfallible teaching, therefore, there are two possible errors. One would be to treat it as if it were infallible. Such an excessive emphasis could overtax the individual's capacity to assent and could lead to a real crisis of faith in the event of a later change of doctrine. The opposite error would be to treat noninfallible magisterial teaching as though it were simply a matter of theological opinion. This would be an error for the reasons already explained. The hierarchy is not just a group of theorists but a body of pastors who are sacramentally ordained and commissioned as teachers of the faith.

Conscientious Dissent

Which of the two errors just mentioned is the greater temptation for American Catholics? In the generation before Vatican II, when they were still something of a foreign enclave, American

Catholics gloried in their obedience to their clergy and to Rome. An exaggerated conformism still persists in certain circles. But the more prevalent danger today is that of excessive distrust. Charles Dickens, in 1842, identified this as an American trait:

> One great blemish in the popular mind of America, and the prolific parent of an innumerable brood of evils, is Universal Distrust. Yet the American citizen plumes himself upon this spirit, even when he is sufficiently dispassionate to perceive the ruin it works; and will often adduce it, in spite of his own reason, as an instance of the great sagacity and acuteness of the people, and their superior shrewdness and independence.[5]

When he remonstrated that this trait had bad effects on public life, Dickens invariably received the same reply: "There's freedom of opinion here, you know. Every man thinks for himself, and we are not to be easily overreached. That's how our people come to be suspicious."[6] Turning a little later to the subject of religious dissent, Dickens observed that it would be impossible to have an established church in America. "I think the temper of the people, if it admitted of such an Institution being founded amongst them, would lead them to desert it, as a matter of course, merely because it *was* established."[7]

Since Vatican II a certain number of Catholics in this country, having become thoroughly Americanized, resent any interference with their freedom to think as they see fit. When confronted by anything less than a solemn dogmatic pronouncement from Rome, they are inclined to respond, "This teaching is not infallible; I do not have to believe it." Such Catholics might do well to ask themselves whether it is really better to believe less rather than more and to be defiant rather than trusting. Do their critical attitudes in fact correspond to the ideals of humility, concord, and submission that are so powerfully commended in the New Testament?

In the normal case conscience and authority are not opposed. Conscience is not a law unto itself but seeks by its very nature to be conformed to the law of God. Conscience therefore bids one to recognize authority, and authority, in turn, educates one's conscience. Only through a perversion of speech does conscience come to be coupled with dissent and authority with abuse. Conscience and authority normally concur because both are given by the same God as helps for knowing what is to be believed and done.

Even when all of this has been said, it still remains true that there are cases in which a person's conscience will permit or require the nonacceptance of some reformable teaching. Vatican II in effect admitted this by employing as prominent experts a number of theologians whose views had been suspect during the pontificate of Pius XII. Without explicitly contradicting previous papal doctrine, the council took many positions that in fact corrected what had been taught.

Did Vatican II teach the legitimacy of dissent from noninfallible teaching? It did so implicitly by its actions, we may say, but not explicitly by its words. The Theological Commission responsible for paragraph 25 of the Constitution on the Church refused to make any statement, one way or the other, about dissent.[8]

A step beyond the council was taken by the German bishops in a pastoral letter of September 22, 1967, which has been quoted on several occasions by Karl Rahner.[9] This letter recognized that in its effort to apply the gospel to the changing situations of life, the church is obliged to give instructions that have a certain provisionality about them. These instructions, though binding to a certain degree, are subject to error. According to the bishops, dissent may be legitimate provided that three conditions are observed: (1) one must have striven seriously to attach positive value to the teaching in question and to appropriate it personally; (2) one must seriously ponder whether one has the theological expertise to disagree responsibly with ecclesiastical authority; (3) one must examine one's conscience for possible conceit, presumptuousness, or selfishness. Similar principles for conscientious dissent had already been laid down by John Henry

Newman in the splendid chapter on conscience in his *Letter to the Duke of Norfolk* (1874).[10]

A year after the German bishops, the United States hierarchy, on November 15, 1968, took up the question of licit dissent from noninfallible doctrine on the part of theological scholars. Their pastoral letter, entitled *Human Life in Our Day,* fundamentally agreed with the German letter except that it went somewhat further in dealing with the expression of theological dissent. It laid down three conditions: (1) the reasons must be serious and well founded; (2) the manner of the dissent must not question or impugn the teaching authority of the church; and (3) the dissent must not be such as to give scandal. The American bishops added, as had the German bishops, that even responsible dissent does not excuse one from faithful presentation of the authentic doctrine of the church when one is performing a pastoral ministry in its name.[11]

In view of collective pastoral letters such as those of the German and American Bishops' Conferences, it now seems impossible to deny that dissent from the noninfallible magisterium is sometimes licit. For to deny such licitness would be to dissent from the teaching of these documents, which lay down conditions under which dissent may be permitted. Anyone who wants to reject the teaching of these documents on dissent is thereby dissenting from the noninfallible magisterium and thus confirming that very teaching!

Types of Dissent

It is by no means accidental that documents such as these two pastorals should have been issued several years after Vatican II, for the council by its doctrinal shifts ineluctably raised the question of licit dissent. These pastorals do not solve all the problems. Difficult questions can arise as to whether a given teaching is fallible or infallible and whether the conditions for legitimate dissent have been met. Distinctions have to be made between internal dissent, private dissent, public dissent, and organized dissent.

It is relatively easy to justify internal (or tacit) dissent, for there are cases in which Catholics of goodwill find themselves simply unable to accept certain teachings of the magisterium. It is more difficult to justify the expression of dissent, but as we have seen, the United States bishops do admit that this can be licit under certain conditions. If the dissent is expressed only privately, for example, the letters or memoranda circulated to a limited number of persons, there is little danger that the faithful will be misled and the public disedified. But there may be occasions when the dissenter has the right, and even the conscientious obligation, to go public. If theologians such as Yves Congar and John Courtney Murray had not publicly manifested their disagreement with certain official teachings, it is far less likely that Vatican II, with their collaboration, would have adopted new positions on subjects such as ecumenism and religious freedom. Another consideration is that in the world of our day it is often difficult to keep one's communications private.

Dissent is said to be "organized" when a deliberate effort is made to mobilize public opinion against a decision of the magisterium. Richard A. McCormick has pointed out that organized dissent of this kind carries with it special risks and hence demands special warrants. Among the risks he lists the following: it tends to polarize scholars and hierarchical teachers in opposition to each other; it tends to undermine the confidence of the faithful in their pastors; it tends to politicize the church and to discourage truly personal reflection; and, finally, it tends to associate theology with the popular media rather than with serious scholarship. The special warrants for such dissent, according to McCormick, are two: (1) other forms of less sensational dissent are ineffective, and (2) the circumstances are such that unopposed error would cause grave harm.[12] Provided that both these conditions are verified, a theologian might feel conscientiously obliged to conduct a campaign of organized dissent, but it is almost inevitable that others would deplore this action and seek to make it ineffective. The church can rather easily tolerate internal or privately expressed dissent, but it can scarcely help but oppose public and organized dissent to the extent that this would in effect set up a second magisterium in opposition to that of the hierarchy.

Some difficult cases regarding dissent arise in connection with theological education. It is often said, with good reason, that the faithful are entitled to have official Catholic doctrine presented to them in a fair and favorable light. But such presentations can be made at various levels. In catechetical instruction the teacher is expected to present the doctrine of the church rather than the opinions of private theologians. But the case is not so simple in higher education. University students, especially at the graduate level, have the right to know the difference between reformable and irreformable teaching. With regard to the former, Francis A. Sullivan of the Gregorian University has recently stated that such students are entitled to know that there are dissenting positions and to know the arguments on both sides.[13] A professor who adheres to the official teaching must be able to present the objections fairly, and one who questions the official teaching must be able to present the official teaching in a favorable light. A professor who fails on either score is deficient by academic standards.

There is always temptation for church authorities to try to use their power of governance to stamp out dissent. The effort is rarely successful, because dissent simply seeks another forum, where it may become even more virulent. Official doctrines may be called into question by anonymous pamphlets or by comments "not for attribution." To the extent that the suppression is successful, it may also do harm. It inhibits good theology from performing its critical task, and it is detrimental to the atmosphere of freedom in the church. The acceptance of true doctrine should not be a matter of blind conformity, as though truth could be imposed by decree. The church, as a society that respects the freedom of the human conscience, must avoid procedures that savor of intellectual tyranny.

Where dissent is kept within the bounds I have indicated, it is not fatal to the church as a community of faith and witness. If it does occur, it will be limited, reluctant, and respectful. Church authorities will quite properly seek to minimize the adverse effects of public dissent. For example, they should not tolerate the presentation of disapproved doctrines as though these were the teachings of the church. But prelates and others who, in their zeal for orthodoxy, would wish to suppress dissent by Draconian measures, might advantageously meditate on the Gospel parable of the good grain and the weeds. When asked by the servants whether the weeds should be uprooted, the Master replied, "No; lest in gathering the weeds you root up the wheat along with them. Let both grow together until the harvest" (Mt 13:28–30). The mistaken doctrines of hierarchical teachers and of theologians can alike be considered weeds, but it is not easy, at any given moment, to discern exactly which doctrines are mistaken. For this reason it is often necessary to allow both to survive and to pray that the Holy Spirit will give clarity of insight so that God's truth may in the end prevail.

7. The Church and Communications: Vatican II and Beyond

Communication might be described as the way in which people are brought to share certain ideas, feelings, attitudes, or styles of action through contact with others. It does not necessarily signify the transfer of articulated thoughts from a teacher to a learner, though this is one prominent form of communication. It can take place equally well through a kind of catalytic action in which ideas or attitudes come to birth through social encounters. More particularly, religious knowledge and attitudes are not passed on like a baton. They are often "maieutically" induced by processes that activate the religious propensities of the "recipients."

The Theology of Communication

The theology of communication does not deal with the entire range of God's saving work but studies in particular how God brings about attitudes, convictions, and commitments connected with religious faith. Since God normally does this by means of the church, the theology of communication is closely connected with ecclesiology. Under one aspect the church may be seen as "a vast communication network designed to bring men out of their isolation and estrangement and to bring them individually and corporately into communion with God in Christ."[1]

New and urgent questions face the church as it seeks to disseminate the Christian message in the postliterate electronic culture now coming into being. This culture is as different from the age of print, to which the church has grown accustomed, as was that age from the oral culture of primitive Christianity. Recognizing this revolution, the World Council of Churches, at its Uppsala Assembly (1968), issued a report, "The Church and the Media of Mass Communication."[2] The Catholic church, especially since Vatican II, has issued an important series of official documents dealing with the media of social communication. The teaching of these documents will provide material for the present chapter.

The Catholic church has always looked upon Jesus Christ as the supreme self-communication of God. Lateran Council IV (1215) gathered up the sense of many New Testament passages when it declared that Jesus Christ as the Incarnate Word manifested the way of life with special clarity (*viam vitae manifestius demonstravit*, DS 801). The Council of Trent in 1546 spoke of the gospel as the source of all saving truth and moral discipline (*fontem omnis et salutaris veritatis et morum disciplinae*, DS 1501). The same council solemnly taught that the gospel is transmitted through Scripture and apostolic traditions. Vatican Council I, in 1870, repeated in substance the teaching of Trent on Scripture and tradition but made significant advances in its pronouncements on revelation, faith, and the magisterium. Not only did Vatican I detail the ways in which revelation is communicated to the faithful in the church; it also spoke eloquently of the Catholic church as a sign raised up among the nations, inviting outsiders to come to faith and at the same time confirming the faith of its own members (DS 3013–14).

When Vatican II addressed the question of how religious knowledge is communicated, therefore, it was able to follow in the footsteps of several earlier councils. In many of its assertions Vatican II simply paraphrased what had been taught in previous centuries, and in all its pronouncements it sought to avoid contradicting what had been previously taught. It would be a mistake, therefore, to read Vatican II in a vacuum or emphasize its innovations as though all its significant teachings were fresh departures.

One would search in vain in the documents of Vatican II for a single theology of communication. The authors of the sixteen documents, each of which was produced by teams of bishops and theologians and amended many times, represented a variety of theological perspectives. It is convenient to distinguish five major outlooks reflected in the council documents.[3]

Five Models of Communication

The first ecclesiology, which I call hierarchical or institutional, is that of the scholasticism that had been dominant in the seminary manuals for some decades before the Second Vatican Council. This approach, as compared with medieval Scholasticism, is rather narrowly concerned with the authority of office and the obligatory character of official doctrine. It tends to view communication, in the theological sense, as a descending process beginning from God and passing through the papal and episcopal hierarchy to the other members of the church. Scripture and tradition are depicted as sources entrusted to the hierarchical magisterium, which is charged to safeguard and interpret the deposit of faith, especially by the issuance of binding decrees. While little is said about the mode of communication, the assumption seems to be that the teaching of the church is contained in clear, concise statements that have been issued by legitimate authority in proper form, and that it is widely available, at least to the clergy, in printed texts.

This point of view, classically set forth by Pius XII in *Humani generis* (1950), was reflected in many of the preparatory documents for Vatican II and continued to be defended by the so-called conservative minority throughout the council. This outlook asserted itself particularly in chapter III of the Constitution on the Church. In his official *relatio* for the 1964 revision of chapter III, Archbishop Pietro Parente told the council fathers, "The structure of the Church is such, already in the ontological order, that the different elements are inseparably united according to a hierarchical subordination, which is that of the faithful to the priests and to the bishops, that of the bishops to the pope, and that of the pope to Christ. No life and no power can be thought of as existing in this organism which does not derive from Christ, the invisible head, so as to pass through Peter and the bishops to the faithful."[4]

The theory of communication implied in the hierarchical model appears most clearly in article 25 of the Constitution— a favorite text of institutionally minded theologians who appeal to Vatican II. This text states the conditions under which the extraordinary and the ordinary magisterium can teach infallibly, and it goes on to assert, in terms reminiscent of *Humani generis*, the obligation of the faithful to assent to the authentic but noninfallible doctrine of the hierarchical magisterium.

As Antonio Acerbi remarks, the doctrine of the magisterium in chapter III of the Constitution on the Church gives the impression that all teaching and ministry originate from above, through the action of the pope and the bishops. The description of the teaching office in this chapter "presents the episcopal magisterium as though the bishops in their teaching role were in no way related as listeners to the faithful people. A minimalistic standpoint remains operative in this section: i.e., the principle of the authentic magisterium and the conditions of validity of its exercise are asserted without attention to the ramifications of such an act in the totality of the Church's faith and the concrete mode of application of the principle (which would place the episcopal magisterium more explicitly in relation to the faith of the community)."[5]

A second ecclesiology present in the documents of Vatican II is what I like to call the herald model. It came into twentieth-century Catholic theology from Protestant biblical theology and Karl Barth's theology of the word. This model, operative in the Dogmatic Constitution on Divine Revelation and in many parts of the Decree on Missionary Activity, has left traces on article 17 of the Constitution on the Church. According to this article, "the Church has received from the apostles as a task to be discharged even to the ends of the earth [the] solemn mandate of Christ to proclaim the saving truth." Hence the church continues unceasingly to send heralds to proclaim the gospel and thereby prepare hearers to receive and profess the faith. Christ is dynamically present in his word when the Scriptures are read in the church and when the biblical message is proclaimed The same point is also made in the Constitution on the Liturgy, *Sacrosanctum concilium* (*SC* 7).

The first and second models share in common the idea that religious communication takes place primarily through the written and proclaimed word and that the proper response to the word is one of submission and faith. The word, moreover, is entrusted to heralds or teachers who are commissioned to disseminate and defend it. Within this larger agreement five points of difference may be noted.

1. The first model is concerned with relationships within the church between those who administer the word and those to whom they minister. The second model looks upon the ministry of the word as a ministry of the church on behalf of outsiders.

2. The first model makes a sharp distinction between the hierarchy as authoritative teachers (*ecclesia docens)* and the rest of the faithful as learners (*ecclesia discens).* In the second model this distinction is less important. Since the whole church is missionary by its very nature (*AG* 2), all baptized believers are bearers of the message. The obligation of spreading the faith weighs indeed most heavily on bishops as successors of the apostles (*AG* 5), but no disciple of Christ is exempt from this responsibility (*LG* 17). The laity, as sharers in Christ's prophetic office, have the right and duty to collaborate in the task of evangelization (*LG* 34; *AA* 2; *AG* 41).

3. The content of the church's authoritative teaching according to the first model is the doctrine of faith and morals contained explicitly or implicitly in the deposit of faith, including whatever is needed to explain or defend the faith. The content of missionary proclamation, on the other hand, is the good news of salvation through the death and resurrection of Christ. The gospel can be summarized in a variety of ways, of which the following, from the Decree on Missionary Activity, may serve as a sample: "It is sufficient [for conversion] that a person be conscious of having been snatched away from sin and of being led into the mystery of the love of God, who issues the call to enter into a personal relationship with him in Christ" (*AG* 13).

4. The hierarchical model, as it has functioned in modern times, presupposes that the official teaching is available in written texts that are accessible to the faithful everywhere, or at least to the pastors. Thus it is tied to communication through print. The kerygmatic model, which has been revived in the twentieth century, harks back to an age in which oral culture was dominant. The gospel message is spontaneously uttered by sincere believers. It may also be summarized in brief creedal or confessional formulas that can be easily committed to memory.

5. The two modes of communication call for different responses. The response to authoritative hierarchical teaching varies according to the nature of the doctrine and the manner of its proposal. It may call for an assent of divine and Catholic faith or for ecclesiastical faith or for a lesser degree of assent called "religious submission of mind" (*obsequium animi religiosum*). The response to missionary proclamation, on the other hand, is a free act of conversion to the Lord, elicited under the influence of the Holy Spirit, who opens human hearts to the message of salvation (*AG* 13, with reference to Acts 16:14). The fundamental act of Christian faith,

by which one entrusts one's whole self to the God who reveals and promises, is more fully analyzed in the Constitution on Divine Revelation (*DV* 5). In summary, one may say that the response to hierarchical doctrine is a submission of the intellect to an authority that commands respect; the response to kerygmatic preaching is an existential adherence of the whole person to the tidings of salvation.

A third ecclesiological model in Vatican II is the sacramental, which predominates in the first chapter of the Constitution on the Church and in the Constitution on the Liturgy. According to this model, religious communication occurs not only through words but equally through persons and events (*DV* 2). Christ himself is seen as the supreme revelatory symbol, the living Image who renders God in some way visible. Christ communicates not only by what he says but even more by what he is and does. The pattern of his life, and especially of his death and resurrection, manifests God's being and intentions on our behalf (*DV* 4).

In many of the council documents the church is described as an efficacious sign or sacrament in which Christ is not only signified but continues to be present and active for the salvation of the world. In this perspective a merely verbal proclamation, while not inappropriate, would be insufficient. The oral witness of the word would lack substance and credibility unless it were backed up by the witness of personal life. Each Christian community, according to the Decree on Missionary Activity, must become a sign of Christ's presence in the world (*AG* 15).

The Vatican I doctrine of the church as a "sign for the nations" is thus taken up in a new and more dynamic context. The church is obliged to become in historical tangibility what in principle it already is by its very existence—a sign and instrument of Christ's living presence (*LG* 1, 48). To the extent that believers fail to live up to their calling "they must be said to conceal rather than reveal the authentic face of God and of religion" (*GS* 19; cf. *UR* 4).

The Constitution on the Liturgy, drawing on the achievements of the liturgical movement in the decades preceding Vatican II, emphasized the communicative aspect of worship. "The liturgy is thus the outstanding means by which the faithful can express in their lives and manifest to others the mystery of Christ and the real nature of the true Church. . . . Day by day the liturgy builds up those within the Church into the holy temple in the Lord . . . To outsiders the liturgy thereby reveals the Church as a sign raised up among the nations (cf. Is 11:12)" (*SC* 2).

The sacramental mode of communication, while it has analogies with symbolic communication as we know it in ordinary human experience, has certain distinctively theological qualities. The sacred signs produce their saving effect thanks to the power of Christ at work in them. He is present when the gospel is proclaimed, when the Scriptures are read, when the congregation prays and sings, and when the sacramental rites are performed (*SC* 7). The liturgy has a transforming impact only on rightly disposed believers, who allow themselves to be taken up into the mystery of the living Christ. The liturgy is not simply an act of the officiating clergy but that of all the members of the assembly according to their distinct roles (*SC* 14).

A fourth ecclesiological model, implying yet another theology of communication, is that of the church as community or communion. The church in this model is viewed as a fellowship of life, charity, and truth (*LG* 9) animated by the Holy Spirit. For the clearest expression of this model one may study the second chapter of the Constitution on the Church, entitled "The People of God." Here the church is said to be composed of many types of persons, having their own distinct abilities and charisms, working together to build up the whole body in love (*LG* 12). Although not much is said here about communications, it is implied that all play an active role and have the obligation both to contribute their own insights and to be receptive to the insights of others. By their mutual union they anticipate the solidarity of the heavenly city and thereby bear witness to the hope that is in them (*LG* 10).

The communion model of ecclesiology, when applied to communication within the Catholic church, favors common witness and dialogue. In its Decree on Ecumenism, Vatican II extended the communion model to relationships between separated churches and ecclesial communities. By virtue of their incorporation in Christ through faith and baptism, as well as other ecclesial elements, Christians of different ecclesiastical allegiances enjoy a real, though imperfect, communion with one another (*UR* 3). From this it follows that members of these separated bodies may appropriately bear common witness to these central beliefs that they hold in common (*UR* 11–12) and engage in respectful dialogue about points that still cause difficulty among them. In such dialogue they may be able to profit from one another's insights and broaden the areas of agreement, thus intensifying their mutual communion. The Decree on Ecumenism, strongly recommending these methods of communication, ushered in a whole new era in the relations between the Catholic church and the other Christian communities. Although a long road still lies ahead, the progress of the past twenty years has been astonishing.

It might seem that the four models already examined would exhaust the ecclesiologies of Vatican II, but there is, in my opinion, yet a fifth. In some passages of the Pastoral Constitution on the Church in the Modern World, and more rarely in other documents, one finds evidences of what I call a secular-dialogic theology. In this approach the non-Christian world is seen not simply as raw material for the church to convert to its own purposes, nor as a mere object of missionary zeal, but as a realm in which the creative and redemptive will of God is mysteriously at work. On this premise the kind of dialogue that we have examined under the heading of communion ecclesiology can be extended to non-Christian religions and even to secular ideologies. In such dialogue the church can hope to gain as well as to give, to learn as well as to teach. There is also the possibility of joint witness with non-Christians for authentic human and religious values.

This fifth theological perspective appears already in the opening paragraphs of the Pastoral Constitution, *Gaudium et spes*. Christians are here described as inextricably involved with the rest of humanity in the process of world history, which at the present time is bringing the whole human family into a common stream. Rapid worldwide communication, according to this document, is having an unsettling effect on previously isolated cultural groups, especially in the traditional societies (*GS* 6). The advent of the new mass culture, disseminated by new media of communication, is fraught with possibilities of disorientation and social conflict or, alternately, of a universal human solidarity (*GS* 53–55). Christians should enter responsibly into this process, casting their influence on the side of justice, peace, and unity.

In order to be of service to humanity, the church finds it necessary to interpret the signs of the times—a term by which the council evidently means "authentic signs of God's presence and purpose in the happenings, needs, and desires in which this People has a part along with other people of our age" (*GS* 11). The discernment of these signs is described as the task of the whole People of God, pastors and faithful together (*GS* 44). In discussing this process the Pastoral Constitution makes it clear that the laity are not to be passively dependent on the hierarchy: "Let the laity not imagine that their pastors are always such experts as to have at hand a concrete solution to every problem that arises, or even to every serious problem, or that such is in fact the pastors' mission. Rather, enlightened by Christian wisdom and giving close attention to the teaching of the magisterium, let the laity take on their own distinctive roles" (*GS* 43). In the later sections of the same document the freedom of the laity to express their views on matters in which they are competent is strongly asserted (*GS* 62). Secular-dialogic theology therefore has repercussions on the kind of dialogue that takes place within the church.

At a number of points the Pastoral Constitution alludes to the intrinsic value of human institutions that have grown up without help from the church. Renouncing any attitude of haughty superiority, the council professes "great respect" for "all the true, good, and just elements found in the very wide variety of institutions which the human race has established for itself and constantly continues to establish" (*GS* 42). This respect includes the readiness of the church to benefit from these advances. "The Church is not unaware of how much it has profited from the history and development of humanity" (*GS* 44). The experience of history and the development of science and culture have opened roads to truth and disclosed new depths in the nature of the human person (ibid.). As an example, the Pastoral Constitution might have referred to the doctrine of religious freedom set forth in the Declaration on Religious Freedom. In its first sentence this Declaration professes to be responding to the sense of the dignity of the human person that has been imposing itself on the contemporary consciousness of humanity. To keep abreast of this unfolding consciousness can therefore be important for the development of Catholic doctrine.

The two-way exchange appropriate to this model is not limited to interlocutors who are formally religious. Based on the common experience of individuals in community, such dialogue can extend to secular ideologies, not excluding atheism (*GS* 21). But this theological model also provides an excellent foundation for interreligious dialogue. According to the Declaration on the Non-Christian Religions, these religions "often reflect a ray of that Truth which enlightens everyone" (*NA* 2). The Pastoral Constitution uses in this context the language of revelation. "All believers of whatever religion," it states, "have always perceived [God's] voice and manifestation in the discourse of creatures" (*GS* 36). Revelation, as seen in this theology, does not begin with Scripture and tradition, or even with Jesus Christ, but with the Word in whom all things have been created. Grace is presumed to operate in the whole of human history. The church, though it is privileged to know God's supreme self-disclosure in his Incarnate Son, can continually deepen its grasp of the divine by dialogue with other religious traditions and by interpreting the signs of the times.

Implications for the Use of the Media

At this point we may turn to the application of the general principles of communication to the several media. I shall draw upon explicit references to the media in the documents of Vatican II and also upon certain postconciliar documents that have sought to apply the principles of Vatican II to the situation of the church today. As an organizing principle for this section I shall follow the five models previously explained. Depending upon one's preferred model of ecclesiology, the relation of the church to the media is variously conceived.

In the institutional model the church is viewed as the authoritative teacher of faith and morals. In the documents of Vatican II that favor this model, little attention is directed to the media as means whereby the hierarchy communicates sound doctrine to the faithful. The assumption seems to be that the traditional channels—such as papal encyclicals, decrees of Roman Congregations, pastoral letters, catechetical instruction, seminary training, and sermons—retain their previous value.

The principal Vatican II document concerning communications is the Decree on the Instruments of Social Communication, *Inter mirifica*. Prepared in advance of the first session, this document was debated in the fall of 1962 and approved, with minor changes, in the fall of 1963. Although it accurately summarizes some important principles from earlier papal teaching, this Decree fails to incorporate the more characteristic themes of Vatican II, such as ecumenism, personal freedom, and dialogue.[6]

In *Inter mirifica* the institutional model of the church as authoritative teacher seems to be taken for granted. The instruments of social communication are described as tools at the disposal of human beings to be used for achieving the supreme goal of all creation, which is the praise of God and the salvation of souls. The church has the tasks of instructing humankind in the worthy use of the media and of using them to bring people to salvation through faith in Christ (*IM* 3). These two tasks are more fully expounded in the doctrinal and pastoral sections of the Decree.

The doctrinal section is preponderantly taken up with the demands of the moral order, including the requirements of truth, justice, and charity, which are in no case to be violated. The communications industry is exhorted to avoid the temptation to exploit the baser desires of its audiences for the sake of monetary gain (*IM* 9). Civil authorities are said to have the duty to intervene where necessary to protect the common good (*IM* 12).

In the pastoral section of the Decree both clergy and laity are exhorted to apply themselves energetically to the use of the media in the apostolate. A number of general directives are given regarding Catholic education, the Catholic press, and the establishment of offices of social communications at the diocesan, national, and universal levels of church governance (*IM* 19–21). Provision is made for the annual observance of World Communications Day (*IM* 18) and for the issuance of a pastoral instruction on communications to be drawn up after the council under the supervision of the proposed office for the media of social communication to be set up at the Holy See (*IM* 23).

More or less in line with the Decree on the Social Instruments of Communication are the passing references to communication in the Decree on Christian Education, *Gravissimum educationis*, which favors the penetration of the educational media with a more Catholic spirit (*GE* 4), and in the Decree on Priestly Formation, *Optatam totius*, which suggests that the new media might be used advantageously to promote vocations to the priesthood (*OT* 2).

The institutional approach to communications in these three documents may be seen as basically sound so far as it goes but as hardly adequate for the total communications situation of the church in the present day. This approach fails to take into account the characteristics of dialogue that were sensitively analyzed in Paul VI's encyclical, *Ecclesiam suam,* in 1964. It also overlooks the radical impact of the new media on communication within the church itself, the importance of two-way communication within and beyond the church, and the need of the pilgrim church to learn from other religions and from secular movements and agencies.

As understood in the second model, to which we now turn, the prime task of the church is evangelization. Several documents of Vatican II in which this ecclesiology is prominent allude in passing to the potential of the mass media for transmitting the Christian message. In the decrees on Missionary Activity and on the Apostolate of the Laity the value of the media for communicating awareness about the work and situation of the missions is mentioned as a source for engendering a livelier missionary spirit among the Catholic faithful (*AG* 36; *AA* 10). The Decree on the Bishops' Pastoral Office in the Church, *Christus Dominus,* which strongly accents the role of the bishop as minister of the word, declares that the various media of communication should be employed for the proclamation of the gospel (*CD* 13). This statement, taken in context, appears to refer both to preaching and to doctrinal instruction.

The teaching of Vatican II on these points was further developed by the Synod of Bishops in 1974 and by the Apostolic Exhortation of Paul VI "On Evangelization in the Modern World," *Evangelii nuntiandi,* issued in 1975 as a reflection on the Synod. The pope here proposes a rather complex concept of evangelization, going beyond the limits of the kerygmatic model and including seven elements: "the renewal of humanity, witness, explicit proclamation, inner adherence, entry into the community, acceptance of signs, apostolic initiative" (*EN* 24). The proclaimed message, he points out, does not reach its full development until it is listened to, accepted, and assimilated through adherence to the ecclesial community, through sacramental worship, and through a committed Christian life. The mass media may and should be used for a kind of "first proclamation" (*EN* 45), sometimes called "pre-evangelization" (51), as well as for catechesis and the further deepening of the faith (45), but to obtain fully personal adherence and commitment it is important for broadcasts to be followed up by personal instruction and direction as well as by active participation in the church's life (23, 46).

Citing the observations of Paul VI in *Evangelii nuntiandi*, the Latin American bishops, at their Third General Conference (Puebla, 1979), advocated greater use of the media of group communication as a supplement to the mass media: "Without neglecting the necessary and urgent presence of the mass-oriented media, it is urgent that we intensify our use of the Media of Group Communication. Besides being less costly and easier to handle, they offer the possibility of dialogue and they are more suited to a person-to-person type of evangelization that will evoke a truly personal adhesion and commitment (*EN* 45–46)."[7]

Passages such as these help to distinguish the Catholic concept of evangelization, which includes personal transformation and the regeneration of society, from the narrower concept of evangelization as mere call to put one's trust in Christ as Savior, which is current in certain Protestant "evangelistic" circles. The two concepts of evangelization have different implications with regard to the media to be used.

The third model, which regards the church as a sacramental embodiment of redemption, particularly stresses the liturgy as the place where the church as sign comes to fullest visibility. The documents of Vatican II that propose this understanding of the church, such as the Constitution on the Liturgy and the Dogmatic Constitution on the Church, reflect an awareness that sacraments are sacred actions performed in a worshiping community and calling for full and active participation. No sacrament achieves its transformative impact when taken simply as a spectacle. The council does not exclude the broadcasting of ecclesial events, and even of the liturgy, but recommends this with suitable reserve: "The broadcasting and televising of sacred rites must be done with discretion and dignity, under the guidance and authorization of a suitable person appointed for this task by the bishops. This is especially important in the case of the Holy Sacrifice" (SC 20).

The council was apparently conscious of the risk that in seeking to create a media event broadcasters might obscure or distort the proper nature of the liturgy. As Karl Rahner had noted in an essay first published in 1953,[8] certain rites of the church can appear ridiculous when projected indiscriminately to unbelievers and persons of no religious background, especially if these spectators are merely curious and lacking in religious sincerity. With respect to television, Rahner argues for the maintenance of something like the ancient *disciplina arcani* ("discipline of the secret"). In this connection it may be of interest to note that the new rites for the Christian initiation of adults, approved bv the Holy See in 1972, provide for the dismissal of catechumens from the liturgy after the service of the word and before the Eucharist proper. These points should be taken into consideration and weighed against the obvious pastoral advantages of having the Mass broadcast on the occasion of papal journeys, for example, or for the benefit of the aged and the infirm.

As the Latin American bishops noted at their Medellín Conference (1968), recent technological developments raise in new form the question of the spiritual efficacy of visual and musical presentations in comparison with the preached and written word. They wrote:

The spoken word is the normal vehicle of faith: *fides ex auditu* (Rom 10:17). In our times the 'word' also becomes image, colors, and sounds, acquiring varied forms from the diverse media of social communication. The media of social communication, thus understood, are a *must* for the Church to realize her evangelical mission in our contemporary world.[9]

Since the early centuries the Catholic church, like the Eastern Orthodox, has constantly defended the use and veneration of images against iconoclasts of many types. The Fourth Council of Constantinople, in A.D. 870, made a bold comparison between holy images and the Holy Scriptures:

We prescribe that the sacred image of Our Lord Jesus Christ should be venerated with the same honor as the books of the holy Gospels. For just as we are all brought to salvation through the letters of Scripture, so by the action of the colors in images all—learned as well as ignorant—equally find profit in what is within reach of all. For painting proclaims and presents in colors the same Scripture (*graphé*) that the word sets forth in letters. (DS 653–54)

Important differences exist, of course, between the cult of holy icons in Eastern Christianity and the use of film and television in the contemporary West, but both raise similar questions regarding the apostolate. Modern communications technology offers instruments of tremendous spiritual power that the Catholic church has scarcely begun to use. As I said on a previous occasion:

Catholicism, as a highly sacramental religion, has an extraordinarily rich heritage on which to draw. It has a splendid variety of liturgical forms, a magnificent musical heritage, an impressive patrimony of religious art and architecture, a long and dramatic history, and a worldwide presence bringing it into contact with diverse races, cultures, and religions. All these features provide precious resources from which to construct vivid, appealing religious programs.[10]

Normally it would not be appropriate to issue a direct call for Christian faith in film and television broadcasts directed to general audiences. But such broadcasts may well serve to break down hostile prejudices, to build up a more favorable image, and to arouse interest on the part of the uncommitted, while at the same time confirming the faith and energizing the commitment of those who already believe. Although such presentations do not fit easily in the category of evangelization characteristic of our second model, they can, in terms of our third model, contribute in important ways to the apostolate.

The fourth ecclesiological model, which depicts the church as a community of free exchange and dialogue, is best suited to spontaneous and informal styles of communication such as talk shows and interviews. The passages of Vatican II favoring this model of the church emphasize free expression and mutual listening but make no reference to the modern media of communication. The communications aspect of this model is explored more amply in the Pastoral Instruction on Communication, *Communio et progessio*, issued by the Pontifical Commission for the Means of Social Communication in 1971[11] in conformity with the directive of Vatican II's *Inter mirifica* mentioned above. Several brief quotations may serve to indicate the general tenor of this Instruction.

Those who exercise authority in the Church will take care to ensure that there is a responsible exchange of freely held and expressed opinion among the People of God. (116)

The free dialogue within the Church does no injury to her unity and solidarity. It nurtures concord and the meeting of minds by permitting the free play of the variations of public opinion. (117)

The normal flow of life and smooth functioning of government within the Church require a steady two-way flow of information between the ecclesiastical authorities at all levels and the faithful as individuals and organized groups. (120)

Also emphasized in this Instruction are the freedom of the Catholic faithful to publish their opinions (118) and the responsibility of the Catholic press to give a true and honest picture of the church (123). The means of social communication are recommended as an aid to fostering dialogue within the church (125).

The United States bishops, in their bicentennial hearings (1975–1976), in the consultations for their pastoral on moral values and for the National Catechetical Directory, and in their recent collective pastoral letters on peace and on the economy, have adopted the dialogic mode of communication recommended in Vatican II's Pastoral Constitution and in *Communio et progressio*. In so doing they have provoked some criticism from theologians favoring a more hierarchical, authoritarian model. Archbishop Rembert Weakland, taking note of this criticism, has correctly identified the root of the problem:

> Underneath this criticism is a definite concept of ecclesiology. Its proponents see a strongly hierarchical model of the Church, where the faithful are taught by the bishops, who are in possession of the gifts of the Spirit needed for such authoritative teaching. The model adopted by the U.S. Conference believes that the Holy Spirit resides in all members of the Church and that the hierarchy must listen to what the Spirit is saying to the whole Church. This does not deny the teaching role of the hierarchy, but enhances it. It does not weaken the magisterium, but ultimately strengthens it. Discernment, not just innovation or self-reliance, becomes a part of the teaching process.[12]

This model of communication has greatly helped to overcome the excesses of clericalism, juridicism, and authoritarianism that became characteristic of Roman Catholicism after the Reformation and especially in the nineteenth century. But we should be on guard against a naive overconfidence in the community model sometimes displayed in the decade of enthusiasm that followed Vatican II. An undirected spontaneous dialogue on the part of church members who have not been thoroughly socialized into the Christian tradition and the Catholic way of life is not necessarily conducive to deeper wisdom and broader consensus. On the contrary, such dialogue may polarize the church, arouse unrealistic expectations, and provoke angry recriminations. These untoward results are intensified when the electronic media purport to give candid portrayals of the present ferment in the church. Because the media have an inbuilt bias toward conflict and contradiction, popular broadcasts of debates, protests, and interviews frequently impair the church's image as a sign of unity and reconciliation. Catholics engaged in the apostolate of the media should seek ways of countering these negative effects.

The fifth ecclesiological model, as mentioned above, makes its appearance in certain sections of the Pastoral Constitution on the Church in the Modern World. It depicts Christians as participating in "the joy and hope, the grief and anguish" of the whole human race (GS 1) and as being in a position to assist the entire human family by "simultaneously manifesting and exercising the mystery of God's love for human beings" (GS 45). In order to serve more effectively, the church must "scrutinize the signs of the times" (GS 4) and profit from the gifts and achievements of those who are not its own members. The Pastoral Constitution notes with satisfaction that modern technological advances are bringing all peoples into closer relations of mutual interdependence, but it also remarks that mere technical progress cannot of itself bring about truly interpersonal dialogue and communion (GS 23).

In greater detail than any of the council documents, the Pastoral Instruction of 1971 spells out the implications of this fifth model for communications. The contemporary world is described as "a great round table" at which a worldwide community is being formed through an exchange of information and cooperation (19, 73). By participating in this universal dialogue, the various religions can move toward a single family under God (98). Through the media Christians are better able to perceive the qualities of the emerging world society and to address its needs and questions in an effective manner (97). Educators seeking to be of service can use the new media for instructing those who lack knowledge in modern methods of agriculture, medicine, hygiene, and community development, as well as for combating illiteracy (20, 48). But training and self-discipline are demanded so that the potential benefits of the new media may be realized and the dangers of blind passion, escapism, and exploitation avoided (21–23).

The Medellín Conference of the Latin American bishops included in its Conclusions a chapter on the mass media, in which the secular dialogic point of view predominates. The media are valued for their capacity to awaken the consciousness of the masses, to promote people's aspiration for a better life, and to manifest the urgency of radical social change (16:2). For reasons given by Vatican II the church must participate in this process: "The involvement of Christians in today's world obliges them to work in the media of social communication external to the Church in keeping with the spirit of dialogue and service which marks the Constitution *Gaudium et spes*. The Catholic professional, called to be the leaven in the dough, will better perform his mission if he integrates himself in these media in order to broaden the contacts between the Church and the world, and at the same time contribute to the transformation of the latter."[13]

The type of polycentric encounter among diverse human groups characteristic of the fifth model can greatly help the church to escape from the cultural isolation and the dogmatic narrowness by which it has at times been afflicted. But these benefits must not blind us to certain concomitant dangers. By exposing the audience to a selected variety of images, problems, programs, and interpretations, communications technology could foment clashes of opinion or could subtly insinuate a hierarchy of values quite alien to the gospel. The connatural tendency of the press and the electronic media to emphasize conflict, change, and novelty could lead to spiritual agitation and undermine the kind of firm and lasting commitment required by Christian faith. Ideally, the faith of Catholics should be nurtured in a relatively stable and propitious environment of trust and discipleship, in which the riches of the tradition can be gradually appropriated. But for persons who do not have an opportunity for such formation in discipleship the church must seek to offer simple and attractive presentations of the core of Catholic Christianity. The ideas and attitudes of the multitudes today are influenced far more by emotionally charged images than by precise and laborious arguments. For this reason the church is compelled to enter into the arena of secular-dialogic communications and to develop communicators skilled in the use of the electronic media.

The pastoral leadership of the church and the theological disciplines have much to learn from communications technology. The effectiveness of the apostolate in every age has depended on the church's ability to make use of the dominant forms of communication. In the words of Paul VI, "The Church would feel guilty before the Lord if she did not utilize these powerful means of communication that human skill is daily rendering more perfect" (*EN* 45). Doctrinal or practical decisions that rested on faulty communications or were incapable of being successfully communicated to earnest seekers of the truth would be pastorally unwise. Yet the criterion of successful communication should not be elevated to the status of an absolute. Not everything that is congenial to the mass media is consonant with the gospel of Christ. Those who wish to preach the message of redemption must be prepared for opposition and ridicule.

In the perspectives of theology, therefore, communications, like every other human reality, has to be interpreted and evaluated in the light of the gospel. Concern with the techniques of communication must always be subordinated to the primacy of the Christian message. Vatican II, while it had little to say directly about the media of communication, provided a theological vision that we do well to ponder. The various ecclesiological models implicit in the council documents are helpful for identifying and appraising the many styles of communication available to the church in our day. They suggest that the church should make use of a large variety of media and methods in its encounter with the different publics that make up its own membership and that of the surrounding world.

8. Vatican II and the Purpose of the Church

Since Vatican Council II the most vigorously debated questions in ecclesiology have been those concerning authority and structures, methods and processes. Such questions are important, and many of them are addressed elsewhere in this book. But even more important is the question, why the church? What is its purpose, importance, necessity? Nothing will be gained by redistributing power or adopting new methods unless those who wield the power and use the methods have a correct vision of what the church is about. Strictly speaking, the question of goal or purpose should be discussed first, for, as the Scholastic philosophers used to say, the end is the first of the causes (*finis est prima causarum*).

The question of the church's finality is not a merely theoretical or speculative one. It has major practical importance. Unless both leaders and members are convinced that the church has an important specific task to accomplish, they cannot be expected to devote great energies or make great sacrifices for its sake. Nor will they be able to reach firm decisions about priorities and the allocation of limited resources.

Should the church, for example, be issuing pastoral guidance on the reform of the economy? Should it be helping undocumented aliens to become citizens? Should it be running hospitals and inner-city schools in which few of the patients or students are Catholics? Should the church sponsor a Campaign for Human Development? Should it patronize philosophy, literature, art, and music, as it has frequently done in the past? Should priests and religious be permitted to engage in politics or surgery, or should such involvements be prohibited by canon law? In this chapter I shall not deal directly with practical questions of this nature, but I shall establish some principles that could throw light on them.

Contrasting Answers

The question, why the church? was regularly treated in the pre-Vatican II scholastic manuals. Authors such as Carlo Passaglia[1] in the nineteenth century and Joseph de Guibert[2] and Ioachim Salaverri[3] in the twentieth spoke for the whole scholastic tradition in identifying the proximate goal of the church as the sanctification of human beings in the present life and its ultimate goal as human salvation in the life to come. Since Vatican II these goals have been less clearly asserted.

A vast spectrum of positions can be discerned in postconciliar Catholic ecclesiology. Jean Daniélou continues to assert that the purpose of the church is to produce saints and to make sanctity possible.[4] Karl Rahner sees the purpose rather as the historical and social embodiment of the grace of Christ, especially through sacramental worship.[5] James D. Crichton speaks in similar terms.[6] Jan Groot holds that the real aim of the church, and indeed of all creation, is to offer worship to God on behalf of all humanity.[7] Robert Sears believes that the purpose of the church is to be present in the world as a living witness to the divine trinitarian love.[8] Andrew Greeley emphasizes the unique capacity of the church to foster intense, intimate personal relationships.[9]

Other authors, inspired by the statement of Paul VI that the church "exists in order to evangelize" (EN 14), formulate the task of the church in terms of evangelization. David Bohr, who takes this position, defines evangelization so broadly as to include proclamation by word and by deed and in fact practically the whole activity of the church. The primary goal of evangelization, he adds, is conversion.[10] Jon Sobrino, a liberation theologian commenting on the same letter of Paul VI, holds that the church achieves its goal when it effectively proclaims the gospel to the poor by word and by deed.[11] Roger Haight holds that the church exists in order to turn outward to the world by participating in the mission of God and of Jesus, especially through evangelization and human development.[12] As an agent of social emancipation, he holds, the church must challenge the sinful patterns of corporate as well as individual behavior.[13]

The sociopolitical dimension of mission receives primary emphasis in secular theology, political theology, and liberation theology. Eugene Bianchi, following some twentieth-century Protestant secular theologians, maintained that human service and reconciliation were the proper business of the church.[14] So too, Richard McBrien, in an early work, vigorously denied that the church should be in what he called "the salvation business." On the contrary, he argued, "The Church must offer itself as one of the principal agents whereby the human community is made to stand under the enduring values of the Gospel of Jesus Christ: freedom, justice, peace, charity, compassion, reconciliation."[15] The German political theologian, Johann Baptist Metz, emphasizes the need to criticize and protest. For him the church's mission is constituted by "creative and militant eschatology," an eschatology that challenges the existing forms of secular society in the name of the promised future of God.[16]

Latin American liberation theologians see the political mission of the church in more positive terms. According to Gustavo Gutiérrez the church in Latin America must be "the visible sign of the presence of the Lord within the aspiration for liberation and the struggle for a more human and just society."[17] Juan Luis Segundo agrees. The very *raison d'être* of the church, he writes, is to be a leaven amid the rest of humanity,[18] fostering "liberative human relationships."[19]

As will be apparent from this cursory overview, recent Catholic literature raises questions such as these: Should the church continue to work for goals that are religious and supernatural? Is eternal salvation attainable without the church? Does a peaceful and just society pertain to the very definition of salvation? Should the church see itself as the servant of secular society? Is the kingdom of God a secular reality, capable of achievement without any recognition of Christ or any religious acts? Does the church have any mission that is uniquely its own, or is it one of a number of agencies devoted to common human betterment? Was the church before Vatican II ecclesiocentric or even narcissistic? Did Vatican II first turn the church into a servant church, a church for others, a decentered church, a church as critic of society?

This line of questioning invites us to engage in a careful examination of the documents of Vatican II. That council provides the most complete discussion of the finality of the church that can be found anywhere in the official utterances of Roman Catholicism or, I suppose, of any Christian church. This teaching, distributed here and there in the 800-odd pages of the council documents, is not easy to assemble and summarize. In any attempt to do so, one must keep in mind the possibility that the council's statements, composed over a period of four years with different purposes, by different groups of authors, might contain different emphases and even, perhaps, some inconsistencies.

The council has been selectively used by social reformers seeking to redirect the energies of the church toward priorities they regard as urgent. They reread the council's documents in the light of postconciliar concerns, such as those generated by secular theology, political theology, and liberation theology. With such motivation, they pick out particular phrases from the conciliar documents, especially those that seemed to open up new directions, and ignore or dismiss other passages as a residue of earlier theology, which is unflatteringly dismissed as pre-Copernican, Ptolemaic, or the like.

This deliberately slanted interpretation of Vatican II has produced mixed reactions. Catholic activists found it stimulating to be asked to make a Christian contribution to the building of the secular city and to work side by side with nonbelievers and believers of other traditions. Regarded as the elite of the postconciliar church, these activists sometimes indulged in a new triumphalism, convinced that their theology could provide solutions to every human problem. But in the course of time, increasing numbers became skeptical about the new secular gospel. Christians did not find that they were in a much better position than others to establish peace and justice in the world. They sometimes felt a certain embarrassment at belonging to a church that had for so many centuries concentrated on spiritual and otherworldly objectives. Meanwhile, Christians who were attracted by the religious heritage of the church felt disillusioned. The Catholic church had seemingly abandoned them and plunged into projects that did not appear to be religious or specifically Christian.

Without attempting to pass judgment on these various reactions, I should like to go back to the council documents and try to reconstruct, as objectively as possible, what they actually do say about the purposes of the church. The experience, I have found, is something like that of a scholar scraping away the surface layer of a palimpsest and discovering, as it were for the first time, the original text beneath it.[20] In the remainder of this chapter I shall attend almost exclusively to the council documents themselves.

Church and Kingdom

The theme of church and kingdom, like other themes, has occasioned a certain myth regarding the achievement of Vatican II. The council is supposed to have discountenanced the view that the church is an end in itself and to have subordinated the church to the kingdom of God, which is an essentially secular reality characterized by peace, justice, freedom, and affluence.

In comparison with other official church teachings of recent centuries, Vatican II is remarkable for its emphasis on the kingdom of God. This biblical concept, so prominent in the synoptic Gospels, is retrieved for the benefit of ecclesiology. While providing for a dynamic and eschatological orientation consonant with the idea of the pilgrim church, the kingdom rhetoric, I would maintain, does not displace the church from its centrality in the total plan of God. This conclusion seems to be supported by the conciliar texts.

The kingdom of God, in its plentitude, is identified with the new heaven and the new earth, in which the whole of creation will be gloriously transformed (GS 39). Since it is the future of the world as well as that of the church, the kingdom is in some sense wider than the church. But the heart and center of the new creation will be the company of the blessed as they praise and worship the triune God (LG 51).

The kingdom of God, in its eschatological completion, is described by Vatican II as the goal of the church (LG 9). When the fullness of the kingdom arrives, the church will attain its full perfection (LG 48) and be everlastingly united to its King (LG 5). Thus the consummation of the kingdom will be the fulfillment, not the disappearance, of the church.

Whether the council saw the kingdom within history as wider than the church may be disputed. The progress of the kingdom is clearly distinguished from earthly progress (GS 39). The church on earth, moreover, is described as the "kingdom of Christ now present in mystery" (LG 3) and as "the initial budding forth of that kingdom" (LG 5).

Certain authors have contended that only some are called to the church, but all to the kingdom. This position is a defensible one if the terms are defined in a particular way, but it is not the position taken by Vatican II. The council documents nowhere state that anyone is in the kingdom without also belonging in some sense to the church, nor do they teach that anyone is called to the kingdom without also being called to the church. On the contrary, the Constitution on the Church asserts that all human beings are called to union with Christ in one body (LG 3). The church, moreover, prays and labors in order that the entire world may be transformed into the people of God, the body of Christ, and the temple of the Holy Spirit (*LG* 17). The growth of the church, and not merely that of the kingdom, is seen as being desirable in itself and as redounding to the glory of God (*LG* 17; *AG* 7 and 9).

In the documents of Vatican II, therefore, the church is not simply a sign or pointer to the kingdom of God, nor is it a mere servant of the kingdom. The church is either identical with or at least central to the kingdom.[21] Whatever contributes to the church by that very fact contributes to the kingdom, and whatever detracts from the church thereby diminishes the kingdom. To say that the goal of the church is the kingdom of God, therefore, is not to deny that the church is, in a certain sense, an end in itself.

The Church and Salvation

Many Catholic theologians since Vatican II have been saying that the church is not a means or instrument of salvation but only a sign or pointer to the saving work of God, which goes on, even without the church, in the world as a whole. According to this line of interpretation the council abandoned the restrictive position that would make affiliation with the church essential to salvation. If this interpretation is correct, it surely follows that the church should not be in the business of salvation. But the actual teaching of the council does not seem to corroborate the position just described. Rather, its teaching may be summarized in the following four points.

First, the council teaches that all human beings are called by God to salvation in the traditional sense of a future sharing in the divine life without diminution or cessation (*GS* 18). There is no suggestion that happiness and prosperity in the present life are constitutive of human salvation.

Second, the conciliar documents affirm that this eschatological salvation, to be fully attained in the world to come, is the ultimate aim of the church (*GS* 40). The mission of the church, according to the Decree on the Apostolate of the Laity, concerns human salvation, which is to be achieved by faith in Christ and by his grace (*AA* 6).

Third, the church is described as being, by its very essence, the universal sacrament of salvation. This description, which holds a prominent place in the Constitution on the Church (*LG* 48), is quoted both in the Decree on the Church's Missionary Activity (*AG* 1) and in the Pastoral Constitution on the Church in the Modern World (*GS* 45). By a sacrament the council evidently means a symbolic reality established by Christ, a sign that contains and confers the grace it signifies. The church, therefore, is not a merely cognitive sign, making known something that exists without it, but an efficacious sign—one that brings about redemption. If it be asked whether all redemption depends upon the church, an affirmative answer seems to be implied by the term *universal* and is confirmed by the further statement that the church is used by Christ "as an instrument for the redemption of all" (*LG* 9).

Fourth, the council documents state on several occasions that the church, like baptism, is necessary for salvation (*LG* 14, *AG* 7). This necessity, however, applies in different ways to those who have been effectively evangelized and to those who, not having been so evangelized, remain in good faith outside the visible structure of the church. Persons of the first category, in order to be saved, are obliged to be baptized, join the church as a socially organized community, and remain in it. Those of the second category are saved if they accept and live by the grace of Christ in whatever form it is accessible to them (*LG* 16; *GS* 22; *AG* 7). Such grace, calling everyone to salvation, always produces a positive relationship or ordination (*ordinatio*) to the church, so that to accept the grace is to be brought into a dynamic connection with the church (*LG* 16). Thus the church is involved in the salvation of all who are saved. It would be contradictory, the council suggests, to affirm the necessity of Christ for salvation and to deny the necessity of his body, whereby he makes himself present in history (*LG* 14).

This teaching of Vatican II on the necessity of the church

does not differ substantively from the teaching of the Holy See since Pius IX. Pius XII in his encyclical on the Mystical Body had spoken of the possibility of being ordered to the church by an unconscious desire and intention (*inscio quodam desiderio ac voto*, DS 3821). A few years later the Holy Office in a letter to Archbishop Cushing of Boston had spoken of the possibility of salvation through an implicit intention (*voto implicito*, DS 3872). The Vatican II Constitution on the Church avoids the subtleties of this scholastic vocabulary and speaks more generally of an *ordinatio* to the church. But this term too implies that grace gives it recipients a positive inclination toward the church, so that all who live by God's grace are in a certain sense affiliated with the church.

The most striking development of Vatican II beyond the previous teaching is to be found in its greater differentiation. Whereas Pius XII in 1943 and the Holy Office in 1949 spoke of a salvific *votum*, conscious or unconscious, on the part of non-Catholics of all categories, Vatican II chose to use the term *votum* only for the explicit desire of the catechumen (*LG* 14). With regard to non-Christians it spoke, as we have seen, of an *ordinatio*. In discussing non-Catholic Christians the council taught that they were "conjoined" (*coniuncti*) to the church by baptism and other ecclesial elements (*LG* 15). These ecclesial elements are said to have an inner dynamism toward the fullness of Catholic unity (*LG* 8). The Catholic church is the "all-embracing means (*generale auxilium*) of salvation" in which alone "the fullness of the means of salvation can be obtained" (*UR* 3). The means of grace available in the separated churches and communities "derive their efficacy from the very fullness of grace and truth entrusted to the Catholic church" (*UR* 3).[22]

In summary, then, Vatican II, like the preconciliar magisterium, teaches that the Catholic church is involved in the salvation of non-Catholic Christians as well as that of non-Christians. No one is saved without being ordered to, joined to, or incorporated in, the Catholic church. While the council does not deny the salvific value of non-Christian religions and of non-Catholic Christianity, it accounts for that value in terms of what the Catholic church possesses and effects.

Some commentators on the council have raised the question whether the church saves simply by being the reality toward which people are oriented or whether it somehow acts to bring about the salvation of such persons. The characterization of the church as "sign and instrument" (LG 1) suggests that the church is actively at work in the salvific process but does not explain by what activities the church accomplishes this result. The nearest thing to an explanation is perhaps supplied by a statement in the Constitution on the Liturgy to the effect that by its prayer and eucharistic sacrifice the church unceasingly intercedes with the Lord for the salvation of the entire world (SC 83).

To summarize, then, we may say that the council repeatedly and emphatically taught that the procurement of salvation is the most important task of the church. Far from doing away with the ancient doctrine that salvation is given only to those united to the church, Vatican II reasserted this doctrine. Of course, it made important distinctions to allow for the salvation of those who are in good faith outside the sociological boundaries of the church, but in this respect the council adhered essentially to the teaching of recent popes, and notably that of Pius XII.

The Church's Inner Life and Worship

According to the postconciliar trend to which we have alluded, the church should no longer be viewed as administering means of grace to its own members. The sacraments are signs intended to remind Christians of what God is doing and wills to have done throughout the world. Worship, therefore, is both a celebration of what is happening everywhere and a summons to the members of the church to measure up to their responsibilities in the building of the kingdom of God. These theses are generally defended with quotations from Vatican Council II.

In my judgment, the council cannot fairly be taken as supporting this doctrine. It did indeed rehabilitate the sign aspect of the church and of its sacraments, and it stressed the links between worship and mission, but it did not for all that minimize the church's ministries as means of grace. As understood by the council, any sacrament is by its very nature both sign and instrument of grace, and the worthy reception of the sacrament is a source of sanctification.

Among the ministries by which the church contributes to salvation, word and sacrament receive special emphasis. The Decree on the Church's Missionary Activity, for example, states that the church leads its members to participation in the mystery of Christ by the example of its life and by its preaching, sacraments, and other means of grace (AG 5). The Constitution on Divine Revelation, because of its subject matter, gives particular prominence to the word of God, which it at one point describes, in Pauline language, as the power of God for the salvation of all who believe (DV 17; cf. Rom. 1:16).

The postconciliar secular theologies are most sharply contradicted by the Constitution on the Liturgy, which singles out the public worship of the church as the activity that most perfectly manifests and accomplishes human sanctification. No other action of the church, says the Constitution, can match the liturgy in its claim to efficacy (SC 7). It is the summit toward which the entire activity of the church is directed and the fountainhead from which all its power flows (SC 10). The goal of apostolic works, we there read, is that all who have been regenerated by faith and baptism should come together to praise God in the midst of the church, to take part in its sacrifice, and to eat the Lord's Supper (ibid.).

The term goal in this passage deserves some comment.[23] Although the liturgy is a means of grace, it is not a mere means, for it is a foretaste of the end to which the church is directed. By celebrating the earthly liturgy we participate in the heavenly liturgy in which the saints and angels eternally sing the praise of God (cf. SC 8). The same idea reappears in the chapter on eschatology in the Constitution on the Church, where we are reminded that the deepest vocation of the church is fulfilled when its children come together as one family and partake, by way of anticipation, in the liturgy of heavenly glory (LG 51). The implication of these passages is that the church is neither a mere token nor a mere means; it already possesses in itself, in seminal form, the reality that it signifies and seeks to bring to maturity.

Vatican II advanced far beyond the average scholastic treatment of the means of grace by treating word and sacrament in a social and ecclesial context. The council repeatedly insisted that by these means the church is constituted as a communal body, and that the individual is sanctified precisely by aggregation to the church. The same emphasis carries through into the Constitution on Divine Revelation, which states that the invisible God out of the abundance of his love chose to speak to human beings as friends and to invite them into fellowship with himself (DV 2). Quoting from the first letter of John, the council affirms that it hands on the message of salvation "in order that you may have fellowship with us, and that our fellowship may be with the Father and with his son Jesus Christ" (DV 1; cf. 1 Jn 1:3).

To summarize the council's doctrine on the internal ministries of the church, we may say that all of them are directed to the sanctification of the faithful and to the glory thereby given to God (SC 10). Sanctification, moreover, is seen in social and dynamic terms as progressive incorporation into the one family of the People of God. Through being a community of truth and love, the church becomes an efficacious sign or sacrament of the universal unity to which all men and women are called. Thus the sacramental worship of the church both expresses and reinforces the sacramentality of the church as a whole. The church achieves its purpose by becoming ever more fully what it already is in germ and in principle.

The Missionary Apostolate

There is a widespread impression that the council downgraded missionary efforts directed at conversion, calling instead for dialogue and collaboration with non-Catholics and non-Christians. The aim of such dialogue and collaboration would allegedly be not the enhancement of the church itself but the development of the larger human community that the church seeks to serve. Such service would presumably be a higher priority than the growth of the church itself.

The position just explained is not entirely without basis in the teaching of Vatican II, but if we read the council documents for themselves we receive a rather different impression. The Constitution on the Church and the Constitution on Divine Revelation strongly emphasize the importance of proclaiming the saving message of the gospel (LG 17; DV 1 and 7). The Decree on Missionary Activity characterizes evangelization and the planting of the church as the specific purpose of missionary work. It adds that when circumstances prevent the direct preaching of the gospel, missionaries must continue to bear witness to Christ by their conduct and works of mercy, thus preparing the way for the Lord and making him in some manner present (AG 6). The following article (AG 7) gives a list of motives for missionary activity in the traditional sense. The list includes obedience to the express command of Christ, the growth of the mystical body, the desire to share with others one's own spiritual gifts, and zeal for the glory of God.

In all these passages there is no minimizing of explicit faith and adherence to the church. The possibility, already mentioned, that persons who are inculpably ignorant of the gospel may be saved by grace does not reduce the importance of spreading the faith and seeking thereby to rescue people from dangerous ignorance and error (LG 17).

Dialogue is indeed promoted by the council, but not as a substitute for the apostolate of conversion. After mentioning that the church rejects nothing that is true and holy in the other religions, the Declaration on Non-Christian Religions goes on to say that the church proclaims and must ever proclaim Christ as "the way, the truth, and the life" (Jn 14:6), in whom is to be found the fullness of religious life and reconciliation with God (*NA* 2).

The Decree on Ecumenism does not advocate dialogue for its own sake, but for the sake of restoring Christian unity and thereby removing a great obstacle to missionary endeavor. The council in this Decree does not place all other churches on a par with Roman Catholicism but declares that, while the elements of truth and holiness in the other churches and religious communities are to be gratefully recognized, the Catholic church alone possesses the fullness of the means of salvation and thus alone qualifies as the all-embracing means of salvation (*UR* 3). Ecumenical dialogue, while it is not the same as the apostolate of conversion, should not interfere with the work of reconciling individuals who desire full Catholic communion (*UR* 4).

Service Toward the World

Since Vatican II many Catholic theologians have taught that action on behalf of justice and the transformation of social structures are no less central to the church's mission than the ministries of evangelization and worship. If this is now understood to be the case, the consciousness of the church must have advanced beyond Vatican II, for in the council documents I can find no such assertion.

The Decree on the Apostolate of the Laity, which emphasized the secular responsibility of the church as much as any of the council's documents, declares,

The mission of the Church concerns the salvation of human beings, which is to be achieved by faith in Christ and by his grace. Hence the apostolate of the Church and of all its members is primarily designed to manifest Christ's message by words and deeds and to communicate his grace to the world. This work is done mainly through the ministry of the word and of the sacraments . . . " (*AA* 6).

In addition to its obligation to dispense the free gifts of divine grace, the church has, of course, a ministry to human needs. The opening chapters of the Pastoral Constitution on the Church in the Modern World call attention to the negative experiences of sin, suffering, and death, and to the inability of science and technology to give satisfactory answers to the deeper religious questions that are asked, in one form or another, by every generation. In response to these human and religious needs the church must administer the saving medicine of redemption. "Through Christ and in Christ," says the council, "light is cast on the riddle of sorrow and death" (*GS* 22). Elsewhere it asserts: "Hence in the light of Christ, the image of the invisible God, the firstborn of every creature, the council wishes to speak to all in order to illuminate the mystery of human existence and cooperate in finding a solution to the outstanding problems of our time" (*GS* 10).

In undertaking to answer the great social problems of the day the council is surprisingly reserved. The Pastoral Constitution quotes with approval the words of Pius XI: "It is necessary never to lose sight of the fact that the objective of the Church is to evangelize, not to civilize. If it civilizes, it is by means of evangelization" (*GS* 58n). A little earlier the same document quoted approvingly from Pius XII:

[The Church's] divine Founder, Jesus Christ, has not given it any mandate or set for it any end of the cultural order. The goal which Christ assigns to it is strictly religious. . . . The Church must lead men to God, in order that they may be given over to him without reserve. . . . The Church can never lose sight of the strictly religious, supernatural goal. The meaning of all its activities, down to the last canon of its code, can only be to contribute directly or indirectly to this goal. (*GS* 42n)

In its own words the Pastoral Constitution declares: "The specific mission (*missio propria*) that Christ entrusted to his church is not in the political, economic, or social order. The purpose which he set before her is a religious one" (GS 42).

The council, however, is aware that the religious mission of the church has ramifications in the temporal sphere. "Pursuing the saving purpose which is proper to it," says the council, "the church not only communicates divine life to human persons, but in some way casts the reflected light of that life over the entire earth" (GS 40). Using other metaphors, Vatican II speaks of the church as "the leaven and, so to speak, the soul of human society as it is to be renewed in Christ and transformed into God's family" (GS 40). "Out of the Church's religious mission," says the Pastoral Constitution, "come a function, a light, and an energy that can serve to structure and consolidate the human community according to divine law" (GS 42). The gospel thus proves itself to be a "leaven of brotherhood, of unity, and of peace" (AG 8). The mission of the church in its full range may therefore be said to include not only the directly religious apostolate but also the penetration of the temporal sphere with the spirit of the gospel (AA 5).

In this connection the council several times comments on the relationship between evangelization and humanization. Evangelization, it states, is aimed at making available the blessings of eternal life, which consists in knowing the one true God and Jesus Christ, whom he has sent (AA 3; SC 9). Humanization of the world is the task of relating all things to humanity as their center and crown (GS 12). Because the gospel has a healing and elevating impact upon the human person, the church believes that it can contribute to making society more human (GS 40). But the church as such is concerned with human progress only under its religious aspect. Thus the council's discussion of the benefits of human culture ends with the statement: "All these values can provide some preparation for the acceptance of the message of the gospel—a preparation which can be animated with divine love by him who came to save the world" (GS 57). While it does not regard the construction of the earthly city as its proper responsibility, the church requires its members to be good citizens and teaches that all the good fruits of human industry will be found again in the heavenly kingdom, "but cleansed from all stain, burnished, and transfigured" (*GS* 39). The council accordingly exhorts bishops to instruct their faithful "that earthly goods and human institutions are ordered, according to the plan of God the Creator, toward human salvation, and therefore can contribute much to the upbuilding of Christ's body" (*CD* 12).

It may seem difficult to reconcile the council's insistence on the social responsibilities of the faithful with its doctrine that the church has no proper mission (*missio propria*) in the social, political, and economic orders. But there is no inconsistency here. By a "proper" mission the council presumably means that which is specific to the church and would remain undone unless the church existed. To preach faith in Christ and to administer the sacraments are in this sense proper to the church. The church was established precisely in order that these activities might be performed. But to erect a just and prosperous society is not, in the sense just explained, the proper business of the church. To contribute to such a society is, however, a responsibility of Christians insofar as they are citizens of the earthly community. Unless they live up to their civic obligations they will be guilty in the sight of God. All Christians, whether clergy or laity, have duties as members of the human community, but to penetrate secular professions and occupations with the spirit of the gospel is preeminently the responsibility of the laity (*GS* 43; *AA* 7).[24]

The council itself, to be sure, set forth official Catholic positions on certain social problems, namely those affecting marriage and the family, human culture, life in its economic, social, and political dimensions, the bonds among the family of nations, and peace (*GS* 46–93). In prefacing this section of the Pastoral Constitution on the Church in the Modern World, the council said simply that it was directing attention to a variety of current problems in the light of the gospel and human experience (*GS* 46). It prayed that Christians might be led by the ideals of the gospel as they searched for answers to these complex questions. The council warned against seeking to impose specific solutions in the name of the gospel itself, as though the authority of the gospel could be appropriated for one human opinion against others (*GS* 43).

Synthesis and Evaluation

At the beginning of this chapter I raised the question whether the council's teaching was internally consistent. We are now perhaps in a position to hazard an answer. I would say that, considering the variety of authors, themes, and dates, the Vatican II documents are remarkably harmonious. Quite naturally, there are varieties of emphasis. For example, the Constitution on the Liturgy, the earliest in date of the council's documents, emphasizes the public worship of the church as the activity that most perfectly anticipates the ultimate goal. The Constitution on Revelation, because of its subject matter, stresses the church's responsibility to herald the word of God and to elicit the response of faith. The Constitution on the Church, especially in its first two chapters, gives prominence to the task of forming the community of the faithful as a symbol or sacrament of God's universal redemptive designs. The Pastoral Constitution on the Church in the Modern World and the Decree on the Apostolate of the Laity give special attention to the church's contribution to the consolidation of the human community. The Decree on Missionary Activity, as one might expect, has much to say about the church's mandate to evangelize all nations. These varying emphases may be considered mutually complementary rather than conflicting.

Notwithstanding these variations one may distill from the council documents as a whole a rather unified body of doctrine on the question of the church's purpose. They establish a hierarchy of ends for the church. The ultimate end that underlies and penetrates all the others is expressed alternatively as the salvation of the human family and as the completion of God's kingdom. Often these two goals are linked, as in the following quotation: "While helping the world and receiving many benefits from it, the Church has a single intention: that God's kingdom may come and that the salvation of the whole human race may come to pass" (*GS* 45). Both these ends are seen as contributing to the glory of God (*LG* 17; *AA* 2; *AG* 7), which is, from one point of view, the ultimate goal of all creation. The church, to be sure, does not achieve the salvation of the human race or the completion of the kingdom of God by its own unaided forces. It depends continuously on God, in whose hands it serves as an instrument (*LG* 9).

Short of the attainment of the ultimate goal, which lies beyond all history, the church has several proximate goals that can be realized even in the present life and are preparatory for that which is to come. The first of these is that human beings may be sanctified (*SC* 10); that they may be delivered from sin and regenerated through faith, hope, and love (*DV* 1; *AG* 8). The church pursues these goals through its direct apostolate and, most importantly, through the ministries of word and sacrament, together with which the good example and virtuous lives of Christians are sometimes mentioned as additional means of grace (*AA* 5; *AA* 6). These ministries come to a kind of culmination in the liturgy and especially in the Eucharist (*SC* 8–10), which make the Author of Salvation truly present in the world (*AG* 8) and proleptically manifest the eschatological kingdom (*LG* 50–51).

In its twofold character as means and fruit of sanctification the church seeks to actualize itself as perfectly as possible within history. By such efforts it becomes more evidently and efficaciously the universal sacrament of salvation. Manifesting in the world the mystery of Christ, it becomes a sign of unity and hope for all who are in search of redemption (*LG* 9).

Finally, the church casts upon the world what the council calls the reflected light of the gospel (*GS* 40). It provides light and energy for the construction of the human community

(*GS* 42). This service to the wider society is essential in the sense that the church cannot absolve its members from social responsibility. But it is not essential if that term is taken to mean that the success of the human enterprise is the proper goal or responsibility of the church as such. In the perspectives of Vatican II, as I understand it, the church's proper and indispensable task is to proclaim and manifest Christ's message and to communicate his grace to the world. This sacred mission, according to the council, is accomplished chiefly through the ministry of word and sacraments (*AA* 6) and only secondarily through the good example of Christians and their loyal participation in the humanization of the world.

It may be objected that the council's teaching, as I have explained it, is ecclesiocentric. In a certain sense this is the case. The council does not regard the world as the center and the church as peripheral, but rather the reverse. As we have said, the material world was made for the sake of humanity (*GS* 12), but human beings exist in order to be brought by grace into the life of the triune God (*GS* 18). Christian revelation irreversibly accomplished a kind of Copernican revolution by presenting the world as taken up into the orbit of Christ and no longer being centered on itself. The church is the place in which the human community participates in the life of God. It is the people of God, the body of Christ, and the temple of the Holy Spirit (*LG* 17).

This outlook does not absolve the church from humble service (*GS* 3). Its aim, like that of its divine Master, is to serve and not be served (*GS* 3). It seeks to liberate rather than dominate, to give rather than take. While the members of the church are summoned to many kinds of giving, depending on their personal talents and assets, the church itself is especially called to render the spiritual service of bringing the world into union with its Creator and Lord. By giving and serving the church builds itself up in love (Eph 4:16) and grows into the full maturity of Christ its head (Eph 4:13–15; cf. *SC* 2; *LG* 30; *AG* 5, 7, and 9).

In our time Christians, and perhaps Catholics more than others, are haunted by the fear of loving the church too much. They find it hard to share Christ's own love for the church (Eph 5:25) and to accept the maxim of St. Augustine, quoted by Vatican II, that "one possesses the Holy Spirit in the measure that one loves the Church of Christ."[25] They fear that love might blind them to the faults of the church and to their own need of self-reform. The council was conscious of this danger and provided remedies against it. In a whole series of texts the council insisted that the church is called to pursue the path of penance and reform (*LG* 8 and 15; *UR* 6). "It does not escape the Church," we are reminded, "how great a distance lies between the message she offers and the human weakness of those to whom the gospel is entrusted" (*GS* 43). God's gifts always bring with them added responsibilities, making their recipients liable to a severer judgment (*LG* 14). The deficiencies of Christians, in fact, have contributed greatly to the rise of modern atheism and unbelief. The actual performance of the church must often be said to conceal rather than to reveal the authentic face of Christ (*GS* 19).

None of these concessions, however, invalidates or undermines the teaching of Vatican II on the purpose of the church. Purpose is a normative, not a descriptive, term. It expresses not what empirically exists but what is intended to be. A statement of purpose can be used critically against the society that professes to live by it as well as defensively to maintain that society's right to exist. The exalted goals of the church set forth by Vatican II constitute a challenge to the church as a whole and to each of its members to become in actuality what they are called to be and to put into practice the principles inherent in their faith.

It should scarcely be necessary to add that Vatican II has not said the final word on this or perhaps any other subject. As indicated in the opening pages of this chapter, many later words have been uttered. Innumerable efforts have been made to go beyond the Council in one direction or another.

Proponents of new positions have sometimes claimed to be governed by the spirit of the council and in other cases have attempted to rectify what they felt was wrong with the council. In either case, the postconciliar views must, I believe, be assessed with the help of the council. On the whole, I would contend, Vatican II embodies greater corporate wisdom and theological maturity than the work of most private theologians since the council.

9. The Church, Society, and Politics

We have seen in the preceding chapter that the proper and primary mission of the church, according to Vatican II, has to do with supernatural salvation that is promised and anticipated in the present life but fully enjoyed only in the life to come. Even if the council did teach this, and was correct in so doing, the question still remains whether the church has a real and important responsibility with regard to the sociopolitical order. This question is affirmatively answered by practically all Catholic thinkers and has been intensely discussed by many theologians since Vatican II. In the present chapter I take up this question in the light of the New Testament, the Catholic tradition, and the contemporary teaching of popes and bishops. I shall devote particular attention to two recent pastoral letters of the United States Bishops' Conference, *The Challenge of Peace* (1983) and *Economic Justice for All* (1986). In my personal reflections I shall show the legitimacy of the church's concern for the social order while at the same time cautioning against any politicization of religion, which would risk making the church an instrument of political parties and ideologies. My positions will be in line with what I understand to have been the thrust of the Hartford Appeal of 1975, to which I shall make reference toward the end of this chapter.

The Gospel and God's New Order

To those who are inclined—as most of us are—to fashion the divinity in the likeness of the human, Jesus responds by proposing a vastly different idea of God. The God of the

Gospels, *pace* Feuerbach, is not a projection of human ideals, nor is divine justice simply human justice writ large. While the God of Jesus is in some respects like a good human father or ruler, he frequently behaves in ways that would be unacceptable in human affairs. In the world disclosed by Jesus divine approval is given to the dishonest manager who craftily reduces the debts owed to his master. In another parable God is likened to an employer who rewards laborers who have worked for a single hour with the same wages as those who have borne the heat of an entire day. Yet again, God is compared to an unjust judge who reluctantly gives in to the demands of petitioners who annoy him by their persistence. God enriches those who are already wealthy and takes away from the poor the little that they have. He severely judges those who scrupulously fulfill their religious duties and liberally forgives tax collectors and prostitutes for the mere asking. He is ready to neglect the many righteous in order to bring back a single individual who has gone astray. God is like a miserly woman who scrapes the floor searching for a lost penny. Throughout the Gospels Jesus seems to be going out of his way to shock those who have constructed their concept of God according to human norms of dignity, virtue, and prudence. God's thoughts are not our thoughts, nor are his ways our ways.

The gospel accordingly presents us with a totally new order of things, quite unlike anything we would suspect from our experience on earth. There is a divine or transcendent order in which certain things are possible and proper that are neither possible nor fitting in worldly affairs. Jesus opens up to his hearers this higher world, asking them to accept it in faith. By his preaching he makes it possible for people to understand reality in a wholly new light. In the world people aspire to health, power, pleasure, family, friends, money, rank, and reputation. All these things are valuable here below, but Jesus teaches that they are of no value for eternity. The only thing of true and lasting importance is our standing in relation to the God whom Jesus makes known. What counts before him is purity of heart, humility, mercy. Even virtues such as honesty, thrift, learning, and industry are not enough. Trusting God, we should make no provision for the morrow. We should have no fear of those who can do nothing worse than kill the body. We should not labor for the food that perishes but only for the bread of eternal life. Not to be rich in the sight of God is the only real tragedy.

Jesus underscores this radical teaching by many sayings and parables that predict a dramatic reversal in the kingdom of God. The first will be last and the last first. The rich will become poor and the poor rich. Those content to be as slaves will be the true masters. Already, by a kind of prolepsis, infants spout wisdom, the blind see, the lame walk. "What is exalted before men is an abomination in the sight of God" (Lk 16:15). All these paradoxes and antitheses are credible only to those who believe; they are visible only to the eye of faith.

Christian dualism bears a certain analogy with Platonism. For Plato the realm of appearances was superficial and unimportant. What counted was the inward reality, known by intelligence. Whoever was truly wise would rather be just and suffer for it than be unjust and escape suffering, for virtue was of greater worth than any external benefits or rewards. For Jesus, likewise, the transitory realm of sense-appearance was unimportant. For him, however, the "really real" was the realm known by faith—the gift whereby one participates in God's own knowledge. True life is bestowed by Jesus and is eternal.

Paul was able to sum up this new perspective by equating the visible with the transitory and the invisible with the eternal. "We look not to the things that are seen but to the things that are unseen; for the things that are seen are transient, but the things that are unseen are eternal" (2 Cor 4:18). For Paul the things that meant most to him before his conversion appear to him in Christ to be no more than rubbish (Phil 3:8).

The wisdom of this world is foolishness in the sight of God (1 Cor 1:18–31).

It is in terms of these stark contrasts that Jesus draws up his concept of discipleship. He calls on his followers to live according to the vision of reality disclosed by faith and thus to seek the very opposite of what the world holds dear. They must be prepared to be poor rather than rich and in this way to accumulate treasure in heaven. They must be prepared to suffer in order to be blessed and to lose their life in this world in order to save it for eternity.

The community of disciples, as Jesus seems to have viewed it, was a "contrast society," into which one entered not by gradual improvement but by a totally new beginning, described as rebirth. The community of the disciples, which was a kind of prelude to the Christian church, had the task of attesting through word and deed the new order disclosed by Jesus. Its first and indispensable task was to evangelize—to proclaim the way of salvation opened up by the only-begotten Son. The church became—and at its best must always remain—what the sociologist Peter Berger calls a "cognitive minority," a faithful remnant of those who forsake worldly benefits in order to follow the crucified and risen Master.

In contrast to Platonism, Christianity proclaims an order that is not timeless. Eternal life has a beginning in time, even though, in principle, it has no end. And the kingdom of God exists not simply in some supercelestial realm, but as a real promise for the future of this earth. With the resurrection of Jesus the glorious transformation of creation has already begun. The church heralds and anticipates the completion of what has been inaugurated; it certifies that the kingdom will in fact be realized. Christians are those who in faith already belong to the ultimate future that now lies hidden in God.

Proclaiming the Christian Way of Life

Although Jesus called for radical transformation, many of his followers remained to a great extent untransformed. Ever since its beginnings the church has been a *corpus mixtum* (Augustine), a net filled with good fish and bad, a field sown with good grain and darnel. The separation of the good from the evil will not occur until the parousia. In the meantime we must not violently uproot the weeds lest in doing so we damage the wheat. The church, while counting sinners in its midst, strives incessantly to purify itself.

Christians constantly face the problem of how to relate the two realms in which they live. By faith they belong to the coming eschatological kingdom, but by experience they are involved in the transitory kingdom of this world. They have involvements with other human beings that do not allow them, except in rare instances, to live consistently by the precepts of the Sermon on the Mount. Lest they be found incapable of completing the tower once begun (Lk 14:28–30), they have to exercise worldly prudence. They must frequently take thought for the morrow, have recourse to law courts, defend their property rights, seek police protection, and sometimes employ military might. They cannot regularly give up their possessions to those who want to rob them nor always turn the other cheek to their assailants.

The primary task of the church is to preserve the message of the gospel in all its novelty and strength. Neither the sinfulness of Christians nor the exigencies of worldly living can exempt the church from this lofty mission. While preaching the gospel by word, the church must seek to embody it in symbolic actions, notably the sacraments. The church, however, cannot pretend to bring about the final kingdom, which God will accomplish when and as he chooses. The promise of the kingdom rests on God's word, which is absolutely reliable, and not on human efforts, which are forever bound by limited possibilities. Although the efforts of human beings, sustained by the grace of God, are by no means useless, such efforts could never bring about the consummation of the kingdom. The church, therefore, must urge its members to put their trust in the power and goodness of God rather than in any created agency, including even the church. God alone can save.

Granted the primacy of evangelization, we must ask whether the church has any further responsibilities beyond holding aloft the transcendent vision proposed by Jesus and confirmed by his resurrection from the dead. I maintain that the church has a second responsibility, from which it can by no means exempt itself. This is to guide its members and all who wish to submit to its influence in behaving according to the gospel. Jesus insists that it is not sufficient to say "Lord, Lord," but that one must put his precepts into practice.

Jesus is strict in his interpretation of the commandments. To relax even the least of them is to make oneself least in the kingdom of God. The practices of fasting and almsgiving are praised; adultery and divorce are roundly condemned. Those who do the will of the Father count as Jesus' brothers and sisters. The evildoer will be cast into the outer darkness and will suffer the torments of eternal flames. Those who beat their fellow servants and make harsh demands on their own debtors will themselves be beaten and severely judged. Most especially will the Son of Man condemn those who close their hearts to the needs of the hungry, the naked, the sick, and the imprisoned.

Faith and Works

The early church was faithful to this aspect of the message of Jesus. Paul, for all his insistence on justification by faith, fully accepted the axiom, rooted in the Wisdom literature of the Old Testament and reechoed in Matthew, that all will be individually rewarded or punished according to their deeds in the flesh (1 Cor 3:8; 2 Cor 5:10). Jews as well as Greeks will receive due retribution for their works (Rom 2:6). Admission to the kingdom will be denied to the envious, murderous, and sexually impure (Rom 1:30). In another list Paul excludes adulterers, practicing homosexuals, thieves, robbers, and drunkards (1 Cor 6:9–10). In a third catalogue, he enumerates impurity, idolatry, enmity, strife, jealousy, anger, drunkenness, and the like as "works of the flesh" that exclude one from inheriting the kingdom of God (Gal 5:19–21).

To hold that people are saved by faith alone regardless of their conduct would be a serious deformation of Paul's actual teaching. Rejecting this pseudo-Pauline position, the letter of James insists that faith without works is dead. Faith is genuine and salvific only if it becomes active through works. John in his first letter calls attention to the deceptiveness of thinking that it is possible to love God without obeying the commandments. The fourth Gospel likewise teaches that those who have done good deeds will experience the "resurrection of life, and those who have done evil, the resurrection of judgment" (Jn 5:29).

It would be superfluous to cite these well-known texts except that it is occasionally asserted that since the church's task is to proclaim the gospel, good works are of little importance. The assumption behind this view is apparently that we are saved by faith alone and not by observing the commandments. A church that insisted on faith alone as a substitute for right conduct would not be proclaiming the gospel of Christ but "another gospel" (cf. Gal 1:6).

I am not trying here to make a polemical point for Catholics against Lutherans. In the eloquent first chapter of his *The Cost of Discipleship* Dietrich Bonhoeffer adroitly defends Luther against the charge of having proclaimed cheap grace, but he does insist, in opposition to some later Lutherans, that "costly grace is the only pure grace, which really forgives sins and gives freedom to the sinner."[1] The only person who has the right to say that he is justified by grace alone, says Bonhoeffer, is the one who has left all to follow Christ. "Those who try to use this grace as a dispensation from following Christ are simply deceiving themselves."[2]

Social Ethics of the New Testament

For the true Christian, the question is not whether obedience and good works are needed, but which works are commanded and are truly good. The New Testament, as I have indicated, gives many lists of virtues and vices, fruits of the Spirit and fruits of the flesh. These lists remain pertinent and helpful for our own day, when anger, lust, and impatience pursue their destructive courses in the world.

It is often said that the New Testament ethic is individualistic. In a certain sense this is true, insofar as the subject of moral behavior is generally regarded as the individual. The commendation or condemnation of nations and races as such is rather rare in the New Testament as compared with the Old. But the New Testament has a social dimension insofar as it accents virtues and vices that affect human interrelationships. In answering the question, "What must I do to inherit eternal life?" Jesus goes immediately to the second table of the law: "Do not kill, do not commit adultery, do not steal, do not bear false witness, do not defraud, honor your father and mother" (Mk 10:19). Paul in Romans gives a similar list of precepts and then adds that all the commandments are summed up in sentences, "You shall love your neighbor as yourself" (Rom 13:9; Gal 5:14). Love, therefore, is "the fulfillment of the law" (Rom 13:10).

Love, as Paul understands it, is not simply a one-on-one relationship. He sees in Christ the inauguration of a new community transcending all divisions of race, sex, nationality, and social status. "Here there cannot be Greek and Jew, circumcised and uncircumcised, barbarian, Scythian, slave, free; but Christ is all, and in all" (Col 3:11). Reconciled to God in Christ, the disciples are reconciled to one another and are sent into the world as agents of Christ's reconciling work.

"Disunity, conflicts, and quarrels among believers," says the Jesuit social ethicist John Coleman, "are a scandal to the unity of the one body of Christ."[3]

The ethical code of the New Testament is drawn primarily from that of ancient Judaism, especially the Decalogue. But in several respects Jesus is more radical. He is intransigent in insisting on monogamous, indissoluble marriage and in disapproving of sexual intercourse outside of marriage. One also finds in the message of Jesus, especially as set forth in Luke, a bias in favor of—or, as it might be called today, a preferential option for—the poor. This is perhaps based on the fact that the poor proved more ready than the rich to accept the good news of the kingdom. However that may be, the poor are considered to be blessed, and riches are regularly portrayed as a danger to salvation. In this respect the Letter of James speaks even more sharply than does Jesus in the Gospels. The rich are bidden to weep and wail over their impending misfortunes. The cries of the poor, whose wages have been withheld, and the complaints of the defrauded harvesters have reached the ears of God (Jas 5:1–6).

Reading these words today, we might imagine that Jesus and the first Christians were social reformers, but of this tendency there is no trace. Jesus does nothing to arouse the poor to struggle against oppression, nor does he instruct his disciples to work for a new social order. As Ernst Troeltsch saw very clearly, "The message of Jesus is not a programme of social reform. It is rather a summons to prepare for the coming of the Kingdom of God."[4] The followers of Jesus must live in such a way that their conduct arouses hope in the imminent coming of the kingdom. By embodying the values of the kingdom they become signs and anticipations of the new creation that is dawning in Jesus Christ.

The Church and Secular Society

Only a naive biblicism, however, could lead us to believe that the social mandate of the church can be adequately settled by an appeal to the practice of Jesus and his first followers. Concentrating on evangelization and personal discipleship, the early generations did what was urgent for their own day, when the Christian movement was just being launched. The church of New Testament times was very small and had no opportunity to shape the order of secular society. There is evidence, too, that the end of the world was believed to be at hand, so that it seemed pointless to plan for the long-term future of society. But as the church grew larger and as the centuries passed, Christians could not help but assume a measure of responsibility for the social order. Their vision of the good society was bound to make a significant impact on public life and institutions. Christian morality, therefore, took on more evidently social and political dimensions.

With the conversion of the Roman Empire to Christianity and the subsequent collapse of the empire of the West, the church was drawn into direct relationships with the political powers. At first the dominant relationship was one of close collaboration bordering on cooption. The emperors used the church to some degree in order to cement the unity of the empire under their own authority. Then, as imperial authority and cultural institutions collapsed in western Europe and North Africa, the church had to move into the vacuum. Churchmen took on political and cultural responsibilities that would not otherwise have come their way. This clericalization of public life continued throughout the Middle Ages.

Medieval theologians, not finding an adequate basis for political theory in the Scriptures, had recourse to Greek philosophy as an additional source. This combination of revealed and natural wisdom, while it did not enjoy the uncontested authority of dogma, provided a solid intellectual basis for reflection on the scope and limits of human government and on the relations between the spiritual and temporal powers. The papacy tended to make exorbitant claims so as to keep the actions of princes and emperors in line with the interests of religion, but these claims were increasingly resisted. The nationalism of the sixteenth century put a definitive end to papal claims of domination, at least in most parts of the world, not excepting Europe.

Since the Enlightenment the church has exercised little direct political power. Its intervention in the social sphere occurs most prominently through statements that are intended to influence the ideas and behavior of Catholics and other receptive readers. The social teaching of the church, as we understand the term today, dates from the mid-nineteenth century. Responding to the disturbances of 1848, Baron Wilhelm von Ketteler (who was to become bishop of Mainz two years later) saw both a challenge and an opportunity. "The world will see," he declared, "that to the Catholic Church is reserved the definitive solution of the social question; for the State, with all its legislative machinery, has not the power to solve it."[5]

In *Rerum novarum* (1891) Pope Leo XIII initiated what has developed into a long series of social encyclicals issued by a succession of popes.[6] These letters, addressing urgent problems of the political and economic order, propound a social philosophy grounded in universal ethical principles that are deemed consonant with, though not directly derivable from, revelation. This social philosophy is in many respects an updating of the ideas of Thomas Aquinas and other medieval theologians.

Thanks to this body of official social teaching, Catholics are generally convinced that there can be no divorce between the moral and the political spheres. The church has to consider the moral aspects of practices such as slavery, torture, genocide, concentration camps, and gas chambers, not to mention more ambiguous phenomena such as war, penal legislation, and divorce. On occasion popes and bishops will find it necessary to condemn certain policies and laws as being incompatible with a correct understanding of the gospel.

This response on the official level, dealing directly with social questions, may be seen as a supplement to, rather than a replacement of, the indirect impact on society of the church's traditional ministries. Through its proclamation of Christ and the kingdom, the church holds up a vision of ultimate religious meaning, and those who accept this vision take a distinctive attitude toward life and death, pleasure and pain, truth and falsehood, wealth and poverty, power and weakness. The Christian view of life serves as a kind of leaven that, through the conduct of committed believers, gradually penetrates and transforms the entire social environment. In a Christianized culture institutions such as schools and hospitals, prisons, slavery, and even war are progressively infused with a spirit of mercy and with loving esteem for each individual. Scholarly studies can trace how the legal and political institutions of Christian countries, including feudalism and the common law, came to be imbued with Christian values. Christian faith, it is sometimes contended, has "helped to supply the ideas through which democratic capitalism has emerged in history."[7] Even anti-Christian movements such as Marxian and Saint-Simonian socialism would not have taken the forms they did had it not been for the social ferment of the gospel.

This does not mean, of course, that the organization and practice of public life in the West were at any time totally Christian. The old Adam with his selfishness survives in every believer, and many who have gone by the name of Christian have failed to put the gospel into practice. The church has never been able to do away with sin and faithlessness in its own members, let alone in society at large. The growing secularization of society since the Enlightenment has put additional barriers in the path of Christianization. But obstacles such as these do not absolve the church from the task of striving to accomplish the evangelization of social institutions.

Two Styles of Magisterial Teaching

While there is always a danger of exaggerating the contrast, it seems undeniable that there has been a shift in the style of Catholic social teaching since the early social encyclicals of Leo XIII and Pius XI. The new style began to emerge with

John XXIII and in certain sections of Vatican II's Pastoral Constitution, *Gaudium et spes,* but is more clearly displayed in Paul VI's letter on the eightieth anniversary of *Rerum novarum, Octogesima adveniens* (1971), and in the document of the Synod of Bishops, *Justice in the World* (1971).

The earlier style of official teaching made a rather sharp cleavage between the church as a supernatural society and the world as the province of natural law. The church was directly concerned with supernatural salvation, but as a teacher of virtue it could authentically interpret the natural law, which was normative for secular behavior. The church, moreover, was seen as a strictly hierarchical society in which the pope and bishops issued doctrinal pronouncements and practical directives that were to be transmitted in the church by parish priests and applied in the world by the laity. The style of speech, accordingly, was didactic and authoritative.

In more recent teaching it seems possible to detect an anthropological shift. All human beings, since they have the same transcendent destiny, are understood as possessing the same basic inviolability and therefore as being essentially equal (*LG* 32). Each, moreover, is ruled by personal conscience, even in religious matters (*DH* 1; *GS* 41). In view of their intrinsic dignity all should, as far as possible, participate responsibly in social and political life (*GS* 73). Within the church, likewise, the active participation of the faithful is appropriate (*SC* 14). In the Decree on the Ministry and Life of Priests, *Presbyterorum ordinis,* ordained ministry is depicted not as a dignity but as a call to humble service (*PO* 3 and 15).

This anthropological shift affects the church-world relationship. The church, rather than being a *societas perfecta* alongside the secular state, is seen as a pilgrim people, subject to the vicissitudes of history, and sharing in the concerns and destiny of the whole human race (*GS* 1). The church is linked to the world as the sacrament of universal unity (*LG* 1), a sign and safeguard of the transcendence of the human person (*GS* 76), a defender of authentic human rights (*GS* 41). In a dynamically evolving world (*GS* 4), social and political liberation pertains integrally to the process of redemption and hence is not foreign to the mission of the church. The 1971 Synod of Bishops went so far as to declare: "Action on behalf of justice and participation in the transformation of the world fully appear to us as a constitutive dimension of the preaching of the Gospel, or, in other words, of the Church's mission for the redemption of the human race and its liberation from every oppressive situation" (*JW* 6). In subsequent synod meetings and papal documents the church's concern for human solidarity, peace, and justice has been strongly reaffirmed, but the statement that social action is a "constitutive dimension" of the gospel has not been repeated.[8]

These anthropological and ecclesiological shifts demanded revisions in the church's methodology and in its official style of speaking about social questions. Beginning with *Gaudium et spes* one notices a much more empirical methodology, which includes a careful phenomenology of the present situation. The magisterium increasingly recognizes the need for its teaching to be adapted to the various situations in different parts of the world. Thus Paul VI in *Octogesima adveniens* declares:

> In the face of such widely varying situations it is difficult for us to utter a unified message and to put forward a solution which has universal validity. Such is not our ambition, nor is it our mission. It is up to the Christian communities to analyze with objectivity the situation which is proper to their own country, to shed on it the light of the Gospel's unalterable words and to draw principles of reflection, norms of judgment and directives for action from the social teaching of the Church. . . . It is up to these Christian communities, with the help of the Holy Spirit, in communion with the bishops who hold responsibility and in dialogue with other Christian brethren and all men of good will, to discern the options and commitments which are called for . . . (*OA* 4)

In its effort to interpret the "signs of the times" and to discern the appropriate response of Christians to concrete situations, the church is beginning to speak in a more tentative style. Maintaining an open dialogue among its own members and with other communities, it strives to be receptive to criticism and to submit its teaching to continuous revision. Infallibility, which retains its value for strictly dogmatic statements, is deemed inapplicable to the new style of social teaching.

The United States Episcopal Conference: Methodology

Not a few regional churches have taken up the challenge that seemed to be contained in the documents just cited. The Latin American bishops, in their general conferences at Medellín (1968) and Puebla (1979), articulated a social doctrine adapted to their own time and situation. The United States bishops, who had begun issuing policy statements as early as 1919, developed a more elaborate technique, notably in their two recent pastoral letters, *The Challenge of Peace* (1983) and *Economic Justice for All* (1986).

From the standpoint of methodology, the introduction to *The Challenge of Peace* merits careful attention. The bishops distinguish three types of statements in their own document: declarations of universal moral principles that are presumably accessible to all through reason and conscience; reiterations of Catholic social teaching as found in papal and conciliar documents; and prudential applications of these principles and teachings to the particular circumstances of the contemporary situation. The bishops are modest regarding the authority of these applications:

When making applications of these principles we realize—and we wish readers to recognize—that prudential judgments are involved based on specific circumstances which can change or which can be interpreted differently by people of good will (e.g., the treatment of "no first use"). However, the moral judgments that we make in specific cases, while not binding in conscience, are to be given serious attention and consideration by Catholics as they determine whether their moral judgments are consistent with the Gospel. (*CP* 10)

Similar disclaimers of obligatory force are enunciated in the pastoral on the economy. The "illustrative topics," say the bishops, are "intended to exemplify the interaction of moral values and economic issues in our day, not to encompass all such values and issues." The document is "an attempt to foster a serious moral analysis leading to a more just economy." (*EJ* 133)

In the following paragraph (*EJ* 134) the bishops are even more explicit:

> In focusing on some of the central economic issues and choices in American life in the light of moral principles, we are aware that the movement from principle to policy is complex and difficult and that although moral values are essential in determining public policies, they do not dictate specific solutions. They must interact with empirical data, with historical, social, and political realities, and with competing demands on limited resources. The soundness of our prudential judgments depends not only on the moral force of our principles, but also on the accuracy of our information and the validity of our assumptions.

This methodological section concludes with an important paragraph on the authority of the pastoral's positions on policy issues:

> Our judgments and recommendations on specific economic issues, therefore, do not carry the same moral authority as our statements of universal moral principles and formal church teaching; the former are related to circumstances which can change or which can be interpreted differently by people of good will. We expect and welcome debate on our specific policy recommendations. Nevertheless, we want our statements on these matters to be given serious consideration by Catholics as they determine whether their own moral judgments are consistent with the Gospel and with Catholic social teaching. We believe that differences on complex economic questions should be expressed in a spirit of mutual respect and open dialogue. (*EJ* 135)

Open dialogue was actually built into the process by which the two pastorals were hammered out. The bishops held extensive hearings in different parts of the country with experts of various points of view. They published preliminary drafts, invited criticisms, and thoroughly revised their own work several times in the light of the feedback. Thus the final statement, although issued in the name of the bishops, was produced with a great deal of input from others, including the laity. The names of the staff, consultants, and witnesses were published. This represents a major development since 1931, when the collaboration of Oswald von Nell-Breuning, S.J., in the drafting of the encyclical *Quadragesimo anno* was kept an absolute secret, which he was not allowed to share even with his provincial and local superiors.[9]

Principles and Applications

Although methodological innovations in the recent pastorals have led to a different style and degree of authority, it would be an oversimplification to imagine that the new method has been substituted for the old. The traditional style of Catholic social teaching remains in place and is illustrated by *Laborem exercens* (1981), an encyclical issued by John Paul II on the ninetieth anniversary of *Rerum novarum*. The American bishops do not seek to distance themselves from the Catholic tradition of social doctrine, which they explicitly invoke and build into their own analysis. In *The Challenge of Peace* the bishops accept and apply the just war doctrine with its norms such as just cause, competent authority, right intention, last resort, probability of success, proportionality, and due discrimination. In *Economic Justice for All* they invoke principles such as respect for human dignity, the common good, the preferential option for the poor, active participation, and subsidiarity. In all of this they rely on the developing body of social teaching contained in Vatican II's *Gaudium et spes* and in the papal encyclicals.

The general principles of social ethics contained in the two pastoral letters aroused only moderate opposition and were to a great extent accepted by the critics. Michael Novak in his alternative peace pastoral, *Moral Clarity in the Nuclear Age*, makes use of almost identically the same just war principles as do the bishops, though his applications are quite different. Another critic, Ernest Fortin, while likewise adhering to the traditional just war doctrine, remarks that the bishops give an excessively juridical or legalistic interpretation to that doctrine, depriving political leaders of the flexibility required to meet unique and unpredictable contingencies.[10]

The criticism of the social principles in the economics pastoral was likewise rather mild. According to Peter Berger, critics such as William Simon and Michael Novak, although they come to very different conclusions about specifics, use the same ethical presuppositions and the same method of reasoning as do the bishops.[11] To be precise, one would have to add that Simon and Novak, in their "lay letter," *Toward the Future*, and in their report, *Liberty and Justice for All* (Nov. 5, 1986), differ from the bishops in their interpretation of economic rights. They also fault the bishops for failing to emphasize liberty as a crucial factor in social justice.

Controversy about the two pastorals has centered less on the principles than on the practical applications, for which the bishops themselves claimed little authority. Regarding the peace pastoral, the critics question, for instance, whether limited nuclear war is in fact an impossibility and whether the United States could prudently commit itself never to use nuclear weapons unless such weapons had first been used by the enemy. With regard to the economy, there is disagreement about whether the minimum wage should be further increased (*EJ* 197), whether affirmative action should be more rigorously enforced (*EJ* 73, 167, 199), whether the tax system should be structured according to the principle of progressivity (*EJ* 202), and whether responsibility for welfare programs should be shifted from the states to the federal government (*EJ* 213). It is occasionally objected that the two pastorals are inconsistent. Can one demand greater reliance on conventional weapons

(*CP* 216) while at the same time calling for a sharp reduction in appropriations for defense (*EJ* 148, 289, 320)? These are only a sampling of the many detailed criticisms that have been, and are being, made.

As we have seen, the bishops do not claim that their practical applications follow inevitably from their convictions as men of faith. They recognize that intelligent and committed Christians may disagree with their concrete policy positions. But the coherence of their document depends upon the existence of some link between the principles and the applications. Otherwise the bishops could scarcely claim in *The Challenge of Peace* that their contribution is pastoral rather than primarily technical or political (*CP*, summary, ii), nor could they maintain, in *Economic Justice for All:* "We write as pastors, not public officials. We speak as moral teachers, not economic technicians" (*EJ* 7). The claim is implicitly made that the bishops' policy positions are more in line with the gospel and with Catholic social philosophy than alternative positions would be.

We may readily admit that people's moral and spiritual attitudes, including their faith outlook, affect what they see and understand about the world in which they live. Selfishness and prejudice can blind people to facts, problems, and solutions. A deep personal conversion to the gospel can be a source of greater discernment in human questions that touch on the order of religion and morality. If individuals can thus derive wisdom from their faith, the same is even more true of a religious community, which is the bearer of corporate moral insights built up through the accumulated reflection of many generations. The bishops could perhaps claim that their situation within the community of faith and their access to the tradition of Christian reflection give them a privileged sensitivity to the moral and religious aspects of the current policy debate.

Yet there are grounds for questioning such a claim. If commitment to the gospel gave the kind of insight embodied in the policy recommendations of the two pastorals, one would

expect that evangelical Christians would be the chief supporters of the bishops and that agnostic liberals would be the
leading opponents. But this does not appear to be the case; if
anything, the opposite is true.

The authors of the pastorals might reply, of course, that
most evangelical Christians, not being formed in the Catholic
tradition, have a distorted view of the gospel. Does the Catholic tradition, then, account for the difference between the
supporters and the opponents of the bishops? This hardly
seems to be so, since many of the bishops' policy positions
are more generally acceptable to nonreligious liberals than to
traditionally oriented Catholics. It may also be noted that the
peace pastoral, especially in its second draft, met with rather
negative reception in western European ecclesiastical circles.
Even after it was amended to avoid open conflict with recent
papal teaching, the pastoral still stood in some tension on the
issue of deterrence with analogous documents issued by episcopal authorities in Belgium, France, Germany, England, and
Wales. The Holy See, and especially the Cardinal Secretary of
State, are still seeking to iron out the inner-Catholic disagreements with regard to the stockpiling and threatened use of
nuclear weapons.[12]

Many critics complain that the true sources of the applications in the pastoral on peace are not to be found in authoritative Catholic teaching but rather in liberal American academic
circles. George Weigel, for instance, asserts, "[H]owever difficult it may be to find the bishops' approach clearly implied by
the norms the bishops establish, it is rather easy to find that
part of the political culture in which the bishops' views have
great resonance—and that is in a fairly narrow band of what
we might call the 'institutional arms control fraternity.' "[13] The
net effect of the pastoral, Weigel concludes, is to "lend the
weight of their [the bishops'] public credibility to factions within
the already existing argument"—factions that, indeed, "seem
to have had an inordinate impact on the bishops' own
reflections."[14]

Similar charges have been leveled at the economics pastoral. Although the bishops speak with great circumspection and repeatedly praise free enterprise, subsidiarity, and "mediating institutions," they are accused of relying too much on government programs and even of adopting "a preferential option for the state" (Simon and Novak). Michael Novak attributes this flaw to the influence of the Catholic tradition in social thought stemming from Wilhelm von Ketteler and Heinrich Pesch. Acknowledging that this tradition has heavily influenced the official teaching of the popes, Novak believes that the defect can be remedied. Just as American Catholicism was the chief catalyst in bringing about a shift in the official Catholic teaching on religious liberty at Vatican II, so too, he maintains, the American experience of capitalism may stimulate a new advance in Catholic social and economic teaching. In Novak's words, "Through the lonely pioneering work of John Courtney Murray, S.J., the experience of religious liberty under democratic capitalism finally, after so much resistance, enriched the patrimony of the Catholic church. So also, I hope, arguments in favor of 'the natural system of liberty' will one day enrich the church's conception of political economy."[15]

Novak is correct, I believe, in saying that the bishops are indebted to a long Catholic tradition that looks primarily to government action to remedy malfunctionings in the economy and that that tradition may be overly dependent on precapitalist and anticapitalist models. Other critics assert somewhat contemptuously that the bishops are "following in the well-worn footsteps of a major segment of official mainline Protestantism"[16] and that although "we now have a generation of experience with liberal social programs . . . the bishops appear to have just discovered them."[17] These particular complaints, besides exaggerating the partisanship of *Economic Justice for All*, fail to recognize that the American Catholic bishops have been pressing for reform of the economy by government intervention ever since 1919, and that the Holy See has generally tended to distrust free enterprise.

Too Specific? Grounds for Caution

The fundamental question in my opinion is not whether the bishops rely on secular sources for their ideas or even whether their policy recommendations are correct, but rather whether they ought to give detailed answers in controverted areas such as nuclear policy, taxation, or welfare programs. John Paul II has frequently stated that the Church as a hierarchical institution should not involve itself in partisan politics. He has declared: "In her social doctrine the Church does not propose a concrete political or economic model, but indicates the way, presents principles."[18]

A number of commentators have faulted the United States Bishops' Conference for having entered too deeply into policy questions of a technical character. Keith A. Breclaw, an instructor in the department of government of Georgetown University, writes about the economics pastoral: "By entering upon the discussion of policy, the bishops choose the weakest possible ground on which to exert their influence, that of economic policy. In doing so, they forego the distinct advantage they would enjoy by confining themselves to the realm of economic philosophy."[19] Similar criticisms have been articulated by Ernest Fortin[20] and Brian Benestad.[21]

The case in favor of making specific applications has been ably argued by J. Bryan Hehir. Moral principles, he contends, must be incarnated in the fabric of a social problem in order for their significance and illuminative power to appear. There is a risk "in stating principles so abstractly that all acknowledge them, then proceed to widely divergent conclusions while claiming support of the principle."[22] A little later he sums up: "I am persuaded from following the commentary on both pastoral letters of the U.S. bishops that neither would have found their way to the center of the national policy debate if they had not pursued basic principles through to contingent but concrete conclusions."[23]

It is undoubtedly true that the bishops gain more national attention by taking specific positions on contentious issues, but when one ponders the price of such specificity it becomes evident that there are good reasons for restraint. An impressive argument from convergence can be constructed on the basis of the following eight considerations:

First, in drawing up pastorals such as those on peace and on the economy the bishops make an enormous investment of time and energy in questions that are also being dealt with, from a very similar perspective, by a variety of foundations, public interest groups, and educational institutions. Is it justified for them to go so far afield when many ecclesiastical matters, for which the bishops have inescapable responsibility, are crying out for greater attention? The impression is given that the bishops are more at ease in criticizing the performance of secular governments than in shouldering their own responsibilities in the church. Few of the American bishops today enjoy a great reputation for their mastery of theology, liturgy, or spiritual direction, yet many of them are known for their views on politics and the economy.

Second, when the bishops devote so much attention to secular affairs they can unwittingly give the impression that what is truly important in their eyes is not the faith or holiness that leads to everlasting life but rather the structuring of human society to make the world more habitable. The church has in the past managed to convey the conviction that poverty and worldly suffering are only relative evils because the wretched of the earth, if they are pure in heart, are loved by God and destined for eternal blessedness. Conversely it has conveyed to the rich and prosperous the warning that if they become proud and use their riches selfishly they must fear divine retribution. Such, as we have seen, was the message of Jesus. The appeal to sociopolitical analysis in recent episcopal teaching, coupled with an almost total lack of eschatological reference, gives the impression that the pastors have little confidence in their spiritual patrimony. By giving such high priority to political and economic questions the bishops reinforce the impression that the church is a satellite institution revolving around the primary world of industry and government.

Third, while there is no doubt that an individual bishop may be well versed in questions of military strategy or economics, the publication of elaborate and highly technical conference statements on nuclear weapons and the economy arouses suspicions that the bishops are exceeding their competence. The entire membership of a national conference can hardly make itself responsible for the details of its own documents, drawn up as they are by staff and committees. When questioned by journalists shortly after issuing their peace pastoral, a number of bishops admitted that they did not really understand certain recommendations contained in their own letter.

Fourth, although the policy positions in these documents are put forth as following (albeit contingently) from the moral and religious principles of Catholic Christianity, the suspicion remains that these positions are heavily indebted to current theories about the efficacy of certain means (such as conventional weapons or government welfare programs) to achieve goals that are shared by practically everyone (peace, prosperity). For the soundness of these theories there are no biblical or theological warrants. Can the bishops properly claim that in making such recommendations they are speaking as spiritual leaders rather than as citizens who accept certain views about political and social science? Are they unconsciously canonizing their own partisan biases?

Fifth, papal documents have recognized "a legitimate variety of possible options" inasmuch as "the same Christian faith can lead to different commitments" (*OA* 50). By taking particular options and by sponsoring elaborate programs to disseminate their pastoral teaching, the bishops seem to restrict the options open to Catholics. Although the bishops are far from excommunicating persons who gainsay their policy statements, a Catholic who wishes to take a different stand than the national hierarchy will inevitably feel somewhat alienated from, or marginalized in, the church.

Sixth, to the extent that dissent from pastoral letters of this type is openly tolerated, factionalism is encouraged in the church. Catholics take up the cry first heard in opposition to Pope John XXIII, *"Mater, si; magistra, no!"* The spirit of criticism and dissent thus unleashed can scarcely be prevented from spreading to strictly religious matters in which the bishops have unquestionable authority in the church. By speaking out on controversial issues of a secular character bishops undermine their authority in areas that clearly fall within the scope of their mission.[24] One conservative lay critic writes, "Forgive me, fathers, but aren't you squandering your moral capital?"[25]

Seventh, as the official church moves from the realm of social teaching to that of concrete policy positions, it becomes entangled in the ambiguities of mundane politics. Practically speaking, for example, there may be a choice between supporting health benefits with entitlement to sterilization and abortions and preventing any benefits from being enacted. In practical politics one frequently has to accept payoffs and compromises. By taking partisan positions on current issues (whether in pastoral letters or in other occasional statements) a bishops' conference can easily fall into the kind of political pragmatism that has proved so harmful to the church's moral standing in traditionally Catholic countries. It is one of the blessings of the American system that the church has rarely endorsed particular political parties or candidates for office. But as it moves into the public policy realm, the risks of entanglement increase.

Eighth, when concrete instructions are issued by the hierarchy on issues of a social and political character, the question arises whether the laity are being deprived of their distinctive responsibility. Vatican II asserted that the renewal of the temporal order is the special responsibility of the laity (*LG* 31; *AA* 7) and that the clergy should not be expected to offer concrete solutions to complex secular questions (*GS* 43). The 1971 Synod of Bishops stated starkly: "It does not belong to the Church, insofar as she is a religious and hierarchical community, to offer concrete solutions in the social, economic, and political spheres for justice in the world" (JW 37).

Already in 1977 a group of American Catholics expressed anxiety over the increasing clericalization of the social apostolate. In their "Chicago Declaration of Concern" they protested:

During the last decade especially, many priests have acted as if the primary responsibility of the Church for uprooting injustice, ending wars, and defending human rights rested with them as ordained ministers. As a result, they bypassed the laity to pursue social causes on their own rather than enabling lay Christians to shoulder their own responsibility. These priests and religious have sought to impose their own agendas for the world upon the laity.[26]

J. Brian Benestad, referring to this and other texts, comments that the American bishops, by frequently issuing policy statements through their conference and its committees, "have effectively adopted the role of the outsider as the model of political action."[27] I agree that it is generally best for the concrete applications of Christian social teaching to be made by lay people who are regularly involved in secular affairs, especially those of the laity who are specialists in the pertinent disciplines.

Grounds for Specificity

From this inventory of disadvantages it does not follow that popes and bishops should never issue concrete directives about social and political questions, but only that they should move cautiously in this field. The United States bishops have exercised commendable restraint, notably in their economics pastoral. They have drawn a clear line of demarcation between their doctrinal teaching and their policy recommendations; they have phrased those recommendations modestly and have explicitly pointed out that the particular policy recommendations are not binding in conscience on those who honestly disagree.

Although I have reservations about the wisdom of certain policy statements that have been issued by the United States episcopal conference in recent years, I do not hold that the bishops should be confined to speaking in airy generalities. I can think of several reasons why ecclesiastical authorities might find it advisable to propose specific policies in the name of the church (rather than simply as citizens or civil officials).

First, they might find it necessary as teachers to indicate how their doctrinal principles might work out in practice, so that the illuminative power of those principles (to repeat Bryan Hehir's term) might more clearly appear. Such concreteness, however, could be achieved by hypothetical or historical examples without it being affirmed that the example is necessarily well chosen. Even for those who reject the specific policies endorsed in *Economic Justice for All*, the applications can serve as valuable illustrations of how a Christian might propose to bring the economy into closer conformity with Catholic social teaching.

Second, the authorities might have reason for pointing out that certain applications are so obvious that no room is left for reasonable disagreement among properly instructed Christians. Whatever may have been true in the past, it seems undeniable that institutions such as slavery and torture are no longer acceptable. It may also be possible to say with confidence that a given act of aggression violates the criteria for a just war. An affirmative judgment that a given war ought to be waged, as positively satisfying all the criteria, is far more difficult to reach.

Third, there can be urgent situations in which it is imperative for Catholics to act in unison in order to prevent an opportunity from being lost. For example, the Filipino bishops may well have been justified when in February 1986 they denounced the irregularities of the presidential election. Or, to give another illustration, the bishops of some country might wish to support one of several acceptable antiabortion bills in order to prevent Catholics from being so divided that all such bills would inevitably be defeated. Since the bishops are the only persons who can effectively direct the Catholic community, they must give moral leadership when united action is necessary. Practical directives of this kind, however, should be distinguished clearly from Catholic social teaching.

A number of recent theologians would wish to add, fourth, that the official leadership of the church should intervene prophetically in certain concrete situations in which there are not sufficient doctrinal warrants for a clear magisterial teaching. As an example, Edward Schillebeeckx suggests issuing a directive that certain large estates in a particular region should be broken up, if necessary, by expropriation. In taking such action, he holds, the official church, functioning under the charismatic guidance of the Spirit, could speak out decisively. Even though the directive in question lay beyond the scope of the church's teaching office, it would merit the obedience due to the church's pastoral function.[28]

In answer to this proposal I can only say that if the hierarchy is indeed moved by the spirit of prophecy, it ought to speak out boldly even on a concrete issue of politics or economics. But I hesitate to make a rule out of the unforeseeable interventions of the Spirit. I think that the charismatic assistance might appropriately be given to the political rather than to the ecclesiastical authorities in a case of this kind. In any case I would want rather clear assurances that purportedly prophetic utterances about contingent secular issues were in fact divinely prompted.

To conclude this discussion of specificity, we may acknowledge that people will continue to disagree about the extent to which the bishops should involve themselves in controversial policy questions. What should not be denied is that moral teaching does call for specific applications. As John Courtney Murray once wrote, "Power can be invested with a sense of direction only by moral principles. . . . But moral principles cannot effectively impart this sense of direction until they have first, as it were, passed through the order of politics; that is, until they have first become incarnate in public policy."[29] The entire question is whether the policy applications are best made by those who authoritatively frame the principles. If the religious teachers attempt to specify how the principles should become incarnate in public policy, they risk falling into a simplistic moralism that could discredit the principles themselves. But the policy makers, if they make the applications, should not feel authorized to ignore moral principles in the name of political realism. The constituencies responsible for policy formation must be motivated to maintain a high level of moral commitment. To the extent that the bishops of this country have aroused public debate, they may have helped to raise the level of moral concern.

Recovery of the Transcendent

As I indicated at the beginning of this chapter, my point of view is in close harmony with that of the Hartford "Appeal for Theological Affirmation," which I helped to draft in 1975.[30] Like the other Hartford signatories, I deplore the instrumentalization of the gospel and the tendency to equate the kingdom of God with the results of human efforts to build a just society. I insist on the utter transcendence of the kingdom and on the primary duty of the church to proclaim the gospel of eternal life. Such proclamation alone can liberate men and women from captivity to innerworldly values and forces.

I maintain with Hartford that God is to be worshiped because of what he is and not for the sake of human self-realization. With Hartford I deny that "emphasis on God's transcendence is at least a hindrance to, and perhaps incompatible with, Christian social concern and action" (Theme 11). I assert, likewise, that "the Church must denounce oppressors, help to liberate the oppressed, and seek to heal human misery" (Theme 10). "Because of confidence in God's reign . . . Christians must participate fully in the struggle against oppressive and dehumanizing structures and their manifestations in racism, war, and economic exploitation" (Theme 11).

The whole problem is how to participate in these endeavors without embroiling the church in partisan politics. Where the sense of the transcendent becomes enfeebled, the church, in attempting to address social concerns, simply reduplicates what a multitude of secular agencies are also doing. It loses the capacity to speak a healing and transforming word. For the church to make its proper contribution it must remind the world that there is more to life than politics and that "the form of this world is passing away" (1 Cor 7:31; cf. 1 Jn 2:17). As a general rule faithfulness to Jesus will incline the ecclesiastical authorities to avoid entanglement in economic and political struggles. Jesus himself set the pattern:

One of the multitude said to him, "Teacher, bid my brother divide the inheritance with me." But he said to him, "Man, who made me a judge or divider over you?" And he said to them, "Take heed, and beware of all covetousness; for a man's life does not consist in the abundance of his possessions." (Lk 12:13–15)

10. The Extraordinary Synod of 1985

Preparations

With reference to Catholic ecclesiology the entire period from 1965 to the present stands under the aegis of Vatican II, which identified the main questions and supplied the basic orientations. The council has undergone different kinds of reception in different parts of the world.[1] In order to measure how the council had been interpreted and implemented in different countries, Pope John Paul II on January 25, 1985, announced that he was convening an extraordinary assembly of the Synod of Bishops to meet from November 25 to December 8, 1985. To allay any fears that he might be distancing himself from Vatican II, the pope at that time stated that it "remains the fundamental event in the life of the modern Church" and that for himself personally it had been "the constant reference point of my every pastoral action."

The pope gave four purposes for the Extraordinary Synod: first, to commemorate the work of the Second Vatican Council on the twentieth anniversary of its conclusion; second, to revive in some way the remarkable sense of ecclesial communion experienced at the council; third, to exchange and examine experiences and information about the application of the council in various regions; and fourth, to promote further study of the incorporation of Vatican II into the ongoing life of the church, "in the light of new exigencies as well."

In preparation for the Synod each episcopal conference was asked to submit a report dealing with thirteen questions—four general questions and nine specific questions. By the opening of the Synod, the general secretariat had received

95 replies out of the 136 requested. Although the reports of the episcopal conferences were in principle intended to be confidential, about a score have found their way into print, and a number of others have circulated in manuscript form.[2] Further elucidated by the oral and written interventions of bishops at the Synod, these reports represent an honest and informative appraisal of the state of the Catholic church all over the world in our day. They should be an extremely valuable resource for ecclesiastical authorities in setting priorities for the years to come. Even if there had been no message or report from the Synod, the replies of the bishops to the secretariat's questionnaire would be an enduring result of the Synod.[3]

Almost universally, the conference reports reflected deep gratitude for the work of the council, thus putting to rest any lingering suspicion that many bishops are unhappy about Vatican II. Reports from certain Third World countries, such as Brazil and Indonesia, and to some degree the Philippines, were full of buoyancy and optimism. Reports from the northern countries, such as Scandinavia, England, Wales, Canada, and the United States, reflected a moderate optimism and a continued desire to follow the liberalizing reforms of Vatican II. Reports from continental Europe (or at least those I have seen from western Europe) represented a more pessimistic view. While calling for courage and confidence in the Holy Spirit, they registered a feeling that the church has been, for some decades, in decline.

Conduct of the Synod

On the first morning of the Synod, the official reporter, Cardinal Godfried Danneels of Mechelen-Brussels, presented a dense and highly schematic summary of the contents of the episcopal conference reports. This summary proved to be a kind of first draft of what became the final report at the close of the Synod.

In a second phase, lasting from Monday afternoon, November 25, to Friday noon, November 29, the Synod listened to 119 brief oral reports from conference presidents and other Synod members.[4] These reports, in turn, were synthesized by Cardinal Danneels in his second report, on Friday, November 29. At that time he also raised the question what kind of document or documents the Synod should issue or mandate.

The Synod then moved to a third phase, the informal discussions in ten small language groups, which met on Saturday, November 30, and Monday, December 2.

In its final phase, from Tuesday afternoon, December 3, to Saturday noon, December 7, the Synod drew up, debated, and approved, by nearly unanimous votes, two documents: a Message to the People of God and a more detailed Final Report. These two reports constitute the most tangible achievement of the Synod.[5]

The Message to the People of God is rather brief, only about five pages. It is a simple, readable document, pastoral and hortatory rather than theological or juridical. It indicates four main topics that the Synod wished to highlight. First, the members of the Synod express their agreement that Vatican II was a great gift of God to the church and one that continues to provide strength and light today. Second, the Message characterizes the church as the mystery of God's love present in human history and not as a sociopolitical organization. Third, it stresses the duty of every Christian to engage in evangelization. Finally, it reaffirms the call of Vatican II for the full participation of Christians in the struggle to build a "civilization of love." By its emphasis on mystery, personal holiness, evangelization, and secular involvement this message picks up some of the major concerns of the Extraordinary Synod.

The Final Report, about twenty pages in most editions, is a tightly compressed synthesis of a vast amount of material from the preliminary reports of the episcopal conferences, the speeches of the conference presidents, and the reports of the language groups. Part I begins with an introduction asserting the abiding value of Vatican II and then sets forth some principles for a proper exegesis of the council documents. These principles may be paraphrased as follows:

1. Each passage and document of the council must be interpreted in the context of all the others, so that the integral meaning of the council may be rightly grasped.
2. The four constitutions of the council (Liturgy, Church, Revelation, and Church in the Modern World) are the hermeneutical key to the decrees and declarations.
3. The pastoral import of the documents ought not to be separated from or set in opposition to their doctrinal content.
4. No opposition may be made between the spirit and the letter of Vatican II.
5. The council must be interpreted in continuity with the great tradition of the church, including earlier councils.
6. Vatican II must be accepted as illuminating the problems of our own day.

These guidelines represent, in my mind, a reaction against the tendency of some earlier commentaries to find oppositions and innovations whenever possible. The Synod, on the contrary, favors harmonizing interpretations. In this way it may be possible to protect the council from being brought into discredit as a revolutionary departure from the authentic tradition or from being dismissed as already obsolete. It is worth stressing that, notwithstanding some real shifts and developments, Vatican II is fundamentally self-consistent, that it stands in substantial continuity with earlier church teaching, and that it remains valuable for illuminating current questions of our day.

The main body of the Final Report (Part II) is organized under four main headings:

A. The Mystery of the Church
B. Sources of the Church's Life

1. The Word of God
2. The Sacred Liturgy
C. The Church as Communion
D. The Mission of the Church in the World

The Synod Documents: Main Themes

These two Synod documents do not report everything that was said at the meeting itself or contained in the preparatory papers. Aiming at universalism, they make no distinction between different parts of the world and thus speak as though all their statements were equally applicable everywhere. Aiming at unanimity, the authors have deliberately omitted not only minority opinions but even majority opinions that encountered significant opposition. For example, they make no reference to problematic issues such as birth regulation, the status of divorced and remarried Catholics, clerical celibacy, the powers of the Synod of Bishops, and the question of Roman centralization, all of which came up for discussion. The question of theological dissent is treated only by a passing recommendation for improved communication and dialogue between bishops and theologians. Although they state that the talents of women should be more effectively used in the apostolate, the Synod documents do not tackle the questions whether women should be installed in official, nonordained ministries (such as lector and acolyte) or whether they might be ordained, at least to the diaconate. Yet these suggestions had been made at the Synod.

Some critics are disappointed that these problem areas are not more openly discussed in the Final Report, but it may be argued that the drafters showed good judgment in not trying to solve everything at once. Some questions are too complex and divisive to be treated with any degree of adequacy at a brief gathering of two weeks, particularly such a large and diverse gathering. Besides, these disputed questions were only tangentially related to the main theme of the Synod, the ecclesiology of Vatican II.

Both in the Message to the People of God and in the Final Report, great emphasis is placed on the theme of the church as Mystery, taken from Chapter I of the Constitution on the Church. In this connection, the Synod makes much of the universal call to personal holiness within the church as a supernatural communion of sacramental life. In speaking of the church's relationship to nonmembers, the Synod gives relatively more weight to missionary witness and evangelization than did the council. The intent is evidently to counteract the tendency in some quarters to accent interfaith dialogue and secular service at the expense of explicit proclamation of the gospel and the expansion of the believing community.

Comparing the Synod documents with Vatican II, nearly all commentators have remarked on the almost total absence of the theme of the church as People of God, which has often been described as the dominant ecclesial image of the council. This term hardly appears except in the title of the Synod Message. Some have suggested that the virtual omission of this theme was due to "some outside agents who have put pressure on the synod to rework the council in this crucially important point."[6] Another commentator calls the near-disappearance of the term *People of God* from the Final Report "an astounding development for a document which warns against partial and selective readings of the Council's texts."[7]

But if one keeps in mind the intention to produce a consensus document, the reticence seems explicable without recourse to conspiratorial theories. Although some of the Synod material was favorable to the image of the People of God, a number of criticisms were voiced. Already in the written conference reports, the Dutch and Belgian episcopates both complained that People of God was being played off against other images, such as body of Christ, with the result that civil democratic thinking was being encouraged in the church. The French episcopal conference likewise reported that Chapter II of the Constitution on the Church had sometimes been subjected to political readings in the light of secular trends. "The presentation of the People of God should be reinserted between the first chapter, which shows the trinitarian grounding of the Church, and Chapter III, which brings out its ministerial structure."[8] Cautions such as these may sufficiently explain why Cardinal Danneels, in his Initial Report, noted, "Above all, the concept of the Church as People of God has been defined in an ideological manner and detached from complementary concepts in the council: body of Christ and temple of the Holy Spirit."[9] This report also took note of the tendency to make false oppositions between the hierarchical church and a "people's church."

At the Synod itself, the direction taken by the Initial Report received considerable confirmation. Archbishop Christian Tumi of Garoua (Cameroon) stated that in his country the concept of People of God had led to confusion regarding the distinction between the common priesthood of all Christians and the ministerial priesthood.[10] In the language group discussions, French-speaking group A and the German-speaking group both remarked that the image of People of God stood in need of being protected against sociopolitical deformations. Thus it is not surprising that the term is practically absent from the final documents. Other terms used—such as body of Christ, family of God, and communion—function, as would People of God, to offset a one-sided concentration on the hierarchical aspect of the church, which the Synod surely did not espouse.

Schools of Thought

It is legitimate to ask whether the Synod documents represent a victory for any particular party or tendency among the bishops. The differences of opinion at the Synod cannot be simplified in such a way as to classify all the members under quasi-political headings such as progressive and reactionary, liberal and conservative. There were many different perspectives, reflecting concerns from a variety of nations and continents. One may, however, call attention to two major schools of thought, each of which had prominent leaders.[11] The first of these, led by figures such as the German cardinals Ratzinger and Hoeffner, had a markedly supernaturalistic point of view, tending to depict the church as an island of grace in a world given over to sin. This outlook I call neo-Augustinian.

These bishops, without opposing Vatican II, were inclined to think that the council had spoken somewhat naively in a situation that no longer exists, when secular society all over the world seemed to be converging toward greater freedom, prosperity, and universal harmony. The signs of the times today, according to these bishops, are almost the contrary. The world is falling into misery, division, and violence. It is manifestly under the power of the Evil One. Catholics who seek friendship with the world easily fall into materialism, consumerism, and religious indifference. Striving for openness to the world, the church in the postconciliar period allowed itself to be contaminated, with the result that much of the faith was called into question. Many priests and religious abandoned their vocations, and few young people felt called to the service of the church.

Under these circumstances, according to the neo-Augustinians, it would be a mistake to persist in the structural reform and modernization that were attempted after Vatican II. In consequence of the efforts already made, they maintain, the church has become excessively bureaucratized. Paralyzed by staff, committees, and agencies, pastors are inhibited in their personal ministry. The church fails to appear as a sign of Christ's love and to beckon its members to the life of evangelical perfection. The church today must take a sharper stance against the world and seek to arouse the sense of God's holy mystery.

The second major school of thought was represented by Cardinal Hume of England and many others, including Bishop James Malone and Bishop Bernard Hubert, the respective presidents of the United States and Canadian bishops' conferences. This group of churchmen, taking their inspiration from Pope John XXIII and Vatican Council II, had a more humanistic and communitarian outlook. Convinced that great progress had been made as a result of the council, they attributed the main difficulties to the failure of conservative prelates to carry through the reforms of Vatican II. If there is disenchantment among youth, these bishops maintain, it is not because excessive attention has been given to structural reform but rather because the necessary reforms have been resisted and partly blocked. The Catholic church has not yet succeeded in giving its laity an adequate sense of participation in and coresponsibility for the mission of the church. The urgent need today is for a further development of collegial and synodal structures so that the church may become a free and progressive society, a sign of unity in diversity, at home in every nation and every sociological group.

These two points of view implied vastly different programs for the future. The neo-Augustinians, putting the accent on worship and holiness, wanted a church more separate from the world, more manifestly united in itself, more taken up with the cultivation of spiritual union with God. The communitarian school—if one may so describe the second orientation—wanted the church to become more internally diversified and more involved in the promotion of peace, justice, and reconciliation. The first group used the term *mystery* as a kind of code word; the second group, *communion*. The first group was eschatological and otherworldly; the second, incarnational and this-worldly.

Not all the bishops and conferences taking part in the Synod could be neatly fitted into one or the other of these two orientations. For example, the leading advocates of liberation theology, coming from Third World countries, shared neither the sacralism of the Augustinians nor the secular optimism of the communitarians. They wanted a politically involved church that was confrontational and militant.

Themes of Final Report

The Final Report of the Synod refrained from taking a definite position in favor of any one of the dominant schools. It preferred to strive for consensus. In certain sections the Final Report seemed to be inclining more toward one school than toward another, but on balance it is difficult to say that any one party was victorious. In its opening sections (Part I and Part II, sections A and B) the Final Report underscores mystery, love for the sacred, and the quest for personal holiness— all themes characteristic of neo-Augustinianism. The section on the sources of faith emphasizes the authority of tradition and of the hierarchical magisterium, the need for mystagogical catechesis, for interiority, and for heroic fidelity even to the point of martyrdom.

Then follows a long section (II.C.) in which the emphasis shifts from mystery to communion. This section begins with the words, "The ecclesiology of communion is a central and fundamental idea in the documents of the council." The following paragraphs celebrate the variety of particular churches and insist on pluriformity as a feature of true catholicity. Then the document goes on to discuss collegiality, affirming that the Synod of Bishops and the episcopal conferences are partial realizations of the collegiality of the episcopate as a whole; that they are signs and instruments of the collegial spirit. The same section then takes up the themes of participation and coresponsibility at all levels in the church, advocating greater collaboration of lay persons in the apostolate and a more adequate use of the distinctive gifts of women. Basic ecclesial communities are here characterized as a positive development offering great hope for the revitalization of the church. In its concluding paragraph this section on the ecclesiology of communion contains a strong endorsement of ecumenism, which is presented as a process that presupposes a measure of communion and aims to achieve full sacramental and ecclesial communion.

In Part II, Section D, the focus of the Final Report shifts again, this time to speak to the concerns of the Third World, especially inculturation, interfaith dialogue, and the church's service toward the poor and the oppressed. All these concerns are encouraged, but only with certain reservations that seem to reflect the outlook I have called neo-Augustinian. In this portion of the Final Report the point is made that the favorable signs of the times, so prominent in the documents of Vatican II, have yielded to the ominous signs already mentioned. It is therefore more necessary than ever to adhere to the "theology of the Cross" (a term reminiscent of Luther but here applied to the struggle for human rights). Strengthened by its Lord, the church must not retreat into itself. In the face of opposition it must fearlessly defend and promote authentic human values, such as personal dignity and freedom from oppression, including the right to life.

Inculturation, according to this section, is desirable but must not be understood as an easy acceptance of whatever cultural forms happen to exist. Interreligious dialogue is accepted and approved with the proviso that it should not be set in opposition to mission and evangelization. Service to the world is encouraged, but only with the caution that it should not infringe on the church's spiritual mission. In Part II, Section A, evangelization had already been identified as the primary mission of the church.

The Final Report thus incorporates many concerns of the neo-Augustinians, who emphasize mystery and sacred authority; of the communitarians, who value communion and participation; and of the liberationists, who prize the option for the poor and the oppressed. So artfully is the Final Report constructed that the reader hardly perceives the transition from one portion to another. All are woven together so that the document reads as a coherent whole. The Vatican II concept of the church as sacrament is used to unify the diverse elements. Sacrament may be seen as a manifestation of mystery, as a source of communion, and as an instrument of transformation. Thus the Final Report can declare, in a pregnant sentence: "The Church as communion is the sacrament for the salvation of the world" (II.D.1.).

In the nature of the case, the Final Report could not have given full satisfaction to the concerns of any party or school. Like the documents of Vatican II itself, it is a compromise. But compromises can often be useful in effecting reconciliation between groups that would otherwise clash. The Final Report, if it is taken as seriously as it deserves to be, can become a unifying and stabilizing factor in a divided and turbulent church. At least some legitimate aspirations of all the major tendencies are affirmed, with suitable cautions to prevent them from becoming mutually antithetical. If the Catholic church has a will to survive—and all the evidence suggests that it does—it would do well to heed the prescriptions of the Synod.

Looking toward the future, the Synod made a number of suggestions. At the end of each section of the Final Report there is a paragraph detailing recommendations growing out of the preceding analysis. The following recommendations may be mentioned by way of sampling: a pastoral plan should be drawn up by particular churches for the better dissemination and implementation of Vatican II; better use should be made of the mass media of communication; more thorough philosophical training should be given to future priests; catechesis is to be oriented toward liturgical life in the church; and the changing signs of the times are to be subjected to continual reexamination.

Among the suggestions of the Final Report four deserve special consideration because of their immediate practical implications for the church as a whole. These are: the early completion of the Code of Canon Law for the Eastern-rite churches, the preparation of a universal catechism or compendium of

196 / THE RESHAPING OF CATHOLICISM

Catholic doctrine, a study of the nature and authority of episcopal conferences, and a study of the applicability of the principle of subsidiarity to the internal life of the church.

Eastern Code of Canon Law

The preparation of a revised Code of Canon Law for all Eastern Catholic churches has been under way since 1972, when Paul VI established a commission to undertake this task.[12] But progress has been slow and difficult. The recommendation in the Final Report may be interpreted in light of the oral intervention of the Melchite Patriarch of Antioch, Maximos V Hakim. He concluded his address with an appeal to the pope:

I ask the Lord to give you the strength, health, and length of life to convoke on the occasion of the jubilee of Vatican II, five years from now, a new Extraordinary Synod. I hope that then all our Eastern Churches and I myself—or my successor, if I am no longer alive— may thank you for having given us at length an Eastern canon law: not any Code at all, but one impregnated with our venerable traditions. May this new code realize the wish of the first President of the Commission for the Reform of Eastern Law, Cardinal Massimo, who said, "You will see that our new Code will be so Oriental that our Orthodox brothers and sisters will be happy to adopt it at the same time as yourselves."[13]

The Final Report expressed great esteem for the institutions, liturgical rites, ecclesiastical traditions, and disciplines of the Eastern-rite churches. Its suggestion that the codification of the law for these churches be completed as soon as possible should be understood in this context.

Pope John Paul II in his closing address at the Synod took up this suggestion. He said that the Code should be according to the traditions of the Eastern churches and the norms of Vatican II. In his annual address to the Roman curia, on June 28, 1986, the pope described this proposal as one of the three priorities for the universal church growing out of the Synod. He stated that the commission charged with drawing up the Code of Eastern Canon Law will be ready, in a relatively short time, to issue "a Code in which they can recognize not only their traditions and disciplines, but also and above all their role and mission in the future of the universal Church and in the broadening of the dimension of the Kingdom of Christ *Pantocrator.*"[14] I take this to be, in part, a warning that any false particularism or anachronistic adherence to the past will be avoided in the forthcoming Code.

The Universal Catechism

The second suggestion that requires our attention has to do with the preparation of a universal catechism or compendium of all Catholic doctrine regarding both faith and morals. The Final Report specified that this work should be a point of reference for all regional catechisms or compendiums, that the presentation of doctrine should be predominantly biblical and liturgical, and that the work should be adapted to the present-day life of Christians.

The idea of a universal catechism had been discussed at Vatican II and rejected in favor of a general catechetical directory (*Christus Dominus,* 44). This was in fact composed after the council and finally promulgated in June 1971. A number of national and regional catechisms, including a catechetical directory for the United States, have been drawn up according to the general directory and approved by Rome.[15]

At the Synod the suggestion for a universal catechism was made rather tentatively in the United States conference report. It was picked up more definitively in the Korean conference document and in the report from the hierarchies of Senegal and Mauritania. In his eight-minute intervention on the Synod floor Cardinal Bernard Law, Archbishop of Boston, stated, "I propose a Commission of Cardinals to prepare a draft of a Conciliar Catechism to be promulgated by the Holy Father after consulting the bishops of the world. In a shrinking world—a global village—national catechisms will not fill the current need for a clear articulation of the Church's faith.''[16] In other interventions Archbishop Joachim Ruhana of Burundi requested ''a model catechism issuing from Vatican II,'' and the Latin Patriarch of Jerusalem, Giacomo Beltritti, called for a single catechism for children to be used by the entire church, adaptable to the needs of various countries.

Cardinal Silvio Oddi, then prefect of the Congregation for the Clergy, apparently gave his support to this movement, which he may have to some extent inspired. At any event the idea of a universal catechism or compendium of doctrine came up in one form or another in six of the nine language-group reports: the Italian, English group A, both French groups, Spanish group B, and the Latin group. The Final Report followed most closely the wording of the Spanish group.

The pope in his closing address picked up this suggestion, which he said corresponded to a real need both of the universal church and of the particular churches. On June 10, 1986, he was able to announce the creation of a special commission composed of twelve cardinals under the presidency of Cardinal Ratzinger, prefect of the Congregation for the Doctrine of the Faith. The two Americans on this commission are Cardinal Baum, prefect of the Congregation for Education, and Cardinal Law, archbishop of Boston.

In his report to the Curia on June 28, the pope further explained that the commission was to prepare, with due consultation, the draft of a true and proper catechism, which should be presented at a forthcoming regular session of the Synod of bishops and promulgated, if possible, on the twenty-fifth anniversary of the close of Vatican II in 1990.

At the October 1987 Synod of Bishops Cardinal Ratzinger presented a progress report on the catechism. He listed the members of the commission of writers (including one American, Bishop William J. Levada of Portland, Oregon) and stated that the catechism would follow the traditional tripartite structure (creed, sacraments, commandments). The intended audience, he said, would be primarily the bishops as the teachers responsible for national and diocesan catechisms. A provisional text is to be circulated to all the bishops through the episcopal conferences in the first half of 1989.[17]

It is too early to predict the precise character of the proposed compendium. Notwithstanding the intervention of Beltritti, who wanted a catechism for children, it appears that, following other suggestions, the commission is preparing a manual of doctrine that might resemble the Catholic Adult Catechism issued by the German Bishops' Conference in 1985. The new document is evidently not intended to be a substitute for national and regional catechisms but to be a sort of model for these—possibly doing for the contemporary church what the Tridentine Catechism did for the church several centuries ago. According to the Final Report the presentation of doctrine is to be "biblical and liturgical" and thus, it would seem, not primarily philosophical or scholastic. Spanish-speaking group B had called not for a detailed catechism but for a common point of reference for Catholics, "an integral synthesis of the doctrine of the Church concerning faith and morals in the new pastoral perspectives of Vatican II."[18] French-speaking group B, in similar fashion, had recommended a catechism or compendium containing the essential doctrines of Vatican II, presenting the "good news" of Jesus Christ as the way of life and not as an ideology.[19] The Latin language group, on the other hand, was especially concerned with orthodoxy. It requested that the new catechism take into account the Credo of the People of God issued by Paul VI in 1968.[20] The Korean hierarchy had called for a new Roman Catechism according to the mind of Vatican II "in order to correct misunderstanding and lessen confusion."[21]

It remains an open question to what degree the special commission will satisfy the intentions of the different groups that had requested the new manual. Will it be a catechism in the traditional sense of the word? Will it be biblical, pastoral, and liturgical in tone, or will it be predominantly doctrinal? Will it leave room for significant pluralism in national and regional catechisms, or will it set a uniform pattern for all?

Status of Episcopal Conferences

The third major project recommended by the Final Report had to do with the episcopal conferences. This institution was welcomed with enthusiasm in many of the conference reports, notably those of Brazil, Canada, England and Wales, France, Indonesia, North Africa, Switzerland, and the United States. Several of these reports asked for greater autonomy for the conferences. At the plenary meeting of the College of Cardinals held immediately before the Synod, Cardinal Jérôme Hamer, prefect of the Congregation for Religious, gave a talk in which he quoted Henri de Lubac and Willy Onclin to the effect that the national and regional conferences were not true instances of collegiality.[22] In their eight-minute presentations the presidents of the conferences of Brazil and the United States strongly favored the growth of the conferences. In the group reports, however, a division of opinion appeared in some of the language groups, such as English-speaking group A. The Latin-speaking group warned against the excessive autonomy of the conferences. Further study of the conferences and their teaching authority was requested by English-speaking group B and by French-speaking group A.

The Final Report commended the conferences as useful and indeed necessary. It called them partial realizations of collegiality and authentic signs and instruments of the collegial spirit. But at the same time the Final Report called for further study of the theological status of the conferences and, in particular, of their doctrinal authority. In his closing address at the Synod Pope John Paul II welcomed this as a valuable suggestion. Then, in a letter of May 19, 1986, he entrusted this study to the Cardinal Prefect of the Congregation for Bishops,

Bernardin Gantin, who was instructed to consult with local churches and to collaborate with the competent organs of the Roman Curia.

The results of this study will be of great importance for the future of the universal church. The subject is a highly controversial one because many regional churches feel that they have not been accorded the freedom and autonomy that seemed to be promised by Vatican II. On the other hand, a number of excellent theologians, together with influential Roman cardinals, fear that the growth of the national conferences could introduce an unhealthy nationalism and separatism within the church. Others have objected that the conferences tend to stifle the pastoral responsibility of the individual bishop for the flock committed to his care. These criticisms will be studied further in the next chapter.

Subsidiarity in the Church

The fourth major suggestion that requires attention in the present context has to do with the principle of subsidiarity. The principle was first set forth by Pius XI in his Encyclical *Quadragesimo Anno* (1931) in the following terms: "It is a fundamental principle of social philosophy, fixed and immutable, that one should not withdraw from individuals and commit to the community what the individuals can accomplish by their own enterprise and industry. So, too, it is an injustice and at the same time a grave social evil and a disturbance of right order to transfer to the larger and higher collectivity functions that can be performed and provided for by lesser and subordinate bodies."[23] The point was therefore that the higher authority is to be seen as a *subsidium* (support) for the lower when the latter is incapable of handling a given problem by its own resources.

Does the principle of subsidiarity apply to the church? Pius XII, in a consistorial allocution of February 20, 1946, after expounding what Pius XI had to say on subsidiarity, added:

"These very enlightening words are valid for social life at all levels and also for the life of the Church, without prejudice to the latter's hierarchical structure."[24] Some interpret this as a positive endorsement of subsidiarity in the church; others regard it as a warning that subsidiarity does not apply to the church without notable qualifications. The first of these interpretations seems preferable in view of the context in Pius XII's address.

At the first meeting of the Synod of Bishops, in 1967, Cardinal Pericle Felici presented ten basic principles for the revision of the Code of Canon Law.[25] The fifth of these was the application of the principle of subsidiarity. When this fifth principle, as formulated by the Code Commission, was submitted to the Synod fathers in 1967 for their reaction, 128 voted affirmative; only one voted negative and 58 voted affirmative with reservations (*placet iuxta modum*).[26] At his press conference on October 5, 1967, Cardinal Giovanni Urbani, president of the Italian episcopal conference, reported that the principle of subsidiarity had been received by the Synod with universal favor.[27]

At the Extraordinary Synod of 1969 the principle of subsidiarity again came up for consideration. In an interview on the eve of the Synod, Cardinal Julius Döpfner of Munich gave a carefully worded formulation of the principle of subsidiarity as applied to the church:

Subsidiarity—an important principle of Christian social doctrine, which holds equally for the Church—signifies that the higher instances and organisms must respect the capacities, competences, and tasks of individuals and communities, in theory and in practice. In this way a healthy and vigorous life, adapted to the different situations, can develop. This holds also for the Church as a whole, for the pope and his curia, for the bishop and his ministers, for the pastor and the government of his parish. On this point much remains to be done on all levels.[28]

At the opening of the Synod of 1969 Paul VI gave a talk in which he cautioned that the principle of subsidiarity should be applied in the Church only with great prudence so as not to compromise the common good.[29] At the Synod the principle of subsidiarity was discussed by Archbishop Carlo Colombo, the theologian Gérard Philips, and Cardinal François Marty, all of whom admitted its applicability to the life of the church. Colombo, however, explained that while the local church has a certain priority in pastoral matters, in which the particular bishops are the first and immediate judges, the reverse obtains for doctrinal matters. "The ultimate judgment in matters of doctrine or in the teaching of the faith and of the moral law, without being withdrawn from the authority of individual bishops, by its nature falls primarily and per se under the competence of the supreme authority of the magisterium," that is, the college of bishops under the direction of the pope, or the pope himself acting as visible head of the universal church.[30]

Cardinal John Francis Dearden, in reporting for the first English-language group on October 21, 1969, declared, "Taking their direction from what is said in *Christus Dominus* no. 8, all admit that, although there are some limits to the power of the bishops imposed by reason of unity of faith and communion and the need for a common ordering of certain matters concerning the whole Church," the principle of subsidiarity nevertheless does apply. "Its actualization, urgently required today, will lead to a radical transformation in the concept and practice of granting faculties."[31]

Summarizing the opinions expressed in the language groups at the 1969 Synod, Giovanni Caprile observes that some preferred not to insist on the term subsidiarity because of the shift of meaning involved in its transfer from civil life to the church. He maintains, however, that in substance the principle was unanimously accepted as valid for the church, suitable, and demanded by the times.[32] Several propositions concerning subsidiarity were subjected to an informal vote, and were approved by a large majority (favorable 98, opposed 7, favorable with reservations 37, abstaining 1).[33]

At the Extraordinary Synod of 1985 the principle of subsidiarity was mentioned favorably in the conference submissions from Brazil, Canada, England and Wales, Indonesia, North Africa, Scandinavia, and (by implication without actual use of the term) Switzerland. In oral reports at the Synod, bishops from Brazil, Kenya, South Africa, and Norway all spoke in favor of the principle and even recommended its extension. The group discussions, however, were less supportive. The German-speaking group asked for further study to determine to what extent the principle was appropriate to describe the life of the church. English-speaking group A was about evenly divided as to whether or not to recommend that ways of furthering subsidiarity in the church be explored. The Latin-speaking group cautioned against understanding subsidiarity in such a way as to imply that local churches should be independent of the primacy of Rome. French-speaking group A observed that any general appeal to subsidiarity was a false trail, since the principle was not applicable to the sacramental and liturgical life of the church. One member of this last group was Cardinal Hamer, who had said at the plenary meeting of cardinals immediately preceding the Synod that subsidiarity does not apply to the church since the universal church is not a mere support (*subsidium*) for the particular church.[34]

Reflecting the general trend of the discussion, the Final Report recommended that a study should be made "to determine whether the principle of subsidiarity in use in human society can be applied to the Church and to what degree and in what sense such an application can and should be made" (II.C.8.). The Report here referred to the 1946 statement of Pius XII quoted above.

In his closing address John Paul II made no reference to the recommendation regarding subsidiarity. In his speech to the Curia on June 28, 1986, he observed that the question of subsidiarity is a complex and subtle one, already treated to some degree at the Extraordinary Synod of 1969 and in connection with the revision of the Code. The revised Code, in the preface to the Latin text, left "to particular legislation or to the executive power that which is not necessary to the unity of the discipline of the universal Church." The Secretariat of the Synod, added the pope, had asked for more time to establish the precise state of the question and the point at issue before embarking on a full study of subsidiarity. In his personal reflections the pope seemed to suggest that, because of the unique nature of the ecclesial society, the principle of subsidiarity as generally understood could not be applied to the church without being modified.[35]

The Unfinished Agenda

The four major agenda items bequeathed by the Extraordinary Synod are instructive. They reflect some of the deepest tensions in contemporary Catholic ecclesiology. A decade ago most American Catholic theologians would have taken it for granted that in fidelity to Vatican II the autonomy of local and regional communities was to be promoted at the expense of the central authority of the universal pastoral office. It was assumed that in the brave new church then emerging there would no longer be any need for a universal "Roman catechism"; that the Eastern Catholic churches should somewhat distance themselves from Rome so as to avoid unhealthy Latinization; that episcopal conferences should become more active in adapting Catholicism to local conditions; and that subsidiarity in the church was authorized and demanded by the spirit if not by the letter of Vatican II.

Today, however, the problems are seen to be more complex. The theological liberalism of the past two decades is no longer triumphant. Efforts are being made to reread Vatican II in the context of the entire tradition. The tensions of our time have made it increasingly evident that for Catholicism to endure in the "global village" visible structures of unity are essential. A vibrant sense of Catholic unity seems to require not only an inner union of spirit but a measure of common catechesis, common legislation, common customs, common symbols, and common ministerial oversight.

The task of the next generation is to safeguard this necessary universalism while still giving due scope to the freedom and initiative of regional and local groups within the church. The extremes of bureaucratic centralism and acephalous federalism are equally unacceptable. Catholicism cannot admit a dilemma between global solidarity and sound inculturation. Ecclesiologies elaborated in the power categories of Western law and politics cannot successfully harmonize the universal and the particular. But there is reason to hope that an ecclesiology of mystery, sacrament, and communion, such as the recent Synod proposed on the basis of Vatican II, may provide the key to the desired solution.

11. The Teaching Authority of Bishops' Conferences

In the last chapter we have seen that the Extraordinary Synod of 1985 called for further examination of two important and interconnected questions: the status of bishops' conferences and the applicability of subsidiarity to the church. As a contribution to the first of these two questions, and, by implication, the second also, I shall now undertake a brief examination of episcopal conferences. My focus will be on the National Conference of Catholic Bishops in the United States, with special reference to its doctrinal authority.

The Controversial Origins

During the period from about 1830 to about 1950 it became customary in many countries of western Europe and the Americas for the national or regional hierarchies to meet about once a year for purposes of consultation and common action.[1] Although encouraged by the Holy See, especially under Leo XIII (1878–1903), these meetings did not as yet have any official status in the general law of the church. They were not included in the 1918 Code of Canon Law. Mentioned in several documents of Vatican II, the conferences first received canonical status in the Decree on the Bishops' Pastoral Office in the Church, *Christus Dominus*. Paul VI, in his *motu proprio*, *Ecclesiae sanctae* (Aug. 6, 1966), ordered that such conferences should be established wherever they did not yet exist and laid down certain norms for their activity.

The United States Catholic Conference had a difficult birth. In 1918 the American bishops set up a National Catholic War

Council to attend to common problems arising out of the country's involvement in World War I. When the war came to an end, many churchmen were convinced that some such organization was still needed to advise the bishops and to promote the concerns of the church on the national level. Cardinal James Gibbons, with some encouragement from the Holy See, set up a committee to study this question. The committee in 1919 proposed the establishment of what was to become the National Catholic Welfare Council. After the idea was approved by Pope Benedict XV, the bishops in September 1919 voted the council into existence and elected a body of officers and an Administrative Committee.

On January 22, 1922, Benedict XV died, and his successor, Pius XI, was elected on February 6. Cardinals William H. O'Connell and Dennis Dougherty, who had come to Rome for the conclave, took the occasion to register their objections to the Welfare Council and found a ready hearing with some of the more conservative cardinals, such as Raffaele Merry Del Val. On February 25, 1922, the Consistorial Congregation issued a decree of dissolution of the National Catholic Welfare Council and a prohibition of the annual meetings of the American hierarchy. This decree was signed by Cardinal Gaetano De Lai, the Secretary of the Congregation, with the approval of the newly elected pope.

Upon receipt of this news, the Administrative Committee, in the United States, sent a cable to Rome pleading for a delay in the publication of the decree and promptly dispatched one of its members, Bishop Joseph Schrembs of Cleveland, to go to Rome to defend the Welfare Council. At Rome Bishop Schrembs found that the opposition to the Welfare Council was based on grounds such as the following: it was against canon law, it was expensive, and it had a tendency, especially through its Social Action Department, to make controversial and divisive statements. Cardinal De Lai added that in his judgment the council would hamper the freedom of individual bishops. To this

Bishop Schrembs replied, according to the summary report, "It's a smoke screen. What they mean is that it is easier to deal with one bishop than with a hierarchy."[2] Cardinal Pietro Gasparri, the Secretary of State, was favorable to the cause of Bishop Schrembs, and the pope himself soon became persuaded that he had been induced to act too hastily. Against the objections of Merry Del Val and De Lai, Pius XI ordered the Consistorial Congregation to cancel its decree. In a new set of instructions the organization was permitted to survive, but its authority was weakened. It was forbidden to make any binding decrees, and its name was to be changed. In place of the word *Council* in the title the bishops eventually settled on *Conference*.

At Vatican Council II, similar debates recurred. Many of the conservative minority, including Cardinals Ernesto Ruffini, Alfredo Ottaviani, Giuseppe Siri, Michael Browne, and James Francis McIntyre, spoke against the upgrading of bishops' conferences. There was sharp division of opinion about the theoretical foundation for such conferences and about the extent of their authority. Because little consensus was achieved, the Decree on the Bishops' Pastoral Office, while authorizing the existence of such conferences, left the theological basis and the powers of the conferences rather vague, and this vagueness has been the occasion of continued disputes down to the present time. The authority of episcopal conferences remains a bone of contention among cardinals and other high ecclesiastics.

One of the prominent theologians currently engaged in the dispute is German Cardinal Joseph Ratzinger, who has been for several years prefect of the Congregation for the Doctrine of the Faith. In 1963, as a young theologian, he published an enthusiastic lecture on the first session of Vatican II in which he attributed "immense ecclesiological significance" to the Constitution on the Liturgy. The "small paragraph which establishes the conferences of bishops as a canonical factor for the first time" he asserted, will in the end have greater significance for the theology of the episcopate and for the universally desired strengthening of episcopal authority than the actual schema dealing specifically with the Church, with all its erudite statements. For here a fact has been established; and the weight of the factual, as history teaches, in a matter of this kind is greater than mere exposition. With little fuss and almost unnoticed by the public, the Council has already taken a fundamental step in the renewal of ecclesiology.[3]

In the following year, Ratzinger published a longer article in defense of bishops' conferences as an appropriate expression on the regional or national level of the principle of collegiality. He explicitly rejected the position that "the bishops' conferences lack all theological basis and could therefore not act in a way that would oblige the individual bishop."[4]

But the senior Ratzinger can be cited on the opposite side of the debate. In 1983, when the American bishops were preparing their pastoral letter on peace, Cardinal Ratzinger, now as prefect of the Congregation for the Doctrine of the Faith, was reported as maintaining that "a bishops' conference as such does not have a *mandatum docendi.*"[5] Again, in August 1984, he gave a lengthy interview to an Italian periodical, *Jesus,* subsequently published in book form as *The Ratzinger Report.* Here the cardinal is reported as making essentially two objections: first, that the conferences are merely practical expedients, lacking any secure theological basis, and second, that their anonymous, bureaucratic procedures tend to undercut the personal teaching authority of the individual bishop.[6] Finally, in October 1985, shortly before the Extraordinary Synod, he published, with a preface by himself, a report of the International Theological Commission (over which he presides). Here a sharp contrast is made between collegiality, which belongs to the church by divine law, and episcopal conferences, which are products of human law. From this the report concludes that to use in connection with the conferences terms such as *college, collegiality,* and *collegial* cannot be acceptable except in "an analogous, theologically improper sense."[7] These various statements attributable to Ratzinger, seen in their mutual tension, bring us to the very heart of the question before us.

The Theological Basis for Bishops' Conferences

Throughout the present century it has been objected repeatedly that whereas the individual bishops and the college of bishops as a whole enjoy an authority of divine right, episcopal conferences cannot claim such legitimation. Similar ideas were voiced at Vatican II, where Bishop Luigi Carli, for instance, contended that bishops' conferences were not authentic embodiments of episcopal collegiality but could be defended only by practical pastoral considerations.[8]

It is beyond dispute that collegiality in the strict sense of the word signifies the universal solidarity of all the bishops with one another and with the pope as the center of communion, in their common responsibility to direct the entire church. Vatican II, however, acknowledged the existence of limited expressions of collegiality. The Constitution on the Church mentions in this context the time-honored practice of summoning several bishops to take part in the consecration of a new member of their body (*LG* 22). In the following article, the Constitution, speaking of the collegial union of individual bishops, adds that modern episcopal assemblies (*coetus episcopales*), like the ancient patriarchates, contribute to the concrete realization of the collegial spirit (*collegialis affectus*, *LG* 23).

A number of theologians have attempted to clarify the relationship between territorial conferences of bishops and the collegiality of the entire episcopal body. Jérôme Hamer, who has since become a prominent curial archbishop, published in 1963 an article in which he defended the thesis that an episcopal conference is "an appropriate manifestation of the solidarity of the episcopal body, which is a reality of divine right in the Church of Christ."[9] To explain this he proposed a helpful analogy. The gospel precept to love one's neighbor, he argued, is universal, but it must be concretely expressed in the love of those who are closest to us and who have a special claim on our love. So, likewise, the concern of the individual bishops for the tasks of the entire episcopate would be deficient it it were not implemented territorially in neighboring dioceses that form, so to speak, natural units within the universal church.

Cardinal Ratzinger, in his 1965 article, carried this line of thought a stage further. It would be contrary to the collegial spirit, he maintained, for the individual bishop to isolate himself as a self-sufficient autocrat in governing a particular diocese. The universal solidarity of all the bishops would be unreal unless implemented by mutual assistance and cooperation on all levels, including the solidarity of bishops in a single region. Collegiality, he contended, "signifies an element of variety and adaptability that basically belongs to the structure of the Church but may be actuated in many different ways . . . The bishops' conferences are, then, one of the possible forms of collegiality that is here partially realized but with a view to the totality."[10]

It is quite true that bishops' conferences are not directly mandated by divine law, but divine law does give the hierarchy the right and duty to establish the structures that are found helpful for the exercise of their divinely given mission as individuals and in groups. Entities such as parishes and dioceses, in their present form, or for that matter the Roman Congregations, are not essential to the church as such, but they have real authority based on the divinely established order of the church. The same may be said for bishops' conferences.

Pope John Paul II has on occasion stressed the close connection between bishops' conferences and the collegiality of the whole episcopate. Speaking to the National Conference of Bishops in Brazil in the summer of 1980, he said that such conferences are "a peculiar expression and particularly appropriate organ of [episcopal] collegiality." He added, "Any utterance at all of a bishops' conference produces greater effect the more it is a reflection of unity as the soul of the episcopal collegiality as concretely incarnated in this group of bishops."[11]

Leaders of the United States Bishops' Conference have frequently spoken in similar terms. The burden of our argument thus far is ably summarized in the words of Cardinal Joseph Bernardin, spoken when he was president of the National Conference in 1976:

We may conclude, then, that our episcopal conference must be far more than a service agency helping the member bishops minister more effectively to their individual churches. In the perspectives of theology, the conference is a concrete embodiment and implementation of the collegiality of the bishops in the United States and thus, indirectly, of the communion by which the local churches are linked to one another in mutual charity and solicitude. By fostering the spirit of brotherly union among its bishop members, the conference helps them fulfill their common apostolic responsibility toward the entire region in which they labor together, as it also helps all of the people of God fulfill their apostolic ministry.[12]

Teaching Authority of the Conference

Granted that the bishops' conferences have a solid theological basis in the principle of collegiality, we may now turn to a second and more difficult question: do they have authority to teach? Ratzinger in 1983, as I have mentioned, was reported as denying that the episcopal conference, as such, has a *mandatum docendi*. By this he presumably meant that its teaching is not juridically binding unless it becomes the teaching of the member bishops individually, or unless it receives recognition from the Holy See after the process prescribed by canon 455.

Vatican Council II, indeed, made no explicit reference to the power of episcopal conferences to teach. Cardinal Henri de Lubac seems to be technically correct when he asserts that the Constitution on the Church "recognizes no intermediary of the doctrinal order between the particular [that is, diocesan] church and the universal Church."[13] *Ecclesiae sanctae*, the document by which Paul VI authorized the establishment of bishops' conferences, does not speak of them as having doctrinal functions, although it does not deny this either.

What about the 1983 revised code of canon law? Peter Hebblethwaite maintains that the new code "does not seem to envisage the episcopal conference as 'teaching' at all."[14] This interpretation would seem to be supported by the group of canons (nos. 447–459) thematically dealing with bishops' conferences. Thus it is understandable how Archbishop John Whealon of Hartford could write, "So far as I can see, a bishops' conference in itself has no teaching authority."[15]

In spite of all this negative evidence, a strong argument can be made in favor of the teaching authority of these conferences. Vatican II in its Decree on the Pastoral Ministry of Bishops speaks of an episcopal conference as "a kind of council (*coetus*) in which the bishops of a given nation or territory jointly exercise their pastoral office in order to promote the greater good which the Church offers humanity . . . " (CD 38). The pastoral office, as defined in this same document, includes the functions of teaching, sanctifying, and governing (CD 11). From this it would seem to follow that the joint pastoral activity of a group of bishops might on occasion include joint teaching.

A confirmation of this position may be drawn from a section of the new code of canon law dealing with the church's teaching function. Canon 753 states, "Although they are not endowed with infallibility in teaching, the bishops in communion with the head and members of the college, whether as individuals or gathered in conferences of bishops or in particular councils, are authentic teachers and instructors of the faith for the faithful entrusted to their care; and the faithful are obliged to adhere to this authentic magisterium of their bishops with religious submission of mind." In other canons the revised code gives considerable responsibilities to episcopal conferences in issuing catechetical materials (canon 775), regulating the catechumenate (canon 788), overseeing the doctrinal content of university teaching (canons 809, 810), authorizing editions of Holy Scripture (canon 825), and establishing procedures for censorship and doctrinal evaluation of books (canons 823, 830).

Even apart from current canon law, it would be difficult to defend the view that there is no teaching authority between the universal magisterium of the popes and ecumenical councils, at one extreme, and that of the individual bishop in his own diocese at the other. The Catholic tradition has always recognized the authority of particular councils, as does the code in the canon just quoted. Bishop Henri Teissier of Oran, chairman of the North African episcopal conference, gives numerous examples from the patristic age, with particular attention to the episcopate of Aurelius of Carthage. He concludes, "All these links between bishops of neighboring churches, within the framework of the historical patriarchates of the East . . . or within that of a regional church (continental in the sense of the age) like that for Roman Africa, expressed a deep-lying conviction that *the bishop could do his duty only in communion with the college of bishops,* beginning with the pastors of those churches which were closest geographically and culturally."[16]

Particular councils have often contributed in important ways to the development of Catholic doctrine. Some illustrations are given by Bishop Francis Stafford, then of Memphis, in a speech delivered on May 27, 1984.[17] The third council of Carthage, in 397, pronounced on the canon of Sacred Scripture. A provincial council of Carthage in 418 issued the first decrees on the subject of original sin. The second council of Orange in 529 rejected what has come to be called semi-Pelagianism. The council of Braga in 675 condemned the Priscillianists. And the eleventh council of Toledo in 675 drew up an important profession of faith. Vatican II, taking note of this history, praised the accomplishments of particular synods and councils "in teaching the truths of faith and ordering ecclesiastical discipline," and it expressed the desire that such organs should flourish with new vigor (CD 36).

The teaching authority of a bishops' conference, to be sure, is not identical with that of a particular council, but such conferences have in fact taken on many of the functions previously performed by particular councils. Several years ago, the Canadian canonist, Francis Morrisey, O.M.I., raised the question whether the conferences should not simply replace the regional councils as their modern successors.[18]

In seeking to assess the teaching authority of episcopal conferences, one should not ignore what such conferences have in fact done. In a complete study, reference would have to be made to western Europe, where the national conferences of Germany and France have engaged in vigorous doctrinal activity. Attention would have to be given to the declaration of the bishops of Zaire, "Our Faith in Jesus Christ" (1975), and to the declarations of the Brazilian hierarchy on human rights. The achievements of the general conference of the Latin American bishops at Medellín (1968) and Puebla (1979) have had worldwide impact, especially with reference to liberation theology.

In the United States, the bishops' conference has attached great importance to its doctrinal activity. Archbishop (now Cardinal) Bernardin, speaking as President of the NCCB in May 1976, insisted on this point: "We have made a number of significant doctrinal statements which have had an impact on our teaching efforts. Consider, for example, the pastoral letters or statements on *The Church in Our Day* (1967), *Human Life in Our Day* (1968), *Basic Teachings for Religious Education* (1972), and *Behold Your Mother* (1974)."[19] He went on to mention the bishops' collective efforts on behalf of the sanctity of human life, both before and after birth, their work in promoting and reviewing the bilateral dialogues, and their involvement in the pastoral on moral values, *To Live in Christ Jesus* (1976), and in the *National Catechetical Directory* (1977), two documents then in preparation. Since that time, of course, the Conference has issued still other documents having a doctrinal aspect, such as the Pastoral Letter on Marxist Communism (1980) and the pastoral *The Challenge of Peace* (1983). At its meeting on

November 11–15, 1984, the conference voted acceptance of an evaluation, made at the request of Rome, of the final report of the Anglican-Roman Catholic International Commission. The conference Committee on Doctrine at this time released a statement entitled "Abortion: A Clear and Constant Teaching." At the same meeting the conference discussed the first draft of its pastoral *Economic Justice for All*, finally adopted in November 1986.

Controversies have occasionally arisen between the bishops regarding the value of their own conference statements. A striking instance was the mixed reaction to the statement *The Many Faces of Aids: A Gospel Response* released by the Administrative Board of the United States Catholic Conference on Dec. 11, 1987.[20] A number of bishops complained that the statement contained ambiguities and gave rise to misinterpretations. Several pointed out that the statement was a document of the administrative board, consisting of forty-eight bishops, and not of the conference, which numbers about 280 active U.S. bishops. Cardinal John Krol of Philadelphia, and Archbishop Anthony Bevilacqua, his successor-designate, declared, "Any part of the statement of the Administrative Board must be understood in the context of the whole document, as well as in the light of both the teaching of the whole body of U.S. bishops and the consistent, authentic teaching of the Catholic Church."[21] Archbishop J. Francis Stafford of Denver, in a letter of December 17, 1987 to the president of the conference, Archbishop John L. May of St. Louis, questioned whether the administrative board of the USCC had authority to issue "seemingly binding prescriptions" on moral education. While these early reactions raise important questions about the internal operations of agencies within the conference, they do not touch directly upon the teaching authority of the conference itself.

By and large, the American bishops themselves have felt that they can do their most effective teaching not as solitary masters in their own dioceses but as members of the national conference.

Archbishop James Hickey of Washington, D.C., at the June 1982 assembly of the American bishops at Collegeville, Minnesota, stressed this point:

One would have to be quite blind and deaf to reality if he denied that the statements of episcopal conferences do have an effective impact on the pastoral life of local dioceses and beyond.. . . . Many of the pastoral letters of conferences play an important role in the life of the church. We have to admit, then, that the conference offers the most effective vehicle nationally for our teaching office. Its statements have impact through the media and through decisions and parochial applications in the life of our country. Our collective exercise of the teaching office is necessary to answer specific challenges that arise for us from the collective life of the nation.[22]

These doctrinal activities of the U.S. Bishops' Conference have been conducted with full approval from the Holy See. In its 1976 Declaration on Sexual Ethics, the Congregation for the Doctrine of the Faith, before Ratzinger became its prefect, felicitated the episcopal conferences that had issued "important documents" conveying "wholesome moral teaching, especially on sexual matters."[23] In 1979 Pope John Paul II, addressing the U.S. Bishops' Conference at Chicago, congratulated the American episcopate on its exercise of the ministry of truth in its collective statements and pastoral letters, notably, *To Live in Christ Jesus.*[24]

In his Apostolic Exhortation on Reconciliation and Penance, *Reconciliatio et paenitentia,* dated December 2, 1984, Pope John Paul II devotes several paragraphs to what he calls the "social magisterium." Catechesis in this area cannot fail to take account, he says, of three types of teaching that have built up "a solid body of doctrine" about social questions. The three are, first, papal teaching, second, the teaching of Vatican II in its Pastoral Constitution on the Church in the Modern World, and, third, "the contributions of the different episcopates elicited by various circumstances in their respective countries."[25] I interpret these words as a papal confirmation of the teaching authority of bishops' conferences.

The Obligation to Assent

The crucial question, as I see it, is whether the determinations of the bishops' conference give rise to an obligation on the part of the bishops and faithful of the territory to concur with what is said. Those who deny that the conference has a mandate to teach are in a sense liberals: they argue for freedom of conscience. But they are not liberals down the line, because they hold that when a person teaches with a *mandatum*, as does the individual bishop in his diocese, the faithful are bound to agree.

In my opinion this line of reasoning is too juridical. Assent is never a matter of sheer obedience, but one of responsible judgment. Whenever anyone teaches without a clear guarantee of infallibility, others must reflectively decide whether or not they can agree. Bishops are qualified witnesses to the word of God and as such enjoy a certain presumption in their favor. But the individual bishop who teaches in isolation has only limited authority. The fact that he happens to be one's own bishop, rather than the bishop of a neighboring diocese, does not necessarily add to his credibility. If the bishops of a whole nation or region, after careful consideration, come to a consensus as to where the truth of the gospel lies, their witness normally has more force than that of the average individual bishop. A statement of a committee or board of the conference would per se have less force than one emanating from the whole membership of the conference.

In assessing the authority behind the statements of a bishops' conference one would have to make many further distinctions. For instance, it would have to be asked: are the bishops reaffirming, perhaps with added emphasis, what is already the received doctrine of the church, expressed in papal or conciliar statements or in a longstanding and unanimous tradition? Or is the conference exploring a new and controverted area, where there is as yet no established doctrine in the church? A further set of questions would revolve around the agreement among the bishops: Are they speaking with or without a solid consensus among themselves? Do the bishops of other nations and the Holy See seem to support their positions? In addition it may be asked what authority the conference attaches to its own pronouncements: does it purport to be teaching the sole view admissible in the church or is it proposing its view as calling only for serious consideration and reflection? Still other questions would center about the subject matter: is the conference speaking strictly of matters of faith and morals, or is it involving itself in social, political, economic, or military questions, or in some other area where churchmen as such enjoy no special competence?

As we have seen in chapter 9, the United States bishops in *The Challenge of Peace* and again in *Economic Justice for All* gave different weight to different passages in their own letters. As Archbishop Weakland pointed out, they introduced an original criterion, which he summarized as follows:

General principles carry with them more certitude when taught by the bishops than practical applications of these same principles. The reason is simply that the application is often contingent upon factual data which may or may not always be verifiable. Such data is often complex and changes rapidly.[26]

Because all these distinctions are important, it makes little sense to ask in the abstract whether the faithful are bound to agree with the statements of their bishops' conferences. The conference does have real doctrinal authority, but that authority varies enormously from one pronouncement to another. The bishops can, and frequently do, indicate what kind of obligation they intend to attach to their words.

The Conference and the Individual Bishop

For reasons that are apparent from the argument thus far, Bishop Stafford is justified in holding that "ordinarily a group of bishops can give stronger witness than an individual one."[27] But this statement is subject to important qualifications. As Cardinal Dearden pointed out in his Collegeville address, the prophetic voice is often a lonely one, that of an individual who sees what is not yet evident to the group as a whole. The conference must therefore take care not to stifle the initiative of individual bishops.[28] Cardinal de Lubac in his study *The Particular Churches* gives a similar warning. The impersonal and bureaucratic style of episcopal conferences should not be allowed to paralyze the personal efforts of the local bishop as a teacher of the faith.[29] Cardinal Ratzinger in *The Ratzinger Report* reiterates this point. He holds that episcopal conferences, with their staffs, committees, and voting procedures, tend to produce rather vapid compromise texts in which the personal insights of individuals are blurred. In this connection he recalls that during the Hitler years the German bishops' conference failed to speak out against the Nazis as firmly and courageously as did certain individual bishops.[30] Cardinal Hamer, in his address to the plenary meeting of the College of Cardinals, November 1985, summarized the difficulties noted by Cardinal de Lubac and ended by asserting the total subordination of the conferences to the particular churches they are intended to assist.

These criticisms call attention to certain real limitations in conference statements—limitations that often show up also in pronouncements of ecumenical councils. Conferences and councils should not attempt to supplant the teaching of individual bishops. John Paul II, in his address to the Brazilian bishops' conference, made this very point. The conference, he asserted, "may not, nor does it claim to, clip, diminish, and even less to do away with and replace the personal responsibility which each bishop assumes, when, together with episcopal ordination, he receives a mission and the charisms necessary for accomplishing it."[31] Bishop James W. Malone, the current president of the United States bishops' conference, made an admirably balanced statement at the November 1984 meeting: "The conference does not substitute for the voice of individual bishops, but it provides a framework within which a coherent theological, moral, and social vision can be articulated and a sense of direction for the church can be determined. The conference is a unique structure, ecclesially and socially, for shaping a consensus on public issues and expressing it."[32]

Proper Sphere of Competence

A further question has to do with the proper sphere of competence of the bishops' conference as a doctrinal agency. In view of its particular responsibility the conference, it would seem, will speak by preference on matters pertaining to faith and morals that are neither internal to a particular diocese nor common to the universal church. The United States bishops' conference, since Vatican II, has quite properly devoted some of its attention to reviewing the orthodoxy of American theological publications and to supervising the work of the ecumenical dialogues sponsored by the conference. But the conference has devoted a major part of its effort to issuing statements on public questions such as abortion, armaments, and poverty.

Informed Catholic critics rarely object, as do some ideological liberals, that the church should keep out of political and social issues. The papal encyclicals and Vatican Council II have made it abundantly clear that the church has a right and duty to concern itself with the moral and religious aspects of sociopolitical questions. The bishops quite properly engage in teaching Catholic social doctrine. As J. Brian Benestad has said in his important study of this question, the spirit of our age demands that special attention be given to themes such as the following: "Morality and public weapons, the just war theory, international human rights, development and integral humanism, the common good, public morality, the equality of human beings, the relation between rights and duties, subsidiarity, the Catholic view of property, detachment from material goods, the social role of the family . . . and the relation of evangelization to the pursuit of a just social order."[33]

While the hierarchy of a given nation or territory should seek to adapt Catholic social teaching to the particular circumstances of the time and place, they must exercise great restraint in seeming to appropriate the church's authority for their opinions on technical questions of policy. Dr. Benestad, in the study just cited, concludes that the American bishops in the period from 1966 to 1980 allowed themselves to be unduly influenced by left-of-center politics and that they acted too much like secular lobbying groups. He particularly blames the staff of the United States Catholic Conference for fostering this quasi-partisan stance.[34]

In chapter 9 I have already indicated my own views on this matter. Generally speaking, I believe, the episcopal conference should devote itself primarily to teaching, leaving the concrete applications, where these are not obvious, to lay persons regularly engaged in secular affairs. Where they do feel obliged to make specific policy statements, the bishops should clearly identify them as such.[35]

Ecclesiastical Nationalism?

A further difficulty, raised by Cardinal Ruffini and others at Vatican II, is that different national conferences might adopt different positions, thus weakening the unity of the universal church.[36] At the 1969 Synod of Bishops, Cardinal Wright warned that the church must be on guard against "immoderate nationalism" in which regional bodies of bishops would establish, so to speak, separate spheres of influence.[37] Cardinal de Lubac sees this danger as thus far remote, but he fears that through a hypertrophy of national and regional conferences the Catholics of different localities might become mutually isolated, forgetting their bonds with the universal Church.[38]

A test case arose in 1983, when several national hierarchies were simultaneously preparing divergent statements on war and peace. The Holy See intervened and called an international meeting at which some of the problems were thrashed out before the American pastoral was put in final form. Even so, however, there were significant differences of approach between the American, French, and German statements. Are such differences harmful?

Cardinal Ratzinger himself, in his 1965 article, spoke out in favor of encouraging a certain diversity of approach among different regional hierarchies. He pleaded for initiatives from various parts of the church—"initiatives that indeed would have to be coordinated, clarified, and supervised by the center," that is, by Rome, but should not be simply replaced by uniform directives. It should be possible, he argued, for "bishops' conferences to address themselves to each other in words of thanks or encouragement or even correction of false ways if such have been followed."[39] In this way, he suggested, the conferences could best contribute to the diversified unity that should characterize the church as a whole.

Looking over the developments that have occurred since Vatican II, I would not say that there has been excessive diversity of teaching between different territorial conferences. Such diversity as there has been may in fact be helpful for offsetting the one-sidedness of certain conference statements. But were it not for the vigilance of Rome, as the apostolic see specially charged with the ministry of unity, the differences could easily become divisive and injurious to the integrity of the faith. The bishops and faithful of a given nation should not regard the solicitude of Rome as though it were an unwarranted intrusion upon their spiritual sovereignty.

The Dialogic Process

In their pastoral on moral values, in their catechetical directory, and especially in the pastorals on peace and on the economy, the responsible committees of the United States bishops' conference have consulted widely, often with hearings, publication of preliminary drafts, and invitations to submit suggestions. This process has inevitably aroused complaints that the bishops have consulted too narrowly or that they have listened to the wrong people, but in my opinion they cannot be fairly faulted on such grounds.

A more fundamental criticism must, however, be mentioned. Certain European theologians, it would seem, have objected that an open, dialogic process of this kind is detrimental to the authority of the hierarchy.[40] The point is apparently that in seeking out the opinions of others the bishops might give the impression of not themselves having the answers. If this is the objection, I cannot share it. Vatican Council II, the most authoritative expression of Catholic doctrine in the twentieth century, called for wide consultation and dialogue within the church. In the Pastoral Constitution on the Church in the Modern World it declared: "Let the laity not imagine that their pastors are always such experts as to have a concrete solution to every problem that arises, or even every serious problem, or that such is in fact the pastors' mission" (GS 43). This recognition was not new with Vatican II. Already in the third century St. Cyprian, bishop of Carthage, laid down the principle: "I have made it a rule, ever since the beginning of my episcopate, to make no decision merely on the strength of my own personal opinion, without consulting you [the priests and deacons] and without the approbation of my people." In another letter Cyprian wrote: "Bishops must not only teach but also learn, for the best teacher is one who daily grows and advances by learning better."[41]

Archbishop Rembert Weakland, addressing the objection just mentioned, correctly identified the root of the problem in words already quoted in chapter 7, above:

Underneath this criticism is a definite concept of ecclesiology. Its proponents see a strongly hierarchical model of the church, where the faithful are taught by the bishops, who are in possession of the gifts of the Spirit needed for such authoritative teaching. The model adopted by the U.S. conference believes that the Holy Spirit resides in all members of the church and that the hierarchy must listen to what the Spirit is saying to the whole church. This does not deny the teaching role of the hierarchy, but enhances it. It does not weaken the magisterium, but ultimately strengthens it. Discernment, not just innovation or self-reliance, becomes a part of the teaching process.[42]

These remarks of Archbishop Weakland suggest a final reflection on the authority of episcopal conferences. If authority means the power to commit the church officially, maximum authority should not always be sought. The bishops do not necessarily wish to commit the church as such to everything they say. They do, however, wish to speak with credibility, so that their words will be taken seriously. If they consult widely and take account of expert criticism, their statements will win a respectful hearing.

In the final analysis authority is only a means to an end, namely, the production of documents that effectively address real and urgent questions. In actual practice the influence of conference documents, like that of encyclicals and even conciliar statements, depends less on the formal authority with which they are issued than on their intrinsic merits. Once a statement has been published it tends to shape its own history. If discerning readers find it persuasive and enlightening, it can produce an impact in excess of its juridical or official weight.[43]

12. Ecumenism and the Search for Doctrinal Agreement

Vatican II formally committed the Catholic church to the ideals and goals of ecumenism. Catholics, therefore, should not become so absorbed in the internal affairs of their own church as to neglect the fostering of positive relationships with other Christian faith communities, with which, according to Vatican II, Catholicism stands in imperfect communion. John Paul II from the very beginning of his pontificate has made it clear that he regards ecumenism as a high priority. The Extraordinary Synod of 1985 affirmed that in the twenty years since the Second Vatican Council "ecumenism has inscribed itself deeply and indelibly in the consciousness of the Church" (II. C. 7.). Our reflections on post-Vatican II ecclesiology, therefore, would be incomplete without some indication of the recent progress of ecumenical discussion.

Generally speaking, we may say that although the relations among the separated churches have vastly improved, the major divisions between Protestants, Catholics, and Orthodox show no signs of disappearing. Since these divisions are generally thought to rest primarily on disagreements about doctrine, a great part of the ecumenical effort has been focused on doctrinal reconciliation. In the past few years distinguished authors such as Yves Congar, Heinrich Fries, Karl Rahner, Joseph Ratzinger, and George Lindbeck have published important books with the aim of helping to overcome the doctrinal impasses. In this final chapter I shall, with some assistance from these works, propose a number of guiding principles in the form of ten theses.

Necessity of Doctrinal Agreement

At the outset it may be useful to close off what I regard as a blind alley, advocated by almost no one seriously engaged in ecumenical work. This would be the proposal to bypass doctrine and unite the churches on a purely pragmatic basis. I call this solution false because the practice of the churches, as they engage in worship, moral teaching, and social advocacy, is intimately bound up with their doctrinal stands. More fundamentally, the church cannot be properly understood simply as a coalition for action. It is first of all a community of faith and witness, and as such it requires a shared vision.[1] Members of a single church must be able to recognize one another's beliefs as being in essential conformity with the teaching of Christ and that of the apostolic community.

Putting what I have just said as a positive principle or thesis, I begin with the assertion that *for church unity a measure of doctrinal accord is a prerequisite.*

A second principle, equally indisputable, is that *complete agreement on all matters of doctrine is unattainable and ought not to be regarded as necessary.* In every church there are certain disputed questions. For example, Roman Catholicism, as indeed most other churches, houses sharply opposed positions about the relationship between divine grace and human freedom. Different theological schools, having their own distinctive tenets, flourish side by side within the same church.[2] The continual search for greater doctrinal clarity and purity is a healthy thing, making for vitality and progress. Unless scope were allowed for original thought and discussion a church could hardly be a living, vibrant community, nor could it keep abreast of the times.

Fundamental Articles

Combining these first two principles, then, let us agree that for church unity one needs a certain measure of doctrinal accord but not absolute agreement on all points of doctrine. According to an ancient formula that Pope John XXIII was fond of quoting, unity is required in essentials, but freedom should be allowed in all other matters.[3] The difficult task, of course, is to draw the line between essentials and nonessentials. Important work on this problem was done by the French Reformed theologian Pierre Jurieu (1633–1713), who held that there was a relatively small number of fundamental articles— that is, contents of the Christian religion that a person must believe in order to be saved and to be called Christian.[4] As examples Jurieu gave the unity of God, the divine character of the revealed word, the messiahship of Christ, and his divine sonship. Jurieu's position, which involved the idea of a church cutting across denominational lines, was contested by some of his contemporaries, including the Catholic bishop Jacques Bénigne Bossuet and the Jansenist Pierre Nicole.

The concept of fundamental articles became especially prominent at the end of the nineteenth century, when certain American Protestants specified the essentials of strict conservative belief. They agreed on the following five fundamentals: the inerrancy of the Bible, the deity of Jesus Christ, the Virgin Birth, Christ's substitutionary atonement, and finally, his physical resurrection and future bodily return. Christians espousing these fundamentals came to be called fundamentalists.

The list just given illustrates how difficult it is to specify the essentials. Drawn up in opposition to liberalism and modernism, fundamentalism represented the particular perspective of one group of Christians, speaking in a time-conditioned situation. Christians of other traditions would have drawn up a markedly different list of fundamentals. The majority would have insisted on the Trinity, the Holy Spirit, the true humanity of Jesus Christ, the primacy of grace, the divine origin of the church, and the value of the sacraments—all of which are missing from the fundamentalist syllabus. Nearly every major Christian community, in fact, would favor a somewhat different list. Lutherans would presumably want to highlight

justification by faith and perhaps, in some sense, the sufficiency of Scripture. Episcopalians would insist on the episcopal office and the early creeds; the Orthodox, on tradition and
the Eucharist; the Roman Catholics, on the papacy.

In *Mortalium animos,* an encyclical published in 1928, Pius
XI rejected the very idea of distinguishing between fundamental and nonfundamental articles.[5] The assent of faith, he declared, since it is motivated by the authority of God the revealer,
must extend without distinction to everything that is divinely
revealed and contained in the deposit of faith. Church unity,
according to the pope, could never be achieved through sub-
scription to a limited number of fundamental articles.

Mortalium animos, however, was not the last word from the
Catholic side. At Vatican Council II, on November 25, 1963,
Archbishop Andrea Pangrazio of Gorizia, Italy, made a speech
in which he observed, "Even though all revealed truths are to
be believed with the same divine faith and all constitutive
elements of the Church maintained with the same loyalty,
nevertheless not all receive and hold the same status."[6] Incor-
porating the substance of Pangrazio's intervention, the Decree
on Ecumenism called attention to the fact that a certain hierarchy of importance exists among church doctrines "since they
vary in their relationship to the foundation of the Christian
faith" (*UR* 11). The Decree went on to exhort all Christians to
profess before the whole world their faith in the triune God
and in the incarnate Son of God, our Redeemer and Lord. The
council was here clearly suggesting that the dogmas of the
Trinity and the Incarnation are central and foundational for
Christianity. Happily, too, these primary doctrines are widely
shared by Christians of many different churches and confessional traditions.

A third thesis or principle, then, is that *there is a hierarchy of
importance in Christian doctrines,* the most central being the
trinitarian and Christological dogmas that are presumably accepted by the vast majority of Christians. In view of the greater
importance of these foundational truths, we may surmise that

the agreements among Christians are, generally speaking, more significant than their disagreements.

Imperfect Communion

The acknowledgment by Vatican II that there is a graded hierarchy of truths, while it did not lead to the conclusion that certain dogmas could be regarded as optional, nevertheless had important ecumenical consequences. The council was able to recognize that Christian communion extends beyond the juridicial frontiers of any given ecclesial body, including the Roman Catholic church. Ecclesial communion includes a real and significant fellowship among Christians of different confessional allegiances. As Yves Congar has noted, the ecumenism of Vatican II is based on an ecclesiology of imperfect communion, which is in need of being further developed.[7] According to the Decree on Ecumenism all baptized believers are somehow incorporated in Christ (*UR* 22). All who believe and are baptized in the name of the triune God "are brought into a certain, though imperfect, communion with the Catholic Church" (*UR* 3). Paul VI would later declare that the Orthodox churches are "in almost complete communion" with the Catholic church.[8]

This doctrine of ecclesial communion has implications for eucharistic sharing. Vatican II looked upon the Eucharist not simply as a sign of achieved unity but as a sign of limited existing unity and as a means for greater unity (*UR* 8). According to the Decree on the Eastern Catholic Churches, *Orientalium Ecclesiarum*, the ecclesial communion between Catholics and Orthodox, although still imperfect, is sufficiently rich so that common worship may occasionally be appropriate (*OE* 27–29). The council, while obviously holding that a measure of communion exists between Catholics and Protestants, did not attempt to specify whether and under what circumstances eucharistic sharing between these groups would be permissible. The present (1983) Code of Canon Law provides for the administration of the sacraments of penance, Eucharist, and the anointing of the sick to Protestants in situations of grave need under conditions that are to be further specified by the local bishop or conference of bishops (can. 844). The provisional regulations issued since the council in different countries and dioceses indicate the difficulty of finding a single formula for all times and places.

To summarize, then, we may lay down a fourth principle, that *where there is agreement in the basic essentials of the Christian faith, and the practice of valid baptism, a considerable measure of ecclesial communion exists,* even though the churches remain canonically separate.

To make this fourth thesis more concrete, we may add a fifth, namely that *in the Scriptures and the ancient creeds* (especially the Apostles' Creed and the Nicene-Constantinopolitan Creed), *the mainline churches, whether Orthodox, Roman Catholic, Anglican, or Protestant, already share in common a large fund of doctrinal materials.*[9] In addition, nearly all such churches accept the trinitarian and Christological decisions of the first four councils of the first five centuries, including the decrees of Chalcedon on the true divinity and true humanity of Jesus Christ.[10] Committed as they are to the New Testament, these churches normally affirm the Incarnation, the resurrection of Jesus, and the central sacraments of baptism and the Lord's Supper. Churches sharing such a wealth of common beliefs and the kind of worship and practice that flow from them ought not to regard one another as strangers.

In spite of these major points in common, however, significant doctrinal differences persist. Eastern and Western Christians are separated, most importantly, by different views on the procession of the Holy Spirit, a doctrine that for the Orthodox, at least, is crucially important. On most doctrinal issues (notably, sacramental teaching and Mariology) the Orthodox are closer to Roman Catholics than to Protestants, but in their rejection of the modern Roman doctrine of the papacy they have a certain affinity with Protestantism.

Protestants and Catholics are divided on a number of issues that have come down from the sixteenth century, such as the sufficiency of Scripture and the doctrine of justification by faith alone, without merits or good works. In addition, the dogmas defined in the Catholic church since the sixteenth century constitute obstacles to reunion. Among these are the papal dogmas of the First Vatican Council and the Marian dogmas defined by the popes in 1854 and 1950 (namely, the Immaculate Conception and the Assumption). Must these dogmas be positively affirmed by Orthodox and Protestants who come into union with Rome?

Noncondemnation of Doctrines

Most theologians have assumed that assent to all defined doctrines is required, but a different view has been advanced by Karl Rahner. In several recent books and articles he argues that, among churches that affirm the Scriptures and the early creeds, union can be effected as soon as each of the partner churches agrees not to condemn the binding doctrines of the other as contrary to the gospel. He further asserts that such an agreement is attainable today, and that therefore God is calling the mainline churches to union at the present time.[11]

The Rahner proposal raises two major questions: First, is it true that the churches are prepared to refrain from condemning each other's doctrines? Second, if they take this step, does it suffice for reunion?

From the Catholic side, I suspect that the first of these questions can be answered in the affirmative. The Orthodox churches, so far as I am aware, teach nothing today as binding doctrine that they did not teach before the breaches of the tenth and eleventh centuries, and hence nothing that the Catholic church needs to anathematize. As for the Protestant churches, they impose very few obligatory doctrines on their members. The Reformation watchwords, *sola scriptura, sola fide,* and *sola gratia,* deeply ingrained in many branches of

Protestantism, are practically equivalent to binding dogmas. But these watchwords can bear an authentically Catholic interpretation. Many contemporary Catholic theologians, including Rahner himself, have written at length on the primacy of Scripture, faith, and grace in the Catholic understanding of Christianity.[12] I would agree that these principles can be understood in a Catholic sense and therefore need not be repudiated by the Catholic church. But I also think that these principles can be interpreted as denying the Catholic doctrines of tradition, good works, and merit. Thus the principles cannot be accepted without qualification.

Bypassing the question whether Orthodox and Protestants could tolerate each other's binding doctrines, let me raise the question whether each of these groups could refrain from condemning the dogmatic positions of the Catholic church. Since the tenth century many Orthodox theologians have contended that the Western formula regarding the procession of the Holy Spirit from the Father and the Son (that is, the *Filioque*) is heretical. But in recent years a number of Orthodox authorities have mitigated their opposition, objecting only to the incorporation of this Western theological theorem into the creed. This position gives rise to the hope that the chief historic barrier to reunion between the Eastern and Western churches might be able to be overcome.[13]

The Orthodox, however, have difficulties with other Catholic dogmas, especially those promulgated since the definitive separation in the eleventh century. It is therefore important to look for ways in which dogmas such as papal infallibility and papal primacy of jurisdiction can be ecumenically handled so as to permit doctrinal reconciliation.

Finally, we must ask whether Protestants are in a position to admit the legitimacy of all the Roman Catholic dogmas. In the dialogues of the past twenty years the Anglicans and Lutherans have greatly moderated their opposition to the pope, formerly depicted as Antichrist, and to the sacrifice of the Mass. Many seem inclined to regard the Catholic forms of devotion to Mary and the saints as permissible rather than idolatrous. Thus they might be in a position to declare that no binding dogma of the Catholic church is unequivocally opposed to the gospel.

A typically Lutheran reaction to the Rahner proposal is that of Eberhard Jüngel.[14] The Roman dogmas, he observes, have at certain times been interpreted by Catholics themselves as excluding the Lutheran doctrine of justification by faith in Christ alone. Under such circumstances, a *status confessionis* arises, calling for prophetic denunciation. But Catholics have recently expounded these dogmas in ways compatible with the gospel of free grace. These dogmas may therefore be tolerated by Lutherans, even though not positively affirmed. Reactions such as Jüngel's give hope that Protestants might be able to accept this aspect of the Rahner proposal.

Our second question about the proposal is whether a statement by each uniting church that the binding doctrines of the others are not manifestly opposed to the gospel would provide a sufficient basis for union. From a Lutheran perspective Harding Meyer indicates that it would be necessary for each church to grant that the doctrines of the others are legitimate interpretations of the gospel, which is something more than not being evidently opposed to the gospel.[15] From the Catholic side Daniel Ols, O.P., in a front-page editorial for the quasi-official *Osservatore Romano*, has objected that a withholding of negative judgment is clearly insufficient.[16] Anyone who is in union with the Catholic church, he maintains, must accept the divine authority of the church's teaching office, which is fully engaged in the proclamation of dogmas. To doubt or deny the truth of a dogma is, in effect, to reject the church's teaching authority and thus to separate oneself from its communion. Ols's position on this point resembles that of Pius XI in response to fundamentalism.[17] I can agree with Ols only subject to various qualifications that will appear in my last four theses.

To this objection I would add another. If Orthodox and Protestant Christians could come into full communion with Rome without positively affirming the modern Catholic dogmas, it would seem that Catholics could not be denied communion in their own church if they voiced the same doubts or denials. Hence all the disputed dogmas would in effect be downgraded to an optional status for Catholics themselves. This would introduce confusion into the Catholic community and weaken its distinctive witness.

In spite of these and other objections, something of the Rahner proposal can perhaps be salvaged. It could be important at the present stage of the dialogue for the various churches to get to the point of not condemning one another's teaching as contrary to the gospel. If this step is feasible, the churches can regard one another not as antagonistically opposed, but as holding the same basic faith, even though they profess to find different implications in it. As a sixth thesis, then, I offer the following: *the different churches can come into closer communion if they recognize that one another's binding doctrines are, if not true, at least not manifestly repugnant to the relevation given in Christ.*

Withdrawal of Anathemas

Is it possible that certain doctrinal norms, formulated in the past, might no longer have such urgency as to require their positive acceptance as a condition for reunion? In replying to this question one should bear in mind that many dogmas are to be understood less as positive declarations of the content of revelation than as rejections of errors prevalent at a certain time. Once the danger of adhering to the heretical party is past, the dogma may perhaps be allowed to lapse into a certain benign neglect. If similar threats to the faith arise in the future, the dogma will be resuscitated in a form directed against the new error.

When one looks over the lists of propositions drawn up by the Catholic magisterium against the Origenists in the sixth century or against Peter Abelard in the eleventh or against the Lutherans in the sixteenth or against the Jansenists in the seventeenth or against the modernists at the beginning of our own century, one finds many propositions that sound, to contemporary Catholic ears, rather harmless. Much the same could no doubt be said by many Lutherans and Calvinists when they contemplate the lists of propositions condemned by their forebears in the sixteenth and seventeenth centuries. Today we are perhaps in a position to judge that the state of emergency—or, in Lutheran terminology, the *status confessionis*—that prompted these declarations has subsided. What is required today is the integral confession of the Christian faith in a manner opposed to the errors to which we ourselves are tempted.

For whatever reasons, rather subtle points of doctrine have been defined at certain points in the past. The Council of Vienne, in the fourteenth century, felt it necessary to teach under anathema that the human soul is the substantial form of the body (DS 902).[18] Today this highly metaphysical doctrine might suitably receive less emphasis, and in practice it does. Some have suggested that a dogma such as the Immaculate Conception of the Blessed Virgin, since it is relatively remote from the center of Christian faith and lacks clear warrants in Scripture and in early Christian tradition, does not need to be taught under anathema.[19] Whatever one may think of this or other examples, at least the principle may be allowed that certain doctrinal concessions may be made for the sake of unity. As Congar has shown, Athanasius, Basil, and Cyril of Alexandria appealed to the principle of economy, as they called it, in allowing for some doctrinal lenience.[20] Already in New Testament times, the Council of Jerusalem laid down the principle: "It has seemed good to the Holy Spirit and us to lay upon you no greater burden than necessary" (Acts 15:28). Vatican II, in its Decree on Ecumenism, alluded to this text and drew the consequence that "in order to restore communion and unity or preserve them, one must impose no burden beyond what is indispensable" (UR 18).

As a seventh thesis, then, I suggest that in the interests of unity *the churches should insist only on the doctrinal minimum required for a mature and authentic Christian faith and that doctrines formulated in response to past historical crises should be reviewed carefully to see whether they must be imposed as tests of orthodoxy today.*

Toward a Hermeneutics of Unity

Since the acceptance of historical consciousness by the churches in recent decades, it has been increasingly recognized that doctrinal formulations are historically conditioned. As the Congregation for the Doctrine of the Faith stated in its Declaration *Mysterium Ecclesiae,* of June 24, 1973, dogmatic pronouncements, which have normally been intended to deal with certain specific questions of their day, have been limited by the amount of background knowledge that was available at a given period. They also show the traces of the thought forms and linguistic usage of their own time. For these reasons dogmatic formulations are sometimes in need of being reinterpreted to make them intelligible, convincing, and relevant in a later age.

A particular problem arises with regard to doctrines defined in view of the historical experiences of a single ecclesiastical body, such as Roman Catholicism, to which other Christians were not a party. This problem was discussed in the context of Catholic-Orthodox relations at several conferences in Graz, Austria, in the 1970s. In 1976 Joseph Ratzinger, before he was named prefect of the Congregation for the Doctrine of the Faith, made a bold and creative proposal that attracted wide attention. With reference to the conditions for reunion between Catholic and Orthodox he stated:

Rome must not require more from the East with respect to the doctrine of primacy than had been formulated and was lived in the first millennium. When the Patriarch Athenagoras, on July 25, 1967, on the occasion of the Pope's visit to Phanar, designated him as the successor of St. Peter, as the most esteemed among us, as the one who presides in charity, this great Church leader was expressing the essential content of the doctrine of primacy as it was known in the first millennium. Rome need not ask for more. Reunion could take place in this context if, on the one hand, the East would cease to oppose as heretical the developments that took place in the West in the second millennium and would accept the Catholic Church as legitimate and orthodox in the form she had acquired in the course of that development, while, on the other hand, the West would recognize the Church of the East as orthodox and legitimate in the form she has always had.[21]

Ratzinger has been understood as here advocating reunion without insistence that the East positively assent to the decrees of the First and Second Vatican Councils on papal primacy and papal infallibility. If this interpretation were correct, he would be subject to the same criticisms that have been directed against Rahner. But Ratzinger expressly disagrees with the Rahner position.[22] He now states that his intention was to assert that the documents handed down from the past must be interpreted according to a certain "hermeneutics of unity." Such a hermeneutics, he explains, "will entail reading the statement of both parties in the context of the whole tradition and with a deeper understanding of Scripture. This will include investigating how far decisions since the separation have been stamped with a certain particularization both as to language and thought—something that might well be transcended without doing violence to the content of the statements."[23]

Ratzinger's conception of a "hermeneutics of unity" has been further developed by Bertrand de Margerie in an article dealing with the degrees of ecumenicity of different councils. In the course of his discussion he proposes that the councils of the first millennium, which met on Eastern soil with little Western participation, should be reread by the Western church in the light of its tradition and that, conversely, the councils of the second millennium, which were almost exclusively Western, should be reread in the East in the light of the Oriental and Syriac fathers. Through a richer biblical and patristic contextualization, de Margerie suggests, the teaching of Trent, for example, on subjects such as transubstantiation and the sacraments could be greatly enriched. Such an enrichment might also succeed in making the decrees of Trent and Vatican I more palatable to the Protestant communities of the West.[24]

Yves Congar advances a similar proposal under the rubric of "re-reception." Doctrines that were too narrowly stated in terms of a given social and intellectual framework often need to be reappropriated in terms of a larger context and a fuller reflection on the testimony of Scripture and tradition. He refers to several historical examples from Roman Catholicism, Lutheranism, and Greek Orthodoxy:

> In particular, I have in mind: in the case of the Catholic Church, some constructions inherited from Scholasticism and the Vatican I Constitution *Pastor aeternus;* in the case of the Lutheran churches, the Augsburg Confession; in the case of the Orthodox Church, Palamism; and these are only examples. These doctrines have been "received," that is to say, the churches recognize their heritage in them and have lived according to them. It is not a matter of abandoning them but of restoring them in the fullness and balance of the biblical witness, what T. Sartory calls "a repatriation of dogmas in the light of the overall witness of Holy Scripture"; it is a matter of thinking them and living them out, taking account of the knowledge we have acquired of the historical, cultural and sociological conditioning of the decision in question, of the current needs of the cause of the gospel which we seek to serve, of the values accumulated since the first reception of the decision or doctrine, and finally of the criticisms and valuable contributions received from others.[25]

In a recent work, *The Nature of Doctrine,* the American Lutheran theologian George Lindbeck distinguishes three types of theory concerning doctrines: first, that they are informative propositions or truth claims about objective realities; second, that they are noninformative and nondiscursive symbols of inner feelings, attitudes, or existential orientations; and third, that they are communally authoritative rules of discourse, attitude, and action.[26] Rejecting the first two theories, Lindbeck adopts almost exclusively the third, or regulative, theory. Although I suspect that Lindbeck unduly minimizes the cognitive and expressive import of doctrines, his analysis is helpful for calling attention to the role of doctrine in shaping the religious orientations of the communities that accept them. In this context he is able to show that controversial theology has in the past reckoned insufficiently with the cultural and linguistic components of religious discourse. The formulas of one church or tradition are often misinterpreted or simply not understood by believers of other traditions, whose experiences have been shaped by a different set of symbols.

Nearly all who have been involved in ecumenical dialogue could certify the difficulty of explaining to members of another confessional body the traditional formulations of one's own. Lutherans, for example, must use extreme care to explain what they mean by the *gospel* and *justification by faith alone,* so that Catholics do not misunderstand them, while Catholics have to struggle long and hard to prevent Lutherans from caricaturing the real meaning of terms such as *transubstantiation* and papal *infallibility.* Through patient dialogue it is often possible to reinterpret such terms in ways that render them intelligible, tolerable, or even acceptable to communities that previously rejected them. In the course of the dialogue each community deepens and refines its own experience, reflection, and expression. This process illustrates what Ratzinger seems to mean by the "hermeneutics of unity" and Congar by "re-reception." As an eighth thesis, then, we may affirm: *through reinterpretation in a broader hermeneutical context, the limitations of controverted doctrinal formulations can often be overcome so that they gain wider acceptability.*

Doctrinal Pluralism

One possible result of the "hermeneutics of unity" is a joint reformulation satisfactory to different parties in the dialogue. But sometimes it does not seem possible to find a single formula that does justice to the experiences and insights of both parties. In this second case, must the parties continue to disagree?

I propose as a ninth thesis the following: *in some cases substantive agreement can be reached between two parties without the imposition of identical doctrinal formulations on each.*

If this principle had been better observed in the past, it might have been possible to avoid certain tragic ruptures, such as the exclusion of the so-called Monophysites from the Catholic communion at Chalcedon in A.D. 451. The Chalcedonian doctrine of the two natures of Christ (DS 302) need not be understood as contradicting the profound intention of the Alexandrian formula, "the one nature of the incarnate Word of God."

Another case in point is provided by the Council of Florence, which in A.D. 1439 declared that the Greek formulation according to which the Holy Spirit proceeds "from the Father *through* the Son" is equivalent to the Latin formulation that the Spirit proceeds "from the Father and the Son" (DS 1301). Regrettably, however, the Council of Florence seemed to interpret the first of these formulas, contrary to the intention of the Greek fathers, as though it gave causal efficacy to the Son, and thus the Decree of Union was perceived in the East as a capitulation to the Latin position. Contemporary theologians such as Congar, addressing the question of the *Filioque* in terms of a more sophisticated epistemology, hold that the mystery of the divine processions eludes adequate statement in any dogmatic formula. Appealing to the authority of Hilary and Thomas Aquinas, Congar asserts that no one expression is adequate to express the mystery apprehended in faith.[27] After an excursus on the theory of complementarity advanced by the physicist Niels Bohr, Congar applies the theory to the theology of the Trinity:

My study of the procession of the Holy Spirit in the Greek Fathers on the one hand and in the Latin tradition on the other has led me to recognize that there are two constructions of the mystery, each of which is coherent and complete—although each is unsatisfactory at some point—and which cannot be superimposed. It is a case for applying Bohr's saying, "The opposite of a true statement is a false statement, but the opposite of a profound truth can be another profound truth." The equivalence affirmed by the Council of Florence between *dia tou huiou* and *Filioque* is not really adequate. More than theology is at stake here. As Fr. Dejaifve has noted, it is at the level of dogma that the two constructions are to be found. However, these are two constructions of the mystery experienced by the same faith.[28]

The Vatican II Decree on Ecumenism suggested the possibility of a certain dogmatic pluralism. It remarked that the differing theological formulations of the Eastern and Western churches "are often to be considered as complementary rather than conflicting." It is not surprising, said the council, "if certain aspects of the revealed mystery are more accurately perceived or more lucidly exposed in one tradition or the other" (*UR* 17). Doctrinal agreement, therefore, need not take the form of a submission by one group to the formulated positions of the other. It may occur by means of a mutual recognition of the complementarity of formulas that cannot be reduced to a common conceptual denominator.

If the mutual complementarity of the Eastern and Western formulations is recognized, both can be tolerated in the church. It might therefore be unnecessary for the Western church in our time to insist on the *Filioque*, which was added to the creed in the Middle Ages partly to guard against certain Arian distortions then current. Congar and Fries, among others, have proposed that if the Eastern churches would concede that the *Filioque* is not heretical, the Western church could withdraw it, for the creed should be acceptable to all who hold the same faith, even though they may not conceptualize it according to the Western tradition. Congar and Fries, however, add that before any such change in the creed is made, the faithful should be pastorally prepared to accept the change.[29]

In the past, doctrinal disputes have usually been conducted as though a choice had to be made between logical contradictories. For example, does the Holy Spirit proceed from the Father alone, or not? Is all doctrine contained in Scripture, or not? Is the Mass a sacrifice, or not? Is the pope fallible or infallible? The ecumenical dialogues of the past few decades have made it clear, at least in my opinion, that the antitheses were never so sharp as appeared, for the two parties were using the same words with different shades of meaning and using different words to mean much the same thing. The meaning itself was richer than the conceptual content of the words.

Qualified Acceptance

This does not mean that the previously opposed parties in every case can be reconciled without any change in their teaching. History shows that Protestants, Catholics, and Orthodox have disagreed sharply over the centuries and have repudiated each other's formulations as false or at least ambiguous. Even if today we can see the possibility of favorably interpreting one another's formulations, we cannot assume without discussion that the most favorable interpretation is the one actually held by the other party. Further dialogue is needed, which might lead to a formula of union stated hypothetically, such as, for example, the following: If faith is comprehensively understood as including not only trust but a grace-inspired assent and a loving commitment, justification may be said to be effected through faith alone. But if faith is understood as a merely intellectual assent to revealed doctrine or as empty human confidence, faith alone does not justify. A nuanced statement such as this can, I think, serve to overcome most of the past differences about the thorny issue of justification by faith.[30]

As my tenth and final thesis, then, I propose the following: *for the sake of doctrinal agreement, the binding formulations of each tradition must be carefully scrutinized and jointly affirmed with whatever modifications, explanations, or reservations are required in order to appease the legitimate misgivings of the partner churches.* This may demand a measure of reformulation.

Unlike Rahner and Fries, who call for immediate union among the mainline churches, I believe that considerable time and effort will be required to achieve the kind of doctrinal agreement needed for full communion among churches as widely separated as the Orthodox, Protestant, Anglican, and Roman Catholic. Such agreement must be accomplished, I believe, in stages. Even now, most of the churches could jointly declare their allegiance to the teaching of Scripture and to the interpretations given to that teaching by the creeds and ecumenical councils of the early centuries. This joint declaration would already ensure a large measure of communion. Second, the churches can gradually advance toward declaring that some or all of the doctrinal positions of the other churches are in their view not contrary to the gospel and hence not liable to condemnation. The ecumenical dialogues of the past twenty years have identified a number of doctrinal disputes that can be treated in this way. Third, the churches can progress to the point of positively accepting one another's binding doctrinal formulations, with whatever added interpretations or explanations are needed to guard against possible deviations. When these three steps have been completed by any two churches with regard to all the obligatory teachings of the other, the doctrinal basis for full communion between them will have been laid.

We have no antecedent certainty that we shall reach the ultimate goal of our ecumenical pilgrimage before the end of historical time. We have the strength to believe, however, that the Holy Spirit is leading us toward a greater measure of unity in the truth. As we allow ourselves to be led by this dynamism, we can enjoy a certain foretaste of the promised goal.[31] Every step toward doctrinal agreement increases the communion among Christians and diminishes the scandal arising from their mutual opposition. The dialogue itself assists the churches to correct their own one-sidedness and to achieve a richer and more balanced grasp of the revelation to which they bear witness. For these results it is not essential that final reconciliation be achieved. The ecumenical effort pays off in rich rewards at every stage of the way.

Abbreviations

Documents of Vatican II are abbreviated according to the two first words of the Latin text.

AA   *Apostolicam actuositatem:* Decree on the Apostolate of the Laity.

AG   *Ad gentes:* Decree on the Church's Missionary Activity.

CD   *Christus Dominus:* Decree on the Bishops' Pastoral Office in the Church.

DH   *Dignitatis humanae:* Declaration on Religious Freedom.

DV   *Dei Verbum:* Dogmatic Constitution on Divine Revelation.

GE   *Gravissimum educationis:* Declaration on Christian Education.

GS   *Gaudium et spes:* Pastoral Constitution on the Church in the Modern World.

IM   *Inter mirifica:* Decree on the Instruments of Social Communication.

LG   *Lumen gentium:* Dogmatic Constitution on the Church.

NA   *Nostra aetate:* Declaration on the Relationship of the Church to Non-Christian Religions.

OE   *Orientalium ecclesiarum:* Decree on Eastern Catholic Churches.

OT   *Optatam totius:* Decree on Priestly Formation.

PO   *Presbyterorum ordinis:* Decree on the Ministry and Life of Priests.

SC   *Sacrosanctum concilium:* Constitution on the Sacred Liturgy.

UR   *Unitatis redintegratio:* Decree on Ecumenism.

Other abbreviations include:

AAS   *Acta Apostolicae Sedis* (Rome, 1909 ff.).

CP   *The Challenge of Peace: God's Promise and Our Response: A Pastoral Letter on War and Peace* by the National Conference of Catholic Bishops, May 3, 1983 (Washington, DC: United States Catholic Conference, 1983).

CSEL   *Corpus Scriptorum Ecclesiasticorum Latinorum* (Vienna, 1866 ff.).

DS   *Enchiridion Symbolorum, Definitionum et Declarationum de Rebus Fidei et Morum*, ed. H. Denzinger, rev. A. Schönmetzer, 36th ed. (Freiburg: Herder, 1976).

EJ   *Economic Justice for All: A Pastoral Letter on Catholic Social Teaching and the U.S. Economy*, by the National Conference of Catholic Bishops (Washington, DC: United States Catholic Conference, 1986).

EN   *Evangelii Nuntiandi: Apostolic Exhortation of Paul VI on Evangelization in the Modern World* (Washington, DC: United States Catholic Conference, 1976).

JW   *Justice in the World*, Document of the Synod of Bishops, 1971, text in *The Gospel of Peace and Justice*, ed. Joseph Gremillion (Maryknoll, NY: Orbis Books, 1976), pp. 513–29.

OA   *Octogesima Adveniens*, Apostolic Letter of Paul VI on the Eightieth Anniversary of *Rerum Novarum*, 1971, text in *The Gospel of Peace and Justice*, ed. Joseph Gremillion (Maryknoll, NY: Orbis, 1976), pp. 485–512.

PG   *Patrologiae cursus completus, series graeca*,   ed. J. P. Migne (Paris, 1857 ff.).

PL   *Patrologiae cursus completus, series latina*, ed. J. P. Migne (Paris, 1844 ff.).

Notes

CHAPTER 1: AMERICAN IMPRESSIONS OF THE COUNCIL

1. William M. Halsey, *The Survival of American Innocence: Catholicism in an Era of Disillusionment (1920–1940)* (Notre Dame: University of Notre Dame Press, 1980).
2. James Hennesey, *American Catholics: A History of the Roman Catholic Community in the United States* (New York: Oxford University Press, 1981).
3. Andrew M. Greeley, "American Catholics: Going Their Own Way," *New York Times Magazine* (Oct. 10, 1982), p. 68.
4. For more detail see Philip Gleason, "American Catholics and the Mythic Middle Ages," chapter 1 of his *Keeping the Faith: American Catholicism Past and Present* (Notre Dame, IN: University of Notre Dame Press, 1987), pp. 11–34.
5. Halsey, *Survival of American Innocence,* p. 98. In his article "A Catholic Defends His Church," *New Republic* 97 (Jan. 4, 1939), Schuster described this minority-itis as a disease consisting in "Catholic resentment against deeply ingrained non-Catholic instinct." He expressed the fear that "our democracy is breaking up into self-conscious mutually antagonistic minorities."
6. John Courtney Murray, *We Hold These Truths* (New York: Sheed & Ward, 1960), p. 41.
7. Ibid., p. 76.
8. Quoted by Hennesey, *American Catholics,* p. 307.
9. New York: Herder and Herder, 1964.
10. New York: Sheed & Ward, 1965.
11. Michael Novak, "American Catholicism after the Council," in his *A Time to Build* (New York: Macmillan, 1967), p. 124; reprinted from *Commentary* 40 (August 1965) 50–58.
12. David J. O'Brien, *The Renewal of American Catholicism* (New York: Oxford University Press, 1972), p. 152.
13. Novak, *A Time to Build,* p. 132.
14. Pope John XXIII, *Ad Petri cathedram* (1959).
15. George A. Lindbeck, *The Future of Roman Catholic Theology* (Philadelphia: Fortress, 1970), pp. 4–5, 8. For a criticism of "the hermeneutics of the new," and of Lindbeck in particular, see Richard John Neuhaus, *The Catholic Moment: The Paradox of the Church in the Postmodern World* (San Francisco: Harper & Row, 1987), pp. 47–50.
16. Robert P. Imbelli, "Vatican II: Twenty Years Later," *Commonweal* 109 (Oct. 8, 1982): 522–26.
17. The names of Andrew M. Greeley, Thomas P. Rausch, and Lawrence S. Cunningham come readily to mind. Other writers will be mentioned in chapter 4.
18. Richard John Neuhaus, *The Catholic Moment,* p. 283.

19. Ibid., pp. 283–88.

CHAPTER 2: THE BASIC TEACHING OF VATICAN II

1. John XXIII, Address to Roman pastors at Passionist Retreat House of Saints John and Paul, Jan. 30, 1959. I cite from the quotation given in *Herder-Korrespondenz* 13 (1958–1959): 274–75. This address was never published in full but only summarized in *L'Osservatore Romano*, Jan. 31, 1959.
2. Text in *Origins* 10 (May 22, 1980): 4–7.
3. James W. Malone, "Diocesan Pastoral Councils: What Makes Them Tick?" *Origins* 1 (June 14, 1971): 71–75; quotation from p. 74.

CHAPTER 3: THE EMERGING WORLD CHURCH AND THE PLURALISM OF CULTURES

1. Karl Rahner, "Toward a Fundamental Theological Interpretation of Vatican II," *Theological Studies* 40 (1979): 716–27. Another translation may be found under the title "Basic Theological Interpretation of the Second Vatican Council" in Rahner's *Theological Investigations* (New York: Crossroad, 1981), 20:77–89. Several other essays in that volume touch on the same theme.
2. Walbert Bühlmann, *The Church of the Future: A Model for the Year 2001* (Maryknoll, NY: Orbis Books, 1986), Epilogue by K. Rahner, pp. 200–34. The Epilogue reproduces with slight changes his article "Perspektiven der Pastoral in der Zukunft," *Schriften zur Theologie* (Einsiedeln: Benziger, 1984), 16:143–59.
3. Some statistics are given by Bühlmann, *Church of the Future* pp. 117–30. For an earlier set of figures see his *The Coming of the Third Church* (Maryknoll: Orbis Books, 1977), pp. 129–40.
4. Rahner insists on the urgency of a comprehensive pastoral strategy in the two papers mentioned in note 2 above.
5. This definition is from William Reiser, "Inculturation and Doctrinal Development," *Heythrop Journal* 22 (1981): 135–48; quotation from p. 135. For a fuller discussion see Ary A. Roest Crollius, "What Is So New About Inculturation?" *Gregorianum* 59 (1978): 721–38.
6. H. Richard Niebuhr in his *Christ and Culture* (New York: Harper & Row, 1951) proposed five models: Christ Against Culture, the Christ of Culture, Christ Above Culture, Christ and Culture in Paradox, and Christ the Transformer of Culture. In his discussion he refers to these respectively as advocating: the rejection of culture, accommodation to culture, the synthesis of Christ and culture, dualism between Christ and culture, and the conversion of culture.
7. See, for instance, Karl Barth, *The Epistle to the Romans* (London: Oxford University Press, 1977), p. 258; cf. pp. 267–68.
8. Paul Tillich, *Systematic Theology* (Chicago: University of Chicago Press, 1951), 1:7.
9. Hilaire Belloc, *Europe and the Faith* (New York: Paulist Press, 1920), p. 261.

10. Paul VI, *Evangelii nuntiandi*, no. 20. Eng. trans., *On Evangelization in the Modern World* (Washington, DC: U.S. Catholic Conference, 1976), p. 16; also available in *Vatican Council II: More Postconciliar Documents*, ed. Austin Flannery. Vatican Collection, vol. 2 (Northport, NY: Costello, 1982), pp. 711–761; here, p. 719. In future references this apostolic exhortation will be abbreviated *EN*.

11. John Paul II, Letter to Cardinal Casaroli establishing Pontifical Council for Culture (May 20, 1982), quoted from *L'Osservatore Romano*, May 21–22, 1982, p. 3.

12. This sentence mirrors the famous definition of culture given by Clifford Geertz: "It denotes an historically transmitted pattern of meanings embodied in symbols, a system of inherited conceptions expressed in symbolic forms by means of which men communicate, perpetuate, and develop their knowledge about and attitudes toward life." *The Interpretation of Cultures* (London: Hutchinson, 1973), p. 89.

13. "By secularization we mean the process by which sectors of society and culture are removed from the dominance of religious institutions and symbols." Peter L. Berger, *The Sacred Canopy* (Garden City, NY: Doubleday, Anchor, 1969), p. 107.

14. "Message to the People of God," *Origins* 7 (Nov. 10, 1977): 324.

15. Ernst Troeltsch, *Christian Thought: Its History and Application* (1923; reprint, New York: Living Age Books, 1975), pp. 42–53.

16. Bernard J. F. Lonergan, "Revolution in Catholic Theology," in his *A Second Collection* (Philadelphia: Westminster, 1974), p. 233.

17. B. Lonergan, *Method in Theology* (New York: Herder and Herder, 1972), p. 327.

18. Ibid., pp. 107–9, 112, 119.

19. Raimundo Panikkar, "The Relation of Christians to Their Non-Christian Surroundings," in *Christian Revelation and World Religions*, ed. Joseph Neuner (London: Burns & Oates, 1967), p. 169. Italics Panikkar's.

20. Some examples are cited by William Reiser in the article referred to in note 5, above. See especially the quotations from Thomas Mampra, p. 144.

21. See, for example, Ishanand Vempeny, *Inspiration in the Non-Biblical Scriptures* (Bangalore: Theological Publications in India, 1973), esp. pp. 188–91.

22. Ary A. Roest Crollius, "Inculturation and the Meaning of Culture," *Gregorianum* 61 (1980): 253–74.

23. David Tracy, "Ethnic Pluralism and Systematic Theology: Reflections," in *Ethnicity*, ed., Andrew M. Greeley and Gregory Baum, *Concilium* 101 (New York: Seabury, 1977), pp. 91–99.

24. John Paul II, *Catechesi tradendae*, no. 53; Eng. trans. in *Vatican Council II: More Postconciliar Documents*, ed. Flannery, p. 794.

25. John Paul II, *Familiaris consortio*, no. 10, ibid., p. 821.

26. Roest Crollius, "Inculturation and the Meaning of Culture," p. 272.

27. John Paul II, *Slavorum apostoli* 27; in *Origins* 15 (July 18, 1985): 123.

28. For these and similar practices see Ludwig Hertling, *Communio: Church and Papacy in Early Christianity* (Chicago: Loyola University Press, 1972).

29. Christopher Dawson, *Religion and Culture* (New York: Sheed & Ward, 1948), p. 48.
30. James Gustafson, *Treasure in Earthen Vessels* (New York: Harper & Row, 1961) p. 42.
31. Robert N. Bellah, "Religion and Power in America Today," *Proceedings of the Catholic Theological Society of America* 37 (1982): 15–25; also published in *Commonweal* 109 (Dec. 3, 1982): 650–55. A similar analysis of American culture, without specific application to Catholicism, is contained in Robert N. Bellah et al., *Habits of the Heart* (Berkeley and Los Angeles: University of California Press, 1985).
32. Cf. Tracy, "Ethnic Pluralism," p. 97.
33. This term is often used by Charles H. Dodd, for example, in *The Bible Today* (Cambridge: Cambridge University Press, 1961), p. 107.
34. Joseph P. Fitzpatrick has recently probed the theme of inculturation with special reference to Catholicism in the United States. See his *One Church Many Cultures: The Challenge of Diversity* (Kansas City, MO: Sheed & Ward, 1987).
35. Wolfhart Pannenberg, "The Place of Creeds in Christianity Today," in *Foundation Documents of the Faith*, ed. Cyril S. Rodd (Edinburgh: T. & T. Clark, 1987), pp. 141–52, esp. pp. 150–52.

CHAPTER 4: THE MEANING OF CATHOLICISM: ADVENTURES OF AN IDEA

1. See Georg W. F. Hegel, *Lectures on the Philosophy of History* (New York: Colliers, 1901), pp. 377–426; idem, *The Christian Religion: Lectures on the Philosophy of Religion*, part 3, *Consummate, Absolute Religion*, ed. Peter C. Hodgson (Missoula, MT: Scholars Press, 1979), esp. pp. 334–44.
2. See Peter C. Hodgson, ed., *Ferdinand Christian Baur on the Writing of Church History* (New York: Oxford University Press, 1968), passim; F. C. Baur, *Der Gegensatz des Katholicismus und Protestantismus nach den Principien und Hauptdogmen der beiden Lehrbegriffe* (Tübingen: L. F. Fues, 1834), esp. pp. 367–438.
3. Friedrich D. E. Schleiermacher, *The Christian Faith* (1928; reprint, New York: Harper Torchbooks, 1963), sec. 24, pp. 103–8.
4. Philip Schaf [sic], *The Principle of Protestantism as Related to the Present State of the Church* (Chambersburg, PA: German Reformed Church, 1845), thesis 83, p. 187.
5. Ernst Troeltsch, *The Social Teaching of the Christian Churches* (1931; reprint Chicago: University of Chicago Press, 1960), 1:91–94. The views of Sohm are conveniently summarized and assessed in Adolf von Harnack, *The Constitution of the Church in the First Two Centuries* (New York: Putnam, 1910), app. 1, pp. 175–258.
6. A. von Harnack, *What Is Christianity?* (1901; reprint New York: Harper Torchbooks, 1957), pp. 63–74.
7. Auguste Sabatier, *Religions of Authority and the Religion of the Spirit* (New York: McClure, Phillips, 1904), p. 15.

8. See Edward B. Pusey, *The Church of England a Portion of Christ's One Holy Catholic Church and a Means of Restoring Visible Unity: An Eirenicon* (New York: Appleton, 1866).
9. A good account of the developments is given in Arthur Michael Ramsey, *An Era in Anglican Theology* (New York: Scribner's, 1960).
10. Norman P. Williams, "The Theology of the Catholic Movement," in *Northern Catholicism*, ed. Norman P. Williams and Charles Harris (London: SPCK, 1933), pp. 130–234.
11. Eric S. Abbott et al., *Catholicity: A Study in the Conflict of the Christian Traditions of the West* (Westminster, UK: Dacre, 1947).
12. Friedrich Heiler, *Der Katholizismus: Seine Idee und seine Erscheinung* (1923; reprint, Munich and Basel: E. Reinhardt, 1970). For the views of Stählin see Wilhelm Stählin, "Katholizität, Protestantismus, und Katholizismus," in *Die Katholizität der Kirche*, ed. Hans Asmussen and Wilhelm Stählin (Stuttgart: Evangelisches Verlagwerk, 1957), pp. 179–204.
13. Hans Asmussen et al., *The Unfinished Reformation* (Notre Dame: Fides, 1961), notably the contribution of Max Lackmann, pp. 66–112.
14. Barth, "Roman Catholicism: A Question to the Protestant Church," in his *Theology and Church* (London: SCM, 1962), pp. 307–33; also in his *Church Dogmatics*, passim.
15. Willem A. Visser 't Hooft, ed., *The First Assembly of the World Council of Churches* (London: SCM, 1949), p. 52.
16. Paul Tillich, "The Permanent Significance of the Catholic Church for Protestantism," *Protestant Digest* 3 (1941): 23–31; also Tillich's *The Protestant Era* (Chicago: University of Chicago Press, 1948), passim; and his *Systematic Theology*, vol. 3 (Chicago: University of Chicago Press, 1963), passim.
17. Jaroslav Pelikan, *Obedient Rebels: Catholic Substance and Protestant Principle in Luther's Reformation* (New York: Harper & Row, 1964), esp. pp. 193–206.
18. Langdon Gilkey, *Catholicism Confronts Modernity* (New York: Seabury, 1975).
19. See the selections from Drey in *Geist des Christentums und des Katholizismus*, ed. Josef R. Geiselmann (Mainz: Matthias-Grünewald, 1940), pp. 83–388. The most important of these selections for present purposes is Drey's essay, "The Spirit and Essence of Catholicism."
20. Ibid., pp. 125–26, a selection from Drey's *Tagebuch* for Jan. 15, 1815.
21. Johann Adam Möhler, *Symbolism; or, Exposition of the Doctrinal Differences Between Catholics and Protestants as Evidenced by Their Symbolic Writings* (New York: E. Dunigan, 1844), p. 333.
22. F. C. Baur, *Der Gegensatz*. The history of the controversy is recounted in Joseph Fitzer, *Moehler and Baur in Controversy, 1832–1838* (Talahassee, FL: American Academy of Religion, 1974).
23. John Henry Newman, *Essay on the Development of Christian Doctrine* (1845; reprint, Garden City, NY: Doubleday, Image, 1960), pp. 59, 110, 310.
24. J. H. Newman, *Apologia Pro Vita Sua* (1864; reprint, Garden City, NY: Doubleday, Image, 1956), p. 323.
25. A. Firmin [Alfred Loisy], "La Théorie individualiste de la religion," *Revue du Clergé français* 17 (Jan. 1, 1899): 212. Loisy reiterates this point against Harnack in his *The Gospel and the Church* (1903; reprint, Philadelphia: Fortress, 1976), p. 165.

26. George Tyrrell, "Reflections on Catholicism," *Through Scylla and Charybdis* (London: Longmans, Green, 1907), chap. 2, pp. 20–84.
27. G. Tyrrell, *Christianity at the Crossroads* (1909; reprint, London: Allen & Unwin, 1963), p. 167.
28. Friedrich von Hügel discusses the characteristics of Catholicism in his *Essays and Addresses on the Philosophy of Religion, First Series* (London: J. M. Dent & Sons, 1921), pp. 227–41, 242–53; *Second Series* (London: J. M. Dent & Sons, 1926), pp. 245–51.
29. F. von Hügel, *The Mystical Element in Religion as Studied in St. Catherine of Genoa and Her Friends*, 2d ed. (London: J. M. Dent & Sons, 1923), 1:50–82; 2:387–89.
30. Karl Adam, *The Spirit of Catholicism* (1929; reprint, Garden City, NY: Doubleday, Image, 1954), esp. chap. 1.
31. Yves Congar, *Divided Christendom* (London: Centenary Press, 1939), pp. 94–95; French original, *Chrétiens désunis* (Paris: Cerf, 1937), p. 117.
32. The Council of Trent in its fourth session (1546) laid down principles for attaining the "puritas ipsa Evangelii" (DS 1501). See Yves Congar, "Comment l'Église sainte doit se renouveler sans cesse," *Sainte Église* (Paris: Cerf, 1964), pp. 152–54.
33. Henri de Lubac, *Catholicism: A Study of Dogma in Relation to the Corporate Destiny of Mankind* (London: Burns, Oates & Washbourne, 1950), p. 153.
34. Medard Kehl and Werner Löser, eds., *The von Balthasar Reader* (New York: Crossroad, 1982), pp. 7–9, 247–61. The latter passage is a selection from von Balthasar, "Die Absolutheit des Christentums und die Katholizität der Kirche" in *Absolutheit des Christentums*, ed. Walter Kasper, vol. 79 of *Questiones Disputatae* (Freiburg: Herder, 1977), pp. 131–56.
35. Leonardo Boff can be understood as holding that without Protestantism as its dialectical counterpart, Catholicism would be unable to overcome its own pathologies. See his *Church: Charism and Power* (New York: Crossroad, 1985), pp. 80–85. The Vatican Congregation for the Doctrine of the Faith, in a notification regarding Boff's book issued on March 11, 1985, criticized Boff for explaining Catholicism and Protestantism as two incomplete mediations, each in need of the other. The CDF's notification may be found in *Origins* 14 (April 4, 1985):683–87.
36. Pius XII, Encyclical *Mystici Corporis Christi* (*AAS* 35 [1943] 193–248, at 225; English translation, *The Mystical Body of Christ* (3rd ed., New York: America Press, 1957), no. 81, p. 35.
37. For a fuller development of certain points in this chapter see Avery Dulles, *The Catholicity of the Church* (Oxford: Clarendon Press, 1985).

CHAPTER 5: VATICAN II AND THE RECOVERY OF TRADITION

1. This text is available in German and Latin in *Glaube im Prozess: Christsein nach dem II. Vatikanum*, ed. Elmar Klinger and Klaus Wittstadt, Freiburg: Herder, 1984), pp. 33–50. A French translation may be found in *La Révélation divine*, ed. Bernard D. Dupuy (Paris: Cerf, 1968), 2:577–87.
2. For Latin and German versions of this see *Glaube im Prozess*, ed. Klinger

and Wittstadt, pp. 51–64. French and Latin versions may be found in *La Révélation divine*, ed. Dupuy, 2:589–98.

3. Umberto Betti, *La Rivelazione divina nella Chiesa* (Rome: Città nuova, 1970), p. 80.

4. The ecumenical document on "Scripture, Tradition, and Traditions" issued by the Faith and Order Commission in 1963 shows some remarkable convergences with Vatican II. See the text in *The Fourth World Conference on Faith and Order*, ed. Patrick C. Rodger and Lukas Vischer (New York: Association Press, 1964), Report of Section II, "Scripture, Tradition, and Traditions," pp. 50–61. The ecumenical import of *Dei Verbum* is considered in articles by Barth, Leuba, Thurian, and Schlink in *La Révélation divine*, ed. Dupuy, vol. 2.

5. Joseph Ratzinger has given an authoritative commentary on Chapter II of *Dei Verbum* in Herbert Vorgrimler, ed., *Commentary on the Documents of Vatican II* (New York: Herder and Herder, 1969), 3:181–98. For an account of the debate on the material sufficiency of Scripture at Vatican II, see Heribert Schauf, "Auf dem Wege zu der Aussage der dogmatischen Konstitution über die göttliche Offenbarung 'Dei Verbum' Art. 9 'quo fit ut Ecclesia certitudinem suam de omnibus revelatis non per solam Sacram Scripturam hauriat," in *Glaube im Prozess*, ed. Klinger and Wittstadt, pp. 66–98.

6. James Hennesey, "All that the Church Is and Believes," *America* 147 (October 9, 1982): 193.

7. Ibid.

8. Robert P. Imbelli, "Vatican II—Twenty Years Later," *Commonweal* 109 (October 8, 1982): 78.

9. Text in Yves Congar, *Challenge to the Church* (Huntington, IN: Our Sunday Visitor, 1976), p. 78.

10. To this general effect see Oscar Cullmann, "The Tradition," in his *The Early Church* (Philadelphia: Westminster, 1956), pp. 55–59.

11. Martin Heidegger, *Being and Time* (London: SCM, 1962), p. 43.

12. See Immanuel Kant, "What Is Enlightenment?" in *Kant's Moral and Political Writings* (New York: Modern Library, 1949), pp. 132–39.

13. Hannah Arendt, *Between Past and Future* (New York: Viking, 1961), p. 26.

14. Michael Polanyi, *Science, Faith, and Society* (Chicago: University of Chicago Press, 1964), p. 52.

15. Alfred North Whitehead, *Science and the Modern World* (New York: Macmillan, 1925), p. 270.

16. Maurice Blondel, *History and Dogma* (New York: Holt, Rinehart & Winston, 1964), especially pp. 264–87.

17. Ibid., p. 274.

18. On the dialectic of dwelling in and breaking out, see Polanyi, *Personal Knowledge* (New York: Harper Torchbooks, 1964), pp. 195–202.

19. Von Balthasar, *A Theology of History* (New York: Sheed & Ward, 1963), p. 105.

20. Blondel, *History and Dogma*, p. 274; cf. pp. 267–68.

21. Ibid., p. 276.

22. This influence could, I think, be documented by comparing the account of Blondel in Congar's *Tradition and Traditions* (New York: Macmillan,

1966), pp. 359–68 with Congar's own formulations in his 1962 schema (note 2 above) and the final text of *Dei Verbum*, chap. II. The French edition of Congar's book appeared in two volumes in 1960 and 1963, and thus did not depend on Vatican II.

23. Congar, *Challenge to the Church*, pp. 47–49, 57.

CHAPTER 6: AUTHORITY AND CONSCIENCE: TWO NEEDED VOICES

1. John Henry Newman, *On Consulting the Faithful in Matters of Doctrine* (1859; reprint, Kansas City: Sheed & Ward, 1985), pp. 53, 71.

2. Ibid., p. 85. Newman quotes from Hilary of Poitiers, *Contra Auxentium* 6 (*PL* 10:613), partly in his own English translation, partly in Latin: "Up to this date, the only cause why Christ's people is not murdered by the priests of Anti-christ, with this deceit of impiety, is, that they take the words which the heretics use, to denote the faith which they themselves hold. . . . *Sanctiores aures plebis quam corda sunt sacerdotum.*"

3. The terms *religiosum animi obsequium* and *religiosum voluntatis et intellectus obsequium* are used in Vatican II, *Lumen gentium*, no. 25, to describe the proper response to noninfallible but authentic magisterial teaching.

4. For a commentary on canon 752 of the 1983 Code of Canon Law, which calls for "religiosum intellectus et voluntatis obsequium" as a response to certain kinds of magisterial teaching, see Ladislas Orsy, "Reflections on the Text of a Canon," *America* 154 (May 17, 1986): 396–99. See also Ladislas Orsy, *The Church: Learning and Teaching* (Wilmington DE: Michael Glazier, 1987), pp. 82–89.

5. Charles Dickens, *American Notes*, chap. 18, "Concluding Remarks" (1842; reprint, London: Oxford University Press, 1957), pp. 244–45.

6. Ibid., p. 245.

7. Ibid., p. 249.

8. In response to several proposed amendments the Theological Commission said that the approved theological authors were to be followed. See *Modorum expensio* of Oct.–Nov. 1964 in *Constitutionis Dogmaticae "Lumen Gentium" Synopsis Historica*, ed. Giuseppe Alberigo and Franca Magistretti (Bologna: Istituto per le Scienze Religiose, 1975), p. 532, esp. *modi* 159 and 160.

9. This text was published by the Secretariat of the Conference of German Bishops in the autumn of 1967 as a semiprivate document and disseminated at the diocesan level. It is most easily accessible in the lengthy quotations given by Karl Rahner in his "The Dispute Concerning the Church's Teaching Office," *Theological Investigations* (New York: Seabury, 1976) 14:85–88. See also K. Rahner, "Magisterium," *Encyclopedia of Theology: The Concise "Sacramentum Mundi"* (New York: Seabury, 1975), pp. 877–78.

10. Newman was concerned to show that assent to authoritative teaching cannot conflict with the rights of conscience. The following quotations from his *A Letter Addressed to the Duke of Norfolk* are illustrative: "Conscience is the aboriginal Vicar of Christ, a prophet in its informations, a

monarch in it peremptoriness, a priest in its blessings and anathemas, and, even though the eternal priesthood throughout the Church could cease to be, in it the sacerdotal principle would remain and have a sway." A little later he added: "So indeed it is; did the Pope speak against Conscience in the true sense of the word, he would commit a suicidal act. He would be cutting the ground from under his feet. His very mission is to proclaim the moral law, and to protect and strengthen that 'Light which enlighteneth every man that cometh into the world.' On the law of conscience and its sacredness are founded both his authority in theory and his power in fact." See *Newman and Gladstone: The Vatican Decrees*, ed. Alvan S. Ryan (Notre Dame, IN: University of Notre Dame Press, 1962), pp. 129, 132.

11. *Human Life in Our Day: A Collective Pastoral Letter of the American Hierarchy Issued Nov. 15, 1968* (Washington, DC: U.S. Catholic Conference, 1968), pp. 18–19.

12. Richard A. McCormick, "Notes on Moral Theology," *Theological Studies* 30 (1969): 651–53.

13. See National Catholic News Service press release of May 6, 1986.

CHAPTER 7: THE CHURCH AND COMMUNICATIONS: VATICAN II AND BEYOND

1. Avery Dulles, "The Church Is Communications," *Catholic Mind* 69 (Oct. 1971): 6–16; quotation from p. 7.

2. Norman Goodall, ed., *The Uppsala Report* (Geneva: World Council of Churches, 1968), pp. 389–401.

3. In what follows I rely on the schematization in Avery Dulles, *Models of the Church* (Garden City, NY: Doubleday, 1974; enlarged edition, 1987). For purposes of this presentation I have inverted the order of Models 2 and 4.

4. *Acta synodalia sacrosancti concilii Oecumenici Vaticani II* (Vatican City: Typis polyglottis, 1971 ff.), vol. III/2, p. 210. Cf. Antonio Acerbi, *Due Ecclesiologie: Ecclesiologia giuridica ed ecclesiologia di communione nella 'Lumen gentium'* (Bologna: Centro Editoriale Dehoniano, 1975), p. 523.

5. Acerbi, *Due Ecclesiologie*, pp. 524–25.

6. A standard commentary, with historical information, is provided by Karlheinz Schmidthüs, "Decree on the Instruments of Social Communication," in *Commentary on the Documents of Vatican II*, ed. Herbert Vorgrimler (New York: Herder and Herder, 1967), 1:89–104. A recent evaluation by David Eley may be found in *The Church Renewed: The Documents of Vatican II Reconsidered*, ed. George P. Schner (Lanham, MD: University Press of America, 1986), pp. 109–124.

7. *The Puebla Conclusions* (Washington, DC: NCCB, 1979), no. 1090, p. 172.

8. Karl Rahner, "The Mass and Television," in his *Mission and Grace* (London: Sheed & Ward, 1963), 1:255–75.

9. Second General Conference of Latin American Bishops, *The Church in the Present-Day Transformation of Latin America in the Light of the Council*, Part 2, *Conclusions* (Bogota: CELAM, 1970), 16:7, p. 239.

10. Avery Dulles, "Mass Evangelization Through Social Media," testimony for U.S. Catholic Conference hearing on communications, March 8, 1979, in *Catholic Mind* 78 (June 1980): 43–49, quotation from pp. 46–47.
11. "Pastoral Instruction on Social Communications," *Catholic Mind* 59 (Oct. 1971): 22–61.
12. Rembert G. Weakland, "Where Does the Economics Pastoral Stand?" *Origins* 13 (April 26, 1984): 758–59.
13. *The Church in the Present-Day Transformation*, 6:12, pp. 239–40.

CHAPTER 8: VATICAN II AND THE PURPOSE OF THE CHURCH

1. Carolus Passaglia, *De Ecclesia Christi: Commentariorum Libri Quinque*, vol. 2, bk. 3, *De Ecclesiae Caussis* (Regensburg: Manz, 1856), chap. 45, "De Fine Institutae divinitus Ecclesiae," nos. 788–807, pp. 840–56. Passaglia's treatment of our question is long, subtle, and nuanced.
2. Joseph de Guibert, *De Christi Ecclesia* (Rome: Gregorian University, 1928), thesis 17, pp. 125–29.
3. Ioachim Salaverri, "De Ecclesia Christi," *Sacrae Theologiae Summa*, 4th ed. (Madrid, 1958), vol. 1, thesis 22, nos. 914–35, pp. 822–30.
4. Jean Daniélou, *Why the Church?* (Chicago: Franciscan Herald, 1974), esp. chaps. 2 and 14; also app. 1.
5. Karl Rahner, *The Church and the Sacraments* (New York: Herder and Herder, 1964); idem, *Theology of Pastoral Action* (New York: Herder and Herder, 1968); idem, "The Church's Commission to Bring Salvation and the Humanization of the World," *Theological Investigations* (New York: Seabury, 1976), 14:295–313.
6. James D. Crichton, "A Theology of Worship," in *The Study of Liturgy*, ed. Cheslyn Jones et al. (New York: Oxford University Press, 1978), pp. 1–29.
7. Jan Groot, "The Church as Sacrament of the World," *Concilium* 31 (New York: Paulist, 1968), pp. 51–66.
8. Robert T. Sears, "Trinitarian Love as Ground of the Church," *Theological Studies* 37 (1976): 652–82.
9. Andrew M. Greeley, *The New Agenda* (Garden City, NY: Doubleday, 1973), chap. 7, "From Ecclesiastical Structure to Community of the Faithful," pp. 233–60.
10. David Bohr, "Evangelization: The Essential and Primary Mission of the Church," *Jurist* 39 (1979): 40–87.
11. Jon Sobrino, *The True Church and the Poor* (Maryknoll, NY: Orbis Books, 1974), chap. 9, "Evangelization as Mission of the Church," pp. 253–301.
12. Roger D. Haight, "The 'Established' Church as Mission: The Relation of the Church to the Modern World," *Jurist* (1979): 4–39.
13. Haight, *An Alternative Vision: An Interpretation of Liberation Theology* (New York: Paulist, 1984), pp. 178–85.
14. Eugene C. Bianchi, *Reconciliation: The Function of the Church* (New York: Sheed & Ward, 1969).
15. Richard P. McBrien, *Do We Need the Church?* (New York: Harper & Row, 1969), p. 229.

16. Johannes B. Metz, *Theology of the World* (New York: Herder and Herder, 1971), esp. pp. 91-97.
17. Gustavo Gutiérrez, *A Theology of Liberation* (Maryknoll, NY: Orbis Books, 1973), p. 262.
18. Juan Luis Segundo, *The Community Called Church* (Maryknoll, NY: Orbis Books, 1973), p. 72.
19. Segundo, *The Sacraments Today* (Maryknoll, NY: Orbis Books, 1974), p. 26.
20. For a brief but accurate presentation, based on the council texts, see Bonaventure Kloppenburg, *The Ecclesiology of Vatican II* (Chicago: Franciscan Herald, 1974), "The Specific Mission of the Church," pp. 97-108.
21. To prevent misunderstanding I must at this point refer to an objection. In his *The Catholic Moment* (San Francisco: Harper & Row, 1987), p. 190, Richard John Neuhaus criticizes my interpretation of Vatican II on the ground that "since we have the church, there would be no point in seeking the Kingdom." I would reply that in the perspectives of Vatican II we do not yet have the church except in its provisional, pilgrim form. The council would insist on the necessity of still seeking the heavenly church, which is central to, if not identical with, the realized kingdom.
22. Did Vatican II hold that non-Catholic Christians have access to salvation through the means of grace available in their own communities or through an implicit *votum* linking them to the Catholic church? The council documents do not seem to recognize any need to choose between these alternatives. The means of grace available outside the Catholic church derive their efficacy from, and possess an inner dynamism toward, the fullness of grace available in the Catholic church alone (*LG* 8 and *UR* 3). Thus Vatican II in effect teaches that the proper reception of the sacraments in a non-Catholic church or community involves an implicit *votum* for the fullness of communion and grace that is objectively available in the Catholic church.
23. In the Latin text the noun *goal* is not found, but the noun in English would seem to be the best translation for the pronoun *id* in the clause "ad id ordinantur ut omnes . . . " (*SC* 10).
24. My interpretation of the scholastic position diverges somewhat from that of Francis Schüssler Fiorenza, who maintains that these theologians rejected the social and political mission as "an improper mission" that would be "reductionistic" and would "substitute natural concerns for supernatural responsibilities." See his *Foundational Theology: Jesus and the Church* (New York: Crossroad, 1984), p. 200.
25. Augustine, *In Ioannem Tract.* 32:8 (*PL* 35:1646), as cited by Vatican II, *Optatam totius*, 9.

CHAPTER 9: THE CHURCH, SOCIETY, AND POLITICS

1. Dietrich Bonhoeffer, *The Cost of Discipleship* (1949; second ed., 1959; reprint, 1963), p. 57.
2. Ibid., p. 55.

3. John Coleman, *An American Strategic Theology* (New York: Paulist, 1982), p. 16.
4. Ernst Troeltsch, *The Social Teaching of the Christian Churches* (1931; reprint Chicago: University of Chicago Press, 1981), 1:61.
5. Quoted in Edward Cahill, "The Catholic Social Movement: Historical Aspects," reprinted in *Official Catholic Social Teaching, Readings in Moral Theology No. 5*, ed. Charles E. Curran and Richard A. McCormick (New York: Paulist, 1986), p. 9.
6. Helpful surveys of the main trends are provided in *The Gospel of Peace and Justice: Catholic Social Teaching Since Pope John*, ed. Joseph Gremillion (Maryknoll NY: Orbis Books, 1976) and, very recently, in Leslie Griffin, "The Integration of Spiritual and Temporal: Contemporary Roman Catholic Church-State Theory," *Theological Studies* 48 (1987): 225–57.
7. Michael Novak, *The Spirit of Democratic Capitalism* (New York: Simon & Schuster, 1982), p. 334.
8. The 1974 Synod in its working paper spoke only of an "intrinsic connection" between evangelization and human promotion. Summarizing the results of the 1974 Synod, Paul VI in *Evangelii nuntiandi* (1975) was content to assert, "Between evangelization and human advancement—development and liberation—there are in fact profound links" inasmuch as the plan of creation cannot be dissociated from the plan of redemption (*EN* 31).
   Charles M. Murphy, after a detailed review of the debate, concludes that the relationship between proclamation and social action may best be understood in terms of the dialectic between gift and task. Evangelization indicates what God is doing, but "the human response is indispensable as the necessary response to the divine initiative." Murphy's article, "Action for Justice as Constitutive of the Preaching of the Gospel: What Did the 1971 Synod Mean?" appears in *Theological Studies* 44 (1983): 298–311; quotation from p. 310.
9. Oswald von Nell-Breuning, "The Drafting of *Quadragesimo Anno*," reprinted in *Official Catholic Social Teaching*, ed. Curran and McCormick, pp. 60–68.
10. Ernest L. Fortin, "Theological Reflections on a Pastoral Letter," *Catholicism in Crisis* (July 1983): 9–12, esp. p. 10.
11. Peter L. Berger, "Can the Bishops Help the Poor?" in *Challenge and Response: Critiques of the Catholic Bishops' Draft Letter on the Economy* (Washington, DC: Ethics and Public Policy Center, 1985), pp. 54–64; quotation from p. 63.
12. See Francis X. Winters, "After Tension, Détente: A Continuing Chronicle of European Episcopal Views on Nuclear Deterrence," *Theological Studies* 45 (1984): 343–51.
13. George Weigel, "The Bishops' Pastoral Letter and the American Political Culture: Who Was Influencing Whom?" in *Peace in a Nuclear Age: The Bishops' Pastoral Letter in Perspective*, ed. Charles J. Reid, Jr. (Washington, DC: The Catholic University of America, 1986), pp. 171–89; quotation from p. 181. Weigel's position is more fully articulated in his important book, *Tranquillitas Ordinis* (New York: Oxford University Press, 1987), pp. 257–85.

14. Weigel, "The Bishops' Pastoral Letter," p. 187. Charles N. Luttwak, in his "Catholics and the Bomb: The Perspective of a Non-Catholic Strategist" (*Peace in a Nuclear Age*, pp. 159–70), writes on p. 169: "When I read the pastoral letter I see, before me, one of those 'faddish' documents that are produced by people who succumb to surrounding social pressures and accept opinions not their own."

15. Michael Novak, *The Spirit of Democratic Capitalism*, p. 28.

16. Peter L. Berger, "Can the Bishops Help the Poor?" in *Challenge and Response*, p. 63.

17. Charles Krauthammer, "Perils of the Prophet Motive," in *Challenge and Response*, pp. 44–53; quotation from p. 52.

18. John Paul II, *Brazil: Journey in the Light of the Eucharist* (Boston: Daughters of St. Paul, 1980), p. 255; quoted by J. Brian Benestad, *The Pursuit of a Just Social Order* (Washington, DC: Ethics and Public Policy Center, 1982), p. 9.

19. Keith A. Breclaw, "From *Rerum Novarum* to the Bishops' Letter: Labor and Ideology in Catholic Social Thought," in *The Deeper Meaning of Economic Life*, ed. R. Bruce Douglass (Washington, DC: Georgetown University Press, 1987), pp. 97–115; quotation from p. 113.

20. Ernest L. Fortin, "Catholic Social Teaching and the Economy," *Catholicism in Crisis* 3 (Jan. 1985): 41–44.

21. J. Brian Benestad, "The Bishops' Pastoral Letter on the Economy: Theological Criteria and Criticisms," *Notre Dame Journal of Law, Ethics, and Public Policy* (1985): 161–77.

22. J. Bryan Hehir, "Church-State and Church-World: The Ecclesiological Implications," *Proceedings of the Catholic Theological Society of America* 41 (1986): 54–74; quotation from p. 69.

23. Ibid., p. 70.

24. Some Catholic authors have argued—wrongly, I think—that the tentative and consultative style adopted by the bishops in their recent social teaching should serve as a model for the revision of doctrines that have been proclaimed in a more binding manner. For instance, Dennis P. McCann, in his *New Experiment in Democracy: The Challenge for American Catholicism* (Kansas City, MO: Sheed & Ward, 1987), puts the question: "If it is possible to consult not just Catholic clergy and laity but also the American 'civil community' as a whole, when reformulating Catholic social teaching on nuclear deterrence and U.S. employment policies, why can't a similar process be used to respond to the current *sensus fidelium* on a host of other sensitive issues like birth control, abortion, divorce, sexual ethics in general, and the role of women in the church in particular?" (pp. 119–20).

25. Philip F. Lawler, "Squandering Moral Capital," in *Challenge and Response*, pp. 71–74; quotation from p. 74.

26. "Declaration of Concern: On Devaluing the Laity," *Origins* 7 (Dec. 29, 1977): 440–42; quotation from p. 441.

27. J. Brian Benestad, *The Pursuit of a Just Social Order* (Washington, DC: Ethics and Public Policy Center, 1982) p. 114.

28. Edward Schillebeeckx, *God the Future of Man* (New York: Sheed & Ward, 1968), p. 163. Somewhat analogous ideas, possibly influenced by Schille-

beeckx, are advanced in Karl Rahner, *The Shape of the Church to Come* (New York: Seabury/Crossroad, 1974), pp. 76–81.

29. John Courtney Murray, *We Hold These Truths* (New York: Sheed & Ward, 1960). J. Bryan Hehir refers to this passage in his article, "Principles and Politics: Differing with Dulles," *Commonweal* 114 (March 27, 1987). I agree with Murray but not with the use Hehir makes of Murray's text.
30. The text of the Hartford Appeal has been printed in many places. It is available with commentaries by some of the signers in *Against the World for the World*, ed. Peter L. Berger and Richard John Neuhaus (New York: Seabury/Crossroad, 1976), pp. 1–7.

CHAPTER 10: THE EXTRAORDINARY SYNOD OF 1985

1. An overview of this process is afforded in *The Reception of Vatican II*, ed. Giuseppe Alberigo, J. P. Jossua, and J. A.Komonchak (Washington, DC: The Catholic University of America Press, 1987).
2. The United States Bishops' Report, presented by Bishop James W. Malone, is in *Origins* 15 (Sept. 26, 1985): 225–33. The report of the episcopal conference of England and Wales is in *The Tablet* (London) 239 (Aug. 3, 1985): 814–19 and in *Origins* 15 (Sept. 5, 1985): 117–86. The most valuable larger collection of synod documents thus far published is *Synode Extraordinaire: Célébration de Vatican II* (Paris: Cerf, 1986).
3. Alberto Melloni writes, "I think that in fact the bishops' replies are paradoxically the most enduring fruit of the Synod . . . " See his article, "After the Council and the Episcopal Conferences: The Responses," in *Synod 1985—An Evaluation*, ed. Giuseppe Alberigo and James Provost, *Concilium* 188 (Edinburgh: T. & T. Clark, 1986), p. 22.
4. For summaries of these interventions see *Il Sinodo della Speranza: Documenti ufficiali della seconda assemblea straordinaria del Sinodo dei Vescovi*, ed. Gino Concetti (Rome: Logos, 1986).
5. The "Message to the People of God" and the "Final Report," together with several important Synod addresses, are published in *Origins* 15 (Dec. 19, 1985). Another translation of the Message to the People of God and the Final Report is given in Xavier Rynne, *John Paul's Extraordinary Synod* (Wilmington, DE: Michael Glazier, 1986).
6. Peter Hebblethwaite, "Exit 'The People of God'," *Tablet* 240 (Feb. 8, 1986): 140–41. He points the finger at Cardinal Ratzinger, who, though hardly an "outside agent," has in fact warned against certain distortions of the image of "People of God." See Joseph Ratzinger, *Principles of Catholic Theology* (San Francisco: Ignatius Press, 1987), pp. 54–55.
7. Joseph Komonchak, "The Theological Debate," in *Synod 1985—An Evaluation*, ed. Alberigo and Provost, p. 55.
8. *Synode Extraordinaire*, p. 201.
9. Initial Report II.3.c. ibid., p. 345. cf. English-language summary in *Origins* 15 (Dec. 12, 1985): 428.
10. Ibid., p. 445.
11. For the following analysis I am in part indebted to Hermann-Joseph

Pottmeyer, "The Church as Mysterium and as Institution," *Synod 1985— An Evaluation*, ed. Alberigo and Provost, pp. 99–109.

12. For a concise survey explaining some of the points at issue see John D. Faris, "The Codification and Revision of Eastern Canon Law," *Studia Canonica* 17 (1983): 449–85.

13. Text in *Synode Extraordinaire*, pp. 391–94; quotation from pp. 393–94.

14. In *L'Osservatore Romano*, Weekly Edition, July 7, 1986, p. 3.

15. On the history of earlier proposals for a universal catechism see Berard Marthaler, "The Synod and the Catechism," *Synod 1985—An Evaluation*, ed. Alberigo and Provost, pp. 91–98.

16. *L'Osservatore Romano*, Weekly Edition, Dec. 9, 1985. This is a summary of Cardinal Law's intervention.

17. Joseph Ratzinger, "Toward a Universal Catechism or Compendium of Doctrine," *Origins* 17 (Nov. 5, 1987): 380–82.

18. *Synode Extraordinaire*, p. 516.

19. Ibid., p. 529.

20. Ibid., p. 541.

21. As quoted in Melloni, "After the Council," p. 19.

22. *Synode Extraordinaire*, p. 601.

23. *AAS* 23 (1931): 2–3; cf. DS 3738.

24. *AAS* 38 (1946): 145.

25. For the ten principles in English translation see James A. Coriden et al., *The Code of Canon Law: A Text and Commentary* (New York: Paulist, 1985), p. 6.

26. *Communicationes* 1 (1969): 100; also René Laurentin, *Le premier Synode* (Paris: Seuil, 1968), p. 305.

27. Quoted in Francesco Salerno, "Canonizzazione del principio de Sussidiarità," in *La Collegialità Episcopale per il Futuro della Chiesa*, ed. Vincenzo Fagiolo and Gino Concetti (Florence: Vallecchi, 1969), pp. 138–39.

28. Quoted from *La Documentation Catholique* 66 (Sept. 7, 1969): 789.

29. *AAS* 61 (1969): 716–21.

30. Quoted in Giovanni Caprile, *Il Sinodo dei Vescovi 1969* (Rome: Civiltà Cattolica, 1970), p. 127.

31. Ibid., pp. 166–67.

32. Ibid., p. 206.

33. Ibid., pp. 216–17.

34. "L'Eglise universelle n'a pas simplement un rôle de suppléance." The text of Cardinal Hamer's speech to the plenary meeting of cardinals is given in *Synode Extraordinaire*, pp. 598–604; quotation from p. 604.

35. In a recent article Jean Baptiste Beyer maintains that while the principle of subsidiarity is valid for civil society, in which the structures of government rest upon the will of the governed, it is not valid for the church, which rests upon the self-impartation of the divine trinitarian life. The total church is immanent in all the particular churches and in every eucharistic community. See "Principe de Subsidiarité ou 'Juste Autonomie'," *Nouvelle Revue Théologique* 108 (Nov.–Dec. 1986): 801–22. Another canonist, Peter Huizing, in an article on "Subsidiarity" (*Synod 1985—An Evaluation*, ed. Alberigo and Provost, pp. 118–23) presents Pius XII and Paul VI as favoring the principle of subsidiarity, notwithstanding their

reservations. Huizing himself concludes rather too hastily that the entire hierarchical structure of the church is subsidiary in nature. I have difficulty in following his argument at this point, since the apostolic office is a constitutive feature of the church itself. If subsidiarity is to be applied to the church, this can be in only a highly analogous sense at the risk of obscuring the original meaning of *subsidium* ("auxiliary").

CHAPTER 11: THE TEACHING AUTHORITY OF BISHOPS' CONFERENCES

1. On the origins and development of bishops' conferences see Bernard Franck, "La conférence épiscopale et les autres institutions de collégialité intermédiaires," *L'Année canonique* 27 (1983): 67–120.
2. Quotation from report of James A. Ryan as given in John B. Sheerin, *Never Look Back: The Career and Concerns of John J. Burke* (New York: Paulist, 1975), p. 78. See also Gerald P. Fogarty, *The Vatican and the American Hierarchy from 1870 to 1965* (Wilmington, DE: M. Glazier, 1985), p. 224.
3. Joseph Ratzinger, "The First Session," *Worship* 37 (1963): 529–35; quotation from p. 534.
4. Joseph Ratzinger, "The Pastoral Implications of Episcopal Collegiality," in *The Church and Mankind, Concilium* 1 (Glen Rock, NJ: Paulist, 1965), pp. 39–67; quotation from p. 63–64.
5. Jan Schotte, "Report on Meeting to Discuss the War and Peace Pastoral," *Origins* 12 (April 7, 1983): 692.
6. Joseph Cardinal Ratzinger with Vittorio Messori, *The Ratzinger Report* (San Francisco: Ignatius Press, 1985), pp. 58–61.
7. Commission théologique internationale, *L'Unique Eglise du Christ* (Paris: Centurion, 1985), no. 5–3, p. 38.
8. Luigi Carli, intervention of Nov. 13, 1963, *Acta synodalia Concilii oecumenici Vaticani II* (Vatican City: Typis Polyglottis, 1973), vol. 2, part 5, pp. 72–75. Cf. Michael Novak, *The Open Church: Vatican II, Act 2* (New York: Macmillan, 1964), p. 249. For a similar approach see Henri de Lubac, *Particular Churches and the Universal Church* (San Francisco: Ignatius Press, 1982), chap. 5, esp. pp. 264–65.
9. Jérome Hamer, "Les conférences épiscopales, exercice de la collégialité," *Nouvelle revue théologique* 85 (1963): 969. Much the same conclusion had already been reached by Karl Rahner in his essay, "On Bishops' Conferences," reprinted in his *Theological Investigations* (Baltimore: Helicon, 1969), 6:369–89.
10. Ratzinger, "Pastoral Implications," p. 64.
11. John Paul II, "Communion, Participation, Evangelization," Address to the Brazilian Bishops, July 10, 1980, *Origins* 10 (July 31, 1980): 131.
12. Joseph Bernardin, "The Collegiality of the United States Catholic Bishops," Address of May 4, 1976, *Origins* 6 (May 27, 1976): 11.
13. De Lubac, *Particular Churches*, p. 265.
14. Peter Hebblethwaite, "Bishops' Groups Draw Fire from Ratzinger," *National Catholic Reporter* 21 (Dec. 14, 1984): 6.

15. John Whealon, Letter to the Editor, *America* 149 (July 9–16, 1983): 40.
16. Henri Teissier, "Bishops' Conferences and Their Function in the Church," in *Synod 1985—An Evaluation*, ed. Giuseppe Alberigo and James Provost *Concilium* 188 (London: T. & T. Clark, 1986), pp. 110–17; quotation from p. 112; italics in original.
17. J. Francis Stafford, "The Conference of Bishops: A New Vision of Leadership and Authority" (Address given May 27, 1984, Cathedral of St. James, Brooklyn, NY), p. 12.
18. Francis Morrisey, "The New Code of Canon Law: The Importance of Particular Law," *Origins* 11 (Dec. 17, 1981): 428. This proposal, it may be noted, was not original with Morrisey.
19. Bernardin, "Collegiality," p. 12.
20. Text in *Origins* 17 (Dec. 24, 1987): 481–89.
21. "Reaction to the AIDS Statement," ibid., p. 493.
22. James Hickey, "The Bishop as Teacher," *Origins* 12 (July 29, 1982): 142.
23. Congregation for the Doctrine of the Faith, "Declaration on Sexual Ethics," *Origins* 5 (Jan. 22, 1976): 487.
24. Pope John Paul II, Address to U.S. Bishops, Oct. 5, 1979, *Origins* 9 (Oct. 18, 1979): 287–91, esp. p. 289.
25. Pope John Paul II, "Apostolic Exhortation on Reconciliation and Penance," *Origins* 14 (Dec. 20, 1984): 448.
26. Rembert Weakland, "Where Does the Economics Pastoral Stand?" *Origins* 13 (April 26, 1984): 758. Cf. "The Challenge of Peace," *Origins* 13 (May 19, 1983): 2–3.
27. Stafford, "The Conference of Bishops," p. 11.
28. John Dearden, "Collegial Sharing in Ministry: Roles of Bishops," *Origins* 12 (July 15, 1982): 120.
29. De Lubac, *Particular Churches*, pp. 267–68.
30. Vittorio Messori, "Colloquio con il Cardinal Joseph Ratzinger," *Jesus* (Nov. 1984), 80; also in *The Ratzinger Report*, p. 61.
31. John Paul II, "Communion, Participation, Evangelization," p. 134.
32. James Malone, "The Intersection of Public Opinion and Public Policy," *Origins* 14 (Nov. 29, 1984): 388. Similar views are expressed in Bishop Malone's address at Collegeville on June 18, 1985. See *Origins* 15 (July 4, 1985): 101.
33. J. Brian Benestad, *The Pursuit of a Just Social Order: Policy Statements of the U.S. Catholic Bishops, 1966–1980* (Washington, DC: Ethics and Public Policy Center, 1982), p. 139.
34. Ibid., pp. 101–2, 111–12.
35. This is the view I articulated in my Foreword to Benestad's book and earlier in "Dilemmas Facing the Church in the World," *Origins* 4 (Feb. 20, 1975): 548–51.
36. Ernesto Ruffini, intervention of Nov. 6, 1963, as reported in *Acta synodalia* (above, n. 8), vol. 2, part 4, p. 477. Cf. Novak, *The Open Church*, pp. 216–17.
37. John J. Wright as quoted in de Lubac, *Particular Churches*, p. 272 n. 25.
38. Ibid., pp. 271–73.
39. Ratzinger, "Pastoral Implications," p. 63.
40. James E. Hug, in his *Christian Faith and the U.S. Economy* (Kansas City,

MO: Leaven Press, 1984), p. 18, refers to an article by Michel Schooyans in *Le Libre Belgique* as embodying this view. I have not seen the article in question.
41. These quotations from Cyprian are taken from Ep. 14:4 and Ep. 74:10 (*CSEL* III/2, 512, 807).
42. Weakland, "Where Does the Economics Pastoral Stand?" pp. 758–59.
43. I have made a similar point in my article "The Teaching Authority of Bishops' Conferences," *America* 148 (June 11, 1983): 453–55. Also on the theme of this chapter see Ladislas Orsy, "Episcopal Conferences: Their Theological Standing and Their Doctrinal Authority," *America* 155 (Nov. 8, 1986): 282–85; Patrick Granfield, *The Limits of the Papacy* (New York: Crossroad, 1987), pp. 97–106.

CHAPTER 12: ECUMENISM AND THE SEARCH FOR DOCTRINAL AGREEMENT

1. This point is well made by Heinrich Fries in Heinrich Fries and Karl Rahner, *Unity of the Churches: An Actual Possibility* (New York: Paulist, 1985), p. 13.
2. Augustine, endorsing the views of Cyprian on this point, laid down the principle that on certain questions one may think differently without sacrificing one's right to communion: "Censuit Cyprianus licet, salvo iure communionis, diversum sentire" (*De Baptismo*, III,3.5; *PL* 434:141–42). Cf. Yves Congar, *Diversity and Communion* (Mystic, CT: Twenty-Third Publications, 1985), p. 24.
3. Pope John XXIII in his Encyclical *Ad Petri Cathedram* (June 29, 1959) quotes the maxim, "In necessariis unitas, in dubiis libertas, in omnibus caritas." For the earlier history of the maxim see Joseph Lecler, "À propos d'une maxime citée par Jean XXIII: *In necessariis . . .*," *Recherches de Science religieuse* 49 (1961): 546–60; idem, "Note complémentaire sur la maxime: *In necessariis . . .*," ibid. 52 (1964): 432–38. The reference is correctly given in Congar's *Diversités et Communion* (Paris: Cerf, 1982), p. 156 n. 4, but the English translation (*Diversity*, p. 206 n. 4) erroneously refers to *Revue des Sciences religieuses*.
4. For the views of Jurieu see Gustave Thils, *Les notes de l'Eglise dans l'apologétique catholique depuis la Réforme* (Gembloux: Duculot, 1936), pp. 166–89. See also Congar, *Diversity*, p. 116.
5. Pius XI, *Mortalium animos* (DS 3683); Eng. trans., *The Promotion of True Religious Unity* (Washington, DC: NCWC, 1928), pp. 13–14.
6. *Acta synodalia sacrosancti concilii Vaticani II*, (Vatican City: Typis Polyglottis, 1973), vol. 2, part 6, p. 34. An English translation may be found in Hans Küng et al., *Council Speeches of Vatican II* (Glen Rock, NJ: Paulist, 1964), pp. 188–92.
7. Congar, *Diversity*, p. 131.
8. Paul VI, Letter to Patriarch Athenagoras of Constantinople, Feb. 8, 1971; text in *Tomos Agapes* (Rome: Polyglot Press, 1971), p. 614.
9. The common biblical and creedal patrimony is indicated by Fries in *Unity of the Churches*, pp. 15–18.

10. The seventeenth-century Lutheran theologian George Calixtus popularized the idea of reunion on the basis of the *consensio quinquesaecularis*. In our own time Max Thurian has advocated the consensus of the first seven ecumenical councils of the first eight centuries as a basis for Christian unity. See Congar, *Diversity,* pp. 113, 121–23, with references.

11. Karl Rahner, in *Unity of the Churches,* thesis II, pp. 25–41, sets forth these positions, which he had previously advocated in *The Shape of the Church to Come* (New York: Seabury, 1974), pp. 102–7, and in "Is Church Union Dogmatically Possible?" *Theological Investigations* (New York: Crossroad, 1981), 17:197–214.

12. See, for instance, Karl Rahner, *Foundations of Christian Faith* (New York: Crossroad, 1982), pp. 359–67.

13. For a recent exploration of the state of the *Filioque* controversy see the articles of Dietrich Ritschl, Michael Fahey, and Theodore Stylianopoulos in *Conflicts about the Holy Spirit,* ed. Hans Küng and Jürgen Moltmann, *Concilium* 128 (New York: Seabury, 1979). Professor Stylianopoulos of the Holy Cross Greek Orthodox Seminary in Brookline, Mass., holds: "The Filioque is not a decisive difference in dogma but a serious difference in the interpretation of dogma which awaits resolution" (p. 30).

14. Eberhard Jüngel, "Ein Schritt voran," Review of Fries and Rahner, *Einigung der Kirchen—Reale Möglichkeit, Süddeutsche Zeitung* (Oct. 1–2, 1983), p. 126.

15. In his review of *Einigung der Kirchen,* Harding Meyer branded Rahner's concept of withholding judgment as a fatal terminological error because church unity cannot be grounded on skepticism; *Theologische Literaturzeitung* 109 (1984): 314. At a Lutheran conference in Chicago, April 16–18, 1985, Meyer proposed to rewrite Rahner's Thesis II to state that the partner churches must recognize each other's binding doctrines "as legitimate interpretations and developments, even though they are not able to accept these as obligatory for themselves" ("als legitime Auslegungen und Entfaltungen anerkannt, auch wenn sie diese nicht für sich selbst als verpflichtend zu übernehmen vermögen"). This alternative thesis of Meyer's has been published in H. Meyer, "Die Thesen von Fries und Rahner—Versuch einer Weiterführung," *Theologische Quartalschrift* (Tübingen) 166 (1986): 290–301, esp. p. 295.

    In his own paper at the Chicago conference, published in *Diakonia* 16 (1985): 365–76, Fries somewhat distanced himself from Rahner's Thesis II.

16. *L'Osservatore Romano* (Roman edition), Feb. 25–26, 1982, 1–2.

17. In an article, "*Einigung der Kirchen:* An Ecumenical Controversy," *One in Christ* 21 (1985): 139–66, Aidan Nichols faults Ols for apparently holding that anyone who does not accept the recent dogmas of the Catholic church cannot have the faith expressed in Scripture and the creeds. Such a judgment, Nichols asserts, would be out of line with Vatican II and the teaching of recent popes (157–58). For his part, Nichols defends the orthodoxy of the Fries-Rahner position but holds that its pastoral imprudence "is so great as to constitute a kind of practical irresponsibility vis-à-vis Catholic doctrine" (166).

18. This example was cited by the Anglican/Roman Catholic Consultation in the United States (ARC) in a statement of Jan. 23, 1972, "Doctrinal Agree-

ment and Christian Unity: Methodological Considerations," in *Documents on Anglican/Roman Catholic Relations* (Washington, DC: U.S.C.C., 1973), 2:49–53, citation from p. 52. The six principles in this paper still retain their validity.

19. Congar cited Heribert Mühlen, J. M. R. Tillard, and Avery Dulles as favoring the removal of the anathemas attached to the dogma of the Immaculate Conception. Congar seems to support these authors as against Bertrand de Margerie. See *Diversity,* pp. 174–75.

20. See Congar's informative note on the term *Oikonomia* in *Diversity,* pp. 54–69, esp. p. 56.

21. Joseph Ratzinger, *Principles of Catholic Theology* (San Francisco: Ignatius Press, 1987), p. 199; cf. Fries and Rahner, *Unity of the Churches,* pp. 40, 70, 77, and 130, where Ratzinger is cited on this point.

22. Joseph Ratzinger, "Luther and the Unity of the Churches," *Communio: International Catholic Review* 11 (1984): 210–26, esp. p. 216.

23. Joseph Ratzinger, "Anglican-Roman Catholic Dialogue: Its Problems and Hopes," *Insight* 1 (March 1983): 2–11; quotation from p. 7.

24. Bertrand de Margerie, "L'Analogie dans l'oecuménicité des conciles, notion clef pour l'avenir de l'oecuménisme," *Revue thomiste* 84 (1984): 425–45. In my summary I have inevitably simplified de Margerie's complex argument, which should be studied for itself.

25. Congar, *Diversity,* p. 171. Translation modified in accordance with French original.

26. George A. Lindbeck, *The Nature of Doctrine: Religion and Theology in a Postliberal Age* (Philadelphia: Westminster, 1984). For discussion of this provocative work see the review symposium in *Thomist* 49 (1985): 392–472. My own reflections on Lindbeck's proposals are more fully set forth in my article "Zur Überwindbarkeit von Lehrdifferenzen—Überlegungen aus Anlass zweier neuerer Lösungsvorschläge," *Theologische Quartalschrift* (Tübingen) 166 (1986): 278–89.

27. Congar, *Diversity,* p. 40.

28. Ibid., p. 76.

29. Congar, *Diversity,* p. 103; Fries, *Unity of the Churches,* pp. 19–20.

30. In "Consensus on the Eucharist?" *Commonweal* 96 (Aug. 25, 1972): 447–50, I have illustrated such hypothetical formulas of union with examples pertaining to the Eucharist. The U.S.A. Lutheran-Catholic Dialogue, in its consensus statement on *Justification by Faith* (Minneapolis: Augsburg, 1985), specifies the conditions under which the Lutheran formula "justification by faith alone," can bear a meaning acceptable to Catholics. See esp. nos. 105–7, pp. 52–54.

31. Congar points out that the ecumenical quest, by virtue of its eschatological orientation, corresponds to the nature of the church itself, which can never be fully understood in static or intrahistorical terms. See *Diversity,* pp. 163–64, with references to Lesslie Newbigin and Paul Evdokimov.

Sources

N.B. All the chapters in the present book are based on previously published articles, trimmed, adapted, and updated. The sources are as follows.

Chapter 1: American Impressions of the Council

Originally given as a lecture on Oct. 21, 1982, sponsored by the Department of Religious Studies of Loyola University in New Orleans in cooperation with the Albert Biever Memorial Lecture Series. With revisions the lecture appeared under the title "Vatican II and the American Experience of Church" in *Vatican II: Open Questions and New Horizons*, ed. Gerald M. Fagin, S.J. (Wilmington, DE: Michael Glazier, 1984), pp. 38–57. Permission from Michael Glazier.

Chapter 2: The Basic Teaching of Vatican II

Developed from a lecture for the diocesan Congress of the Diocese of Rockville Center, N.Y., delivered at South Huntington, Long Island, April 6, 1984. The lecture was printed under the title "Vatican II Reform: The Basic Principles" in *Church* 1 (Summer 1985): 3–10, published by the National Pastoral Life Center, 299 Elizabeth Street, New York, NY 10012. Permission from the editor, *Church*.

Chapter 3: The Emerging World Church and the Pluralism of Cultures

Given as the keynote address on June 13, 1984, for the 39th Annual Convention of the Catholic Theological Society of America, under the title "The Emerging World Church: A Theological Reflection." It appears in the *Proceedings of the C.T.S.A.* 39 (1984):1–12. Permission from the editor.

Chapter 4: The Meaning of Catholicism: Adventures of an Idea

First published, with some sections here omitted, as "The Essence of Catholicism: Protestant and Catholic Perspectives" in a *Festschrift* for Yves Conger, O.P., in *The Thomist* 48 (1984):607–33. Permission from the editor, *The Thomist*.

Chapter 5: Vatican II and the Recovery of Tradition

Initially composed for a *Festschrift* for Karl Rahner, S.J., under the title "Das Zweite Vatikanum und die Weidergewinnung der Tradition," and published in *Glaube im Prozess: Christsein nach dem II. Vatikanum*, ed. Elmar Klinger and Klaus Wittstadt (Freiburg: Herder, 1984), pp. 546–62. Permission from Verlag Herder.

Chapter 6: Authority and Conscience: Two Needed Voices

Developed from a lecture for the Brooklyn *Tablet* Forum given on May 22, 1986, and published under the title "Authority and Conscience: Two Needed Voices in the Church" in *Church* 2 (Fall 1986): 8–15. Permission from the editor, *Church*.

Chapter 7: The Church and Communications: Vatican II and Beyond

Written under the title "Vatican II and Communication" for volume 3 of René Latourelle, ed., *Vatican II: Assessment and Perspectives*, to be published in English by Paulist Press, Mahwah, NJ, in 1988. Permission from Paulist Press and from the editor.

Chapter 8: Vatican II and the Purpose of the Church

Delivered as the 1985 William L. Rossner Visiting Scholar Lecture at Rockhurst College, Kansas City, MO, on Nov. 7, 1985. The lecture was printed under the title "Vatican II and the Church's Purpose" in *Theology Digest* 32 (Winter 1985): 341–52. Permission from the editor, *Theology Digest*.

Chapter 9: The Church, Society, and Politics

First composed as a response to a paper by Peter Berger at a conference, "The Ordering of Our Life, Temporal and Eternal," sponsored by the Rockford Institute Center on Religion and Society in New York, NY. The paper was printed in full in *Origins* 16 (Feb. 19, 1987): 637–46. In that form it will also appear in *Different Gospels: The Meaning of Apostasy*, to be published by William B. Eerdmans Publishing Company, Grand Rapids, MI, in the fall of 1988. Sections in the original paper referring to Berger's presentation have been deleted in the version here printed. Permission granted by The Rockford Institute Center on Religion and Society.

Chapter 10: The Extraordinary Synod of 1985

Written as an Appendix for the English-language edition of Giuseppe Alberigo, Jean-Pierre Jossua, and Joseph A. Komonchak, eds., *The Reception of Vatican II*, (Washington, DC: The Catholic University of America Press, 1987), under the title "The Reception of Vatican II at the Extraordinary Synod of 1985," on pp. 349–63. Permission from The Catholic University of America Press.

Chapter 11: The Teaching Authority of Bishops' Conferences

Adapted from a lecture for the Serra Colloquium given on Jan. 3, 1985, in Washington, DC. That lecture was printed under the title, "Bishops' Conference Documents: What Doctrinal Authority?" *Origins* 14 (Jan. 24, 1985): 528–34.

Chapter 12: Ecumenism and the Search for Doctrinal Agreement

Expanded form of the Edwin T. Dahlberg Ecumenical Lecture at Colgate Rochester Divinity School, Rochester, NY. In a form similar to that here printed, the chapter appeared as an article "Paths to Doctrinal Agreement: Ten Theses" in *Theological Studies* 47 (1986):32–47. Permission from the editor, *Theological Studies*.

Gratitude is hereby expressed to the respective editors and publishers who have granted the author the necessary rights.

Index